Jacob B. de Liefde

The Great Dutch Admirals

Jacob B. de Liefde

The Great Dutch Admirals

ISBN/EAN: 9783337309695

Printed in Europe, USA, Canada, Australia, Japan

Cover: Foto ©ninafisch / pixelio.de

More available books at **www.hansebooks.com**

THE

GREAT DUTCH ADMIRALS

BY

JACOB DE LIEFDE

With ILLUSTRATIONS by TOWNLEY GREEN and others

LONDON
HENRY S. KING & CO., 65 CORNHILL
AND 12 PATERNOSTER ROW
1873

CONTENTS.

	PAGE
JACOB VAN HEEMSKERK	1
PIET HEIN	30
MARTEN HARPERTS TROMP	60
WITTE CORNELIS DE WITH	119
MICHIEL ADRIÁNSZOON DE RUYTER	148
JOHAN EVERTSEN	268
CORNELIS TROMP	296

ILLUSTRATIONS.

	To face Page
HEEMSKERK'S SAILORS ATTACKED BY BEARS	10
THE SLAUGHTER OF THE BEAR	17
'BOYS, FOLLOW ME INTO THE BOATS'	38
'WILL YOU NOT REVENGE MY FATHER'S DEATH?'	62
BATTLE BETWEEN TROMP AND BLAKE OFF DOVER	95
TROMP AND DE WITH SETTLING THE PLAN OF BATTLE	128
THE FLUSHING PEOPLE STARING AT DE RUYTER ON THE TOP OF THE CHURCH TOWER	150
CAPTURE OF NYBORG (*from an old Dutch Engraving*)	182
DE WITT AND DE RUYTER CONSULTING THE MAP OF LONDON	233
'DOES ANYONE KNOW THE ADMIRAL'S HANDWRITING?'	255
THE ENGLISH BOARDING THE 'PHŒNIX'	303

THE GREAT DUTCH ADMIRALS.

JACOB VAN HEEMSKERK.

THE other day I came across a curious map of Europe published in the year 1600. Every country in it is represented by a figure, which, although very absurd, denotes with great truth the then actual state of each nation. There is England as a chubby little fellow making mud-pies at the sea-side, and looking very happy and contented. There is France as a school-boy cutting himself all over with a sharp knife. There is Italy, dressed as the Pope, with a high crown on his head, holding a chain in one hand and a crucifix in the other. There is also, in a small corner opposite England, a little dwarf with a beard, standing in a washing-tub full of water: in one hand he holds an axe, in the other a pistol, while he has a sword between his teeth. This little mannie is looking up to a tremendous giant, who stands with one foot on Spain and the other on Belgium, and is trying all he can to press the little fellow down in his tub. The giant is the King of Spain, the little dwarf is the young republic of the Netherlands, and the two are having a desperate fight together, for the King is determined to kill the little man, and the little man is equally determined not to be killed. Now you will say that when a giant fights with a dwarf the giant is certain to get the best of it; yet it was not so. The whole of Europe was looking on while this fight lasted, and the whole of Europe was astonished and delighted with the pluck of the little fellow. Again and again the giant King of Spain got hold of him, and nearly pressed him down or upset his tub: but every time he managed to jump aside, kicking and biting and hitting the giant so tremendously that he howled with pain.

For you must know that in those days there were in the Netherlands a number of men who loved their little watery country very dearly, and were determined to make it free, or die in the struggle. I could give you a long list of heroes who fought both on land and sea, most of whom died in some battle, and whose memory is dearly loved by every Dutch boy and girl. Their wonderful deeds are always read at school, and well do I remember, when our master described how they fought against this giant, that we were all as quiet as mice, and could have listened for hours. I propose to tell you something about a number of these men who fought at sea; and if you do not say with me, after having read my stories, that they were splendid fellows, it will be my fault and not theirs.

The first of these was Jacob van Heemskerk. He was born in the city of Amsterdam in the year 1567. His father was a man of very good family and considerable wealth, but I have not been able to find out whether he was engaged in business or was himself a soldier. His father's brother was a man of great note, being at different times counsellor, sheriff, and accountant-general of North Holland. Now many of the inhabitants of Amsterdam were Roman Catholics, and in those days the Catholics were intolerant and cruel, as you will no doubt know from the history of Queen Mary. Heemskerk's family belonged to the Protestant religion, and they were consequently exposed to no end of dangers, persecutions, and hardships. Nevertheless, young Jacob received from his father, who was a God-fearing man, an excellent education, as the history of his later years will show. It must not be imagined, however, that his school-days were passed as quietly as they would be nowadays, or might have been had he been educated as an English lad in London under good Queen Bess.

With such things going on all over the country, it was not possible that some of the excitement of the rebellion, some of the hatred between Protestants and Catholics, between Dutchmen and Spaniards, should not penetrate into the schools; and I have read in more than one old book that the boys used to have most terrible fights in the streets and the market-squares, belabouring each other with heavy sticks and stones, and that their fights often assumed so alarming a character, that the watchmen of the town had to interfere, and drag two or three of the ringleaders before the magistrate. The greater number of the boys at school were generally Catholics; but this would not have caused so serious a disturbance, had it not been that the Catholic fathers generally favoured the Spaniards. The Protestant and patriotic boys were always in the minority, but they felt strongly for the good cause. They incessantly taunted the others with being the enemies of their country, and were always ready at any moment of the day to give battle to their opponents.

In those days, moreover, there were plenty of other things to stir boys' hearts. As Amsterdam lies on the shore of a large bay, the merchant-vessels were enabled to come right up to the town, and anchor alongside the quay, which was lined by the houses of the merchants; and as the town was intersected by numerous canals into which these vessels could be dragged, there was scarcely a merchant who did not have his own ships loading or unloading in front of his door, at which he could sit and look while taking his breakfast or dinner. Now, as many of the skippers and their sailors were right patriotic fellows, whatever their masters may have been, they generally carried two or three small guns in their vessel, and each man was armed with arquebuss and cutlass. When the

Spaniards in Amsterdam saw these arms, and asked what they were for, the skippers were bound to answer that they were bought as a protection against the pirates; and such, no doubt, was the case, for the North Sea and the Channel swarmed with the pirates of Dunkerque and Ostend. But when the Spaniards had turned their backs, and Heemskerk with his boy-comrades crept on board, the skipper, knowing them to be patriotic fellows, would tell quite another tale: how he had attacked a Spanish vessel in the Zuyder Zee, taken it, and sold it in the nearest port for the benefit of the Prince of Orange and the good cause; or how he had filled his vessel with bread and meat and cheese, and under cover of the night sailed into some town which was besieged by the Spaniards, the inhabitants being reduced to eat cats and dogs. And they would then hear of such horrible cruelties done by the foreign soldiers to their friends in other towns, that their blood would boil in their veins, and they promised each other to avenge these wrongs as soon as they were old enough to carry arms.

Nothing certain is known about the earlier years of Van Heemskerk; but we may be very sure that after he left school he would either become a soldier, in the army of the Prince of Orange, or, what was more likely, go to sea in one of the merchant vessels that sailed from Amsterdam. The first that we hear of him is in the year 1595, when he was twenty-seven years old, and went with an expedition to the North Pole. 'To the North Pole?' you will say. 'What in the world did he go there for? That surely is not a place for merchant-ships to go to.' I acknowledge that it was a queer place to go to, but it was a splendid expedition nevertheless. It came about in this wise. The Spanish King had gone from bad to worse. Seeing that he could not kill the little Dutchman, or get him out of his tub, he became most cruel and wicked. He sent into the country a strong army under the cruel Duke of Alva, who killed, and robbed, and imprisoned everybody who would not pay him great sums of money and go to the Roman Catholic Church. Then he sent a wretched man to the Prince of Orange, who had sold all his estates and his silver to help the country, and when that wretched man had murdered the prince, the king paid him 5,000*l.* as a reward, or would have done it had he not been seized and executed by the Dutch.

When that did not help him he took away all the Dutch ships he could find on the seas, or in the ports all over the world. This you may imagine was a great blow to the Dutch. There are no coal-mines, or iron-mines, or gold-mines in Holland as in other countries; and the people are, therefore, compelled to live by trade. Lying close to the sea, their ships could sail all over the world, and bring coffee, spices, silk, ivory, timber, and a host of other things to Amsterdam and other cities, where they were sold to the French, Germans, and Russians who came to Holland to buy them. Now these things had to be fetched from countries far away. From America, and Africa, from Italy, Turkey, Greece, and Egypt; but whenever the Dutch came close to Spain there was sure to be some great Spanish galleon, the crew of which quietly seized them, threw all the sailors overboard, and took the ship away. For some time the people of Holland were very despondent, for they feared they were all going to be ruined. Presently, however, some of them looked at the map, and rubbed their hands with delight. 'Why,' they said, 'we need not go past Spain to get to China or America. Look at this map. There is a large sea above Norway, where nobody has ever been yet. Now, there is no doubt that this sea goes somewhere; and if the earth is round, and we sail far enough, we must at last get out on the other side, and get that way to China and America. We will provide the ships. Who will go and try this new route?' They needed not to ask very long. There were plenty of men to risk their lives in this undertaking, for everybody felt that the existence of the country was at stake.

On the 2nd of July, 1595, a small fleet of seven vessels, the largest of which was only a cutter of one hundred tons, set sail from Texel for the Arctic regions, determined to find their way to China. The fleet was led by the 'Greyhound' of Amsterdam. The captain was William Barends, a most courageous and experienced seaman, and the super-cargo, or commissioner on behalf of the Amsterdam merchants, was our old friend Jacob van Heemskerk.

On the 19th of August they arrived safely in the

Straits of Waygatz, but the hopes which had inspired them seemed to sink at the sight of the land. They went on shore, but not a person was to be seen. There was nothing but snow and ice, glittering in the sun, and surrounding them on all sides. It floated on the water in thin sheets, it covered the land, it seemed even to fill the heavens. They had before landing seen some figures ashore, but when they approached the spot they found nothing but a few sledges, loaded with reindeer skins and leather bags full of oil—the owners having fled in terror. In order to allay the fears of the natives they left everything untouched, put some bread and cheese by the side of the sledges, and returned to their ships. This had the desired effect. Next day, when they went on shore, a whole party in sledges drawn by reindeer came to meet them, and, having got out, approached them with many smiles and curtsies, which betokened friendship. Happily there was amongst the crew one man who could speak the native language, and who put many questions to them. One amongst the Samoyedes, for that was the name of the people, told him of many countries and rivers, and described how, if they sailed far enough, they could get from a cold sea into a warm sea until they reached a new land. The savages, who were dressed in skins, received many presents, and they parted the best of friends.

This information was exactly what Heemskerk and his friends wanted, and they consequently returned to their ships in very high spirits, determined to make their way through this cold sea to a warmer climate. But next morning, what a disappointment! The sea was full of immense blocks of ice, as hard as steel, a dense fog prevented them from seeing each other, a strong wind began to blow, and they were at their wits' end which way to turn. For three days they tried their utmost to sail in the direction indicated by the Samoyedes, but the ice was too strong for them. On the 6th of September the sailors on Heemskerk's ship asked permission to land on the island they were passing, to gather some beautiful crystals; and about thirty of them set out in a boat for that purpose. Now these crystals were only to be found in the crevices and splits of the rock, wherefore it was necessary for the sailors to throw themselves down and insert their hands in the opening. While two of them were thus engaged, talking of home, and how pleasant it would be to sell the crystals for a large sum of money, one of them suddenly uttered a sharp cry. The other pulled his hand back out of the rock, and looked at his mate in astonishment, when to his horror he found him in the grasp of a terrific animal, twice as big as himself, whose powerful limbs were crushing his comrade to death. Half dead himself with fright, the sailor ran down the rock to where he had left his comrades, shouting to them all the while. Hearing the cries of their mate, the others ran towards him, wondering what could be the matter. Breathless with excitement and terror the poor fellow told his story, pointing at the same time towards the rock where he had lately been; and there sure enough a huge animal was doing something they could not make out. In an instant everybody was ready to go to the rescue. Some ran to the boat and got out the heavy oars, others seized the boat-hooks, others, again, had brought spears with them, some had swords, some axes, everybody was armed somehow, and eager to save their comrade. They divided in three groups, and approached the rock. As they drew nearer they saw with horror that the monster was sitting on his haunches, sucking the poor fellow's blood. They gave a yell. The bear looked up quietly, and, having eyed his enemies, went on with his occupation. This gave the party courage, and they approached from different sides. Suddenly the bear jumped up. He was a gigantic animal, and his jaws when he opened them were full of strong teeth. He uttered a low growl, and ran towards the strongest party. A panic seized them, and they fled towards the boat. The others followed, trying to attack the bear; but he suddenly turned round, and rushed at them, growling all the time. They too were seized with fear, and bolted for the ship, while the third party, who were now left alone, dodged him and got out of his way as well as they could. One of them, however, who could not run very fast, stumbled, fell, and before he could get up and escape the bear had seized him with his terrific claws, and killed him. The party returned to shore as soon as they could fetch their muskets, and managed to shoot the monster, after a combat of

HEEMSKERK'S SAILORS ATTACKED BY BEARS.

half-an-hour, when he was found to be larger than the largest ox, with terrific jaws and teeth. They skinned him, and took the hide to Amsterdam; but the death of the two poor fellows was always remembered with great sorrow. It may have been this untoward circumstance which determined them to give up the attempt for that year at least. At all events two days afterwards there was a council of war, and although both Barends and Heemskerk urged that two of the ships should remain for the winter, nobody seemed to like the notion; and what with the ice, the fogs, the bears, the tempests, and the coming winter, it was resolved to return to Amsterdam, whither they arrived in the end of October, bringing with them no Chinese tea or silks, but a bear-skin and a few bright crystals.

Although this result was certainly not very encouraging, Heemskerk and Barends were resolved that they would not allow the scheme to drop before they had made one more effort. Almost everybody was against them. The merchants said they did not like to lose their money and their ships. The States-General said they could not support the enterprise, there being so little chance of success; and the sailors said they did not care to go because they might be eaten up by the bears. During the winter Heemskerk, who had resolved to make another trial, went from one person to another, and spoke so hopefully and bravely that people began to have faith in the young and handsome captain, who was willing to leave his comfortable home and his friends for such an undertaking. The States-General were induced to promise that they would give two thousand pounds and some valuable privileges to the owners of the ships that could find the way to China. Some Amsterdam merchants fitted out two small ships, and William Barends, J. Ryp, and Heemskerk, who undertook to guide the expedition, now set about providing themselves with those things which they would require on a journey which they now knew must be exceedingly difficult and perhaps fatal. They bought a great quantity of salted meat and dried fish, three hundred barrels of flour and ships' biscuits, ten barrels of cheese, bacon, oil, wine, and also some parcels of broadcloth, velvet, and other manufactures, which they thought might be acceptable to the foreign people. It was somewhat difficult to find sailors, but Heemskerk was now so well known as a man of honour, piety, and knowledge that they at last succeeded in getting together a good crew. And a good crew it was beyond any doubt. A braver, hardier, or finer set of men I do not think ever trod the deck.

On the 10th of May, 1596, the two ships sailed from Amsterdam, accompanied by the prayers and blessings of their friends. The first three weeks presented nothing worthy of note. But during the night of the 1st of June, as Heemskerk was lying in bed, one of the men who had the watch on deck came softly into his cabin and called him.

'There's something the matter with the sun, sir.'

'With the sun!' exclaimed Heemskerk, rubbing his eyes; 'what can be the matter?'

'He won't go down, sir,' replied the man; 'it is past midnight, and he is still above the horizon!'

It was certainly very light in the cabin for midnight, and on going on deck there was the sun just peeping above the horizon, as if he would say, 'I'm looking at you.' From that day for six weeks they never had an hour's darkness.

Three days afterwards they saw something more startling still. It had been snowing slightly, so that at one time the sun was obscured. When the snow ceased everybody uttered an exclamation of surprise, for there, before them, they saw not one but three suns, several rainbows with the most gorgeous colours crossing each other round these, while the largest and actual sun looked as though he stood upside down. The men gazed at each other in astonishment, and thought they had reached some enchanted land, but Heemskerk, who was on deck, explained to them the mystery, so that, although they saw it more than once afterwards, they were no longer astonished at the sight.

The following day their ship was surrounded with ice; as far as their eyes could reach the water was covered with the white and glittering substance. From that moment it never left them for eight months; but as Heemskerk and Barends were prepared for it, they steered through it manfully, and braced themselves for the hard battle with the cold enemy which they knew they must now fight. Knowing exactly which way they had to go, they steered into the midst of it; but as they came more and more north, they began to perceive that their enemy was stronger than they had bargained for. The ice, which had hitherto been flaky and thin, became compact and firm. Towards the end of July the icebergs —vast mountains more than a hundred feet above and two hundred feet under the water—came sailing down upon them like immense giants, ready to crush their tiny vessel to pieces. At night, when the wind howled, and the small ice bumped against the side of the ship, when the large bergs creaked, and tore and split up with terrific and horrible sounds, and when the bears could be heard growling ashore, the poor sailors lay in their hammocks trembling with cold and fright, and wishing they were well out of it, and at home.

It was now the middle of August. They had already been away for three months, but they had not come one mile nearer the end they sought. The ice was increasing in size, the cold was becoming intense, they were frequently surrounded by a dense fog, and whenever they went on shore they had to fight with bears, until at last some of the men went to Heemskerk, and asked him respectfully to let them go home. To this he consented, but it was now too late. On the last day of August, early in the morning, they found that during the night the ice had come round them everywhere. They tried all they could to get away; they rowed, they tugged, they hoisted all their sails, but in vain. The huge masses of ice closed round them, the ship creaked and groaned, went first over on one side and then on the other, as though it would burst and split, and fall asunder. When evening came they were immovably fixed, with the ice for miles and miles around, and hundreds of miles from any human being to help them.

What was to be done? In this terrible hour everybody looked to Heemskerk and Barends. These noble men had worked as hard as the rest, directing the united efforts, running up the mast to get a better view, or flying from bow to stern to encourage the men; but it was all of no avail. The night was passed in anxious watching, the ice groaning and creaking and wedging closer. Part of the company had lugged the boats on to the ice with some barrels of biscuits and wine. Over these they were obliged to watch all night, and burn a large fire, as the bears were prowling round, ready to seize them all. Next morning their last hope died away. The ice had become like a rock, and the ship was not to be moved. There was nothing for it but to build a hut and pass the winter, until warmer weather should come and liberate the ships. To pass more than half a year in the company of bears without seeing any friends, or hearing any music save the creaking of the ice—to live in this glaring wilderness of whiteness, with no food but biscuits and salted meat, seemed indeed a horrible idea! But not a murmur was heard. Heemskerk cheered them up, and told them that it was God's will, and that it was now their duty to do the best under the circumstances. So they set about building their hut. Happily enough a couple of men who had gone inland reported that about two miles further on there were large quantities of fallen trees which they could use. With incredible labour and diligence they dragged these trees over four miles of rock, snow, and ice on rude sledges to their ship, and began to build their hut. It was made large enough for the whole party, with very thick walls and floor. An empty barrel was put on the top for a chimney, and the berths for sleeping were made as cosy as possible.

Heemskerk pointed out that it would be well to make some large space for their firewood inside the hut, as they might possibly be snowed in altogether for days. When the men heard this they looked at each other in blank amazement, but they acted on the suggestion, and it was well that they did so. Heemskerk also managed to turn their enemies the bears to some good use. These monsters were always lurking about the ship and hut, to seize any of the men unawares, so that they were all compelled to work with their arms lying beside them, ready to fly to each other's assistance. Hitherto they had merely killed the animals and preserved the hides, but as Heemskerk saw that the days would become very short and the nights very long, and that the oil

THE SLAUGHTER OF THE BEAR.

could not last for ever, he showed them how to preserve the bears' grease and use it for the lamps. When the men found out that these animals might be made useful, they went out in large parties and hunted them; and had on more than one occasion the most terrible fights.

It was now October, and the cold was becoming awful. Each man had to put on three or four suits of clothes and run about to keep himself warm. Half the ship had been broken up to cover the hut, and as it was now very evident that they would never be able to use the ship again, everything had been fetched out and put in the hut. They employed their time in making coats from the bear-skins and repairing their shoes, in setting traps for the foxes, and in playing at quoits and golf on the ice. But gradually the days became shorter and shorter, and on the 4th of November they woke up from their sleep, and enquiring of each other in the darkness what time it might be, found out that it was mid-day. One of them ran to the door, and opened it; but there was only just enough light to show him that the sun had not risen. It never rose again for eleven weeks, during all which time they were in perpetual darkness, and had to do their reading and work by lamp-light. There was one comfort in this—that the white bears remained away from that very day; but a tremendous storm buried their hut entirely under the snow, which was packed so closely that they were not able to dig an opening for several days.

During all that time they heard some peculiar scratching on the roof of their hut, as if animals were running over it, and on getting into the open at last, they saw a whole troop of white foxes running away across the snow.

You may easily imagine that the little party was as nearly miserable as they could be, and would have been wholly so but for Heemskerk and Barends. These two, knowing that laziness and want of occupation were the worst things possible, kept them continually at work, sawing wood, digging traps, mending clothes, hunting foxes, or even wrestling and racing with each other. They did not know night from day or day from night; there was a dim, unchangeable twilight for eleven weeks. Their watches had stopped, but they took great care to turn their sand-glass every half-hour, so as to note the time, and each day was dutifully marked off on the calendar. Thus came Christmas and New Year. The thoughts of the beloved ones at home made them all somewhat sad, for no one believed in his inmost heart that he would ever live through this terrible ordeal, and regain his fatherland. So there was no rejoicing on Christmas or New Year. The customary chapter of the Bible was read, and as they all lay in their berths, each had to tell a story until they fell asleep. But on Twelfth Day some of the men came up very respectfully to Heemskerk, and hoped that in all their sorrow he would allow them to be merry for one evening. Of course Heemskerk and Barends were very willing, so they lighted an additional lamp, soaked some biscuit in a little wine, took some of the paste they had taken with them to make cartridges, and baked a few pancakes. Then they wrote tickets and drew lots, and the boatswain, De Veer, was chosen King of Nova Zembla. He was put in a high seat at the head of the table, a paper crown was put on his head, and what with the warm wine and the pancakes, and the songs they sang, and the stories they told, they were as happy that night as if they were snug at home again.

They hoped that they had now seen the worst part of their misery; but they were mistaken. The cold became so intense that they could not keep themselves warm. The beer froze in the barrels and burst them. The immense wood fires could not keep them from shivering. When they put their feet before the flame their socks were singed, but the feet remained cold. The ice covered the walls of their hut and their very berths, an inch thick. Their shoes became so hard that they could not use them, and had to walk on wooden sandals. One evening, when it had become so cold that they were afraid they would all be dead in the morning, they made a large fire of coal in the grate, stopped up the chimney and the doors, and went to bed. This seemed to help them. A delicious warmth filled the hut. Everybody began to feel comfortable; they chatted together for many hours by the glow of the fire, and at last one by one turned over on one ear, and fell cosily asleep. Half an hour afterwards, Heemskerk awoke with a strange feeling in his head; he could scarcely breathe—his limbs were stiff. He called out, but nobody answered him; everything was silent as death. With difficulty he jumped out of bed, dragged himself to the door, pushed it open, and as the cold air rushed in, he fell senseless on the snow outside. Presently the cold awakened some of the others. They too felt horribly sick, and seeing the door open, ran outside. It was their preservation. The coal-damp had stupefied them all, and lulled them to sleep; had not Heemskerk opened the door, they must all have been suffocated. Although life was almost unbearable, this escape showed them that there was still some hope; and when they had all recovered with the aid of some wine, they earnestly thanked God for his mercy in allowing them to live.

Barends had made his calculations as to the reappearance of the sun, and concluded that they must wait at least another six weeks; but a fortnight after the above occurrence Heemskerk and some of the men had gone out to look at the fox-traps. Presently they came running back, breathless and beaming with joy. 'The sun, the sun!' they exclaimed. 'It can't be,' said the skipper, who was ill in bed; but the others ran out, and sure enough there was the harbinger of new hope. Everybody felt as though he had received new life. Tears were in their eyes, they pressed each other's hands with a new strength, and thought once more that they would see their friends at home. And yet there were many hard days in store for them. With the sun the bears returned also, and proved more ferocious than ever. The cold remained intense; their wood was all done, and they were forced either to burn the dangerous coal or go a long distance to fetch wood, fighting all the way with their enemies. When they got to the wood they were too weak to drag it along, and wept with disappointment; but returning next day they managed, with great difficulty, to procure a supply sufficient for three or four days. At last, after three months' anxious waiting, the weather became bright and warmer. The boats had been buried under the snow, and had to be dug out. A way had to be cut from the ship to the sea; the two small boats had to be fitted out for a perilous journey, and the men were all the time so weak that they could sometimes scarcely stand. Every man took his turn to occupy the barrel-chimney, and look out for bears; others patrolled about with muskets, and the rest worked. And thus, labouring steadily, they got their boats ready, and having hung up a short account of their adventures in the chimney, set sail for home on the 14th of June. After many curious adventures, which I may relate some other day, they arrived in the Meuse on the 29th of October. Barends and another man died in the boats on the journey. Of the sixteen who had set out only twelve landed in Delft, and when these appeared next day, dressed in their bearskin coats, their caps of fox-hides, and their wooden sandals, the whole of Amsterdam ran out to see those who had been lamented as dead long since. When it became known what they had gone through, the fame of Heemskerk and his brave men spread throughout Europe; for everybody was amazed that so small a company could have travelled and lived where no human being had ever gone before.

It is impossible for me to attempt anything like a full description of Heemskerk's life. I must therefore content myself, and endeavour to satisfy you, by describing as shortly as possible the last and greatest of his deeds. Seven years after his return from Nova Zembla, when he was in the prime of his manhood, and had become the most famous sea-captain of the republic, Heemskerk died for his country. He could not have done more. He might have done less, without weakening the gratitude of the nation, or losing the respect of his men; but he resembled those heroic Greek and Roman warriors, who, knowing that somebody must die for the common good, were proud to be the victims. During these years the enmity of Spain had become more and more fierce. In every possible manner that country attempted to oppress the inhabitants, to stamp out the liberties, and to ruin the commerce of the Netherlands. But the King of Spain had reckoned without his host. Such men as Heemskerk and Barends it was not easy to conquer, and now that war at sea was as practicable as on land, every captain who went to sea prepared himself to fight the Spaniards wherever he met them, not waiting to be attacked, but sailing up to them boldly, and pounding away at them until either they or he had to give in or fly. In many cases, of course, the Dutch vessels were defeated, and taken captive; for the Spanish ships were generally five or six times larger and splendidly fitted out for war, whereas the Dutch vessels were very small, and crammed full of cargo; so that there was but little room left for guns and ammunition. The Dutch, however, had one advantage: their ships, being so very much smaller, could be much more easily manœuvred; so that the little Dutchmen very often sailed round and round their opponents, pouring shot into them from all sides, while the heavy Spanish galleons lay like logs in the water. One of the results of this bravery of the Dutch seamen was that the natives of the strange countries to which they sailed began to like them for their courage, the more as they made it a sacred principle never to tell a falsehood or cheat, whatever they might gain by it for the moment. Another result was that the Spaniards became more furious than ever, maltreated and executed the Dutchmen whenever they caught them, and took away so many ships that the country was beginning to feel the losses very seriously. The Spanish fleet was accustomed to wait quietly in some small port until a large number of Dutch vessels, who knew nothing of their presence, were in the neighbourhood, when they would suddenly sail out, pounce upon them, and take them away.

In the beginning of 1607 the States-General resolved to aim a great blow at this practice, and a fleet of twenty-six vessels was equipped for the purpose of seeking the enemy and giving him a drubbing. It was the first war-fleet the young republic had ever sent out. The ships were all merchantmen with a double allowance of cannon. The captains and crew were picked out as the bravest from hundreds of ships that lay in the ports. There was the 'Æolus,' the 'Black Bear,' the 'White Bear,' the 'Gold Lion,' the 'Star,' the 'Tiger,' the 'Leopard,' and a host of other ships commanded by sturdy fellows. But who would command the fleet? Everybody turned to Heemskerk, and Heemskerk modestly accepted. But he would take no money. He refused a salary of five hundred pounds as admiral, being desirous to serve his country out of pure love; but after much pressing he consented that if the prizes he took amounted to more than forty thousand pounds he would accept as his share thirteen per cent. of the surplus. With this Heemskerk took leave of his friends, went on board the 'Æolus,' and sailed for Spain on the 25th of March. He had already been informed that the great Spanish fleet had run up the Tagus to Lisbon; so, when he arrived near the mouth of that river on the 10th of April, he sent one of his men in an English vessel to reconnoitre. The man returned presently with the intelligence that the great fleet had run out again, and was lying, true to its practice, like a spider in his web, somewhere about the Straits of Gibraltar, knowing that about this time of the year many Dutch vessels would be returning from Italy, Turkey, and Egypt. Here was a glorious chance. Exactly the thing they wanted. Immediately they steered for Gibraltar. On the 22nd, while they were sailing forward with a sharp look-out, they met a Dutch vessel which had just miraculously escaped the Spaniards, having sailed right into the midst of them during the night. This was splendid news; for they were now on the right track. Two nights more and they met a Frenchman, who told them that the fleet lay before Gibraltar, and was twenty-one vessels strong. Now the decisive time had come. Heemskerk sent for all the captains, and told them how things stood. Although he was perhaps the youngest of them all, his courage, his energy, his patriotism inspired them, and the eloquent words with which he addressed them stirred their hearts. He pointed out that the Dutch were by far the better sailors, and the more courageous, and that they had now an opportunity of doing what would gain them the gratitude and blessing of those at home, and the admiration of the whole world. Then he told them his plan of battle. They were to divide in pairs, and each pair was to steer alongside one of the Spaniards right and left, and pound him until there was nothing left to pound. Heemskerk had reserved for himself and Captain Lambert the admiral's ship, and promised to lead the attack. Having commended them to God, and urged them to uphold the honour of their country, he shook hands with them all round. Every one of them swore to obey his orders until death, and left the ship. Then the fleet sailed towards Gibraltar. Next morning, the 25th of April, the Spanish fleet appeared in sight, lying in a half-circle in front of the quay. Their position was magnificent. The quay of the city was armed, the castles on either side were bristling with guns, and the galleons of the Spaniards carried twice the number of cannon on the Dutch ships. Besides this they had prepared for the contest by crowding their ships with more than four thousand soldiers, and also manning one German, three Dutch, and four French vessels which they had captured. Notwithstanding all this the Dutch fleet came sailing on quietly, with Van Heemskerk in the van. The Spanish admiral, Don Juan Alvarez d'Avilla, on seeing this extraordinary approach, called one of the captured Dutch captains and asked him whether that little fleet actually meant to fight him.

'It looks like it,' answered the Dutchman.

'Why, this is absurd,' exclaimed the admiral; 'one of my galleons can lick the lot.'

'We'll see presently,' said the prisoner, and they did see.

The Dutch fleet came gliding into the bay like a flock of swans. On every ship the captain collected his men, and told them the order. He exhorted them to piety, as not many of them would come out of this deadly conflict. They all knelt down, and offered up a short prayer; a cup of wine was handed round for a farewell draught, and then the work began. In the most death-like silence Heemskerk's ship led the way. He himself stood on the upper deck, helmet on head, and in full harness. At his bold approach the Spanish admiral, who lay first, cut his anchor, and drifted behind the other ships nearer the town. The vice-admiral's ship then came first.

'Shall we attack him, sir?' asked the captain of the 'Æolus.'

'No,' said Heemskerk; 'follow the admiral. Do not fire a shot until you are alongside of him; do not drop your anchor until you hear it go 'crack;' and a hundred dollars for the man who fetches me down the flag.'

On he went, passing the vice-admiral on his left, and closely followed by Lambert. When the Spanish admiral saw that there was no help for it, he resolved to fight, and opened fire out of his two stern-pieces. The first shot went through the forecastle, and did but little damage. Then Heemskerk turned to his men, and gave the word to fire. At the same time the ships touched with a 'crack,' und the anchor dropped. Then the Spanish admiral fired his second stern-piece. The shot cut a young musketeer in two, and Heemskerk fell by his side. The blood streamed over the deck. His left leg was smashed, and he felt that death was near. Captain Verhoeff ran towards him, and threw himself on his knees by his dear friend's side. Van Heemskerk pressed his hand faintly, exhorted those around him to go on as they had begun, and obtain the victory at any price. He then commended his soul to God, and died.

At that moment the other ships had all reached their respective opponents, and the battle was raging everywhere. The whole were soon intermingled in deadly conflict, and enveloped in one vast and lurid cloud of sulphur. The earth trembled under the terrific cannonade. The very sea heaved in mighty billows when one of the largest Spanish galleons blew up with a terrific explosion, and flung the fragments a hundred feet into the air. The water was covered with the bodies of the dead, or the wounded who endeavoured to escape; the air was filled with the cries of war, and ship after ship of the Spaniards caught fire, and threw a terrible glare over the scene. Those who had begun so proudly now begged for mercy; but the Dutch were furious. They were fighting ten to one, and they would give no quarter. Their patience had long since been exhausted, and they must teach the tyrant their power. Ship after ship was blown up or burned. When the evening fell, the whole Spanish fleet had disappeared. The two admirals' ships, three galleons, one large man-of-war, and two foreign vessels had been burned; two galleons had been blown up, one was shot under water, and sank; two were chased ashore, and rendered useless. The admiral was killed, his son and fifty others taken prisoners; the vice-admiral, many officers, and two hundred men were wounded; and the dead—so the historian tells us—were so numerous that they could not be counted, but floated about the bay in numbers. The Dutch lost nearly a hundred killed, and fifty to sixty wounded, but not a single ship. When it was known that Heemskerk had fallen, the grief in the fleet was profound; for his courage, his piety, and his disinterestedness had inspired all. His body was immediately embalmed, and sent to Amsterdam on the following day by one of the ships. The city honoured him with a public and magnificent burial in the old church of Amsterdam. I have often stood before the tomb where his deeds are recorded, and I have felt that but for him, and men like him, Holland would never have been the free country it is; and I wish I could more thoroughly render the beauty of the words which the poet Hooft wrote under his name—

> Here lies a man of noblest courage and device,
> Heemskerk, who cut his way through iron and through ice.
> His fame is ours. His life, which he in gaining gave,
> Found in Gibraltar's bay its climax and its grave.

PIET HEIN.

It will, I hope, be remembered by my readers that in a previous memoir I related how the personal influence of the brave Heemskerk, and his determination not to think of death in the hour of greatest danger, so inspired all those around him with courage that they performed a feat, which, when done, was long looked upon as a wonder. I now come to a man whose name is perhaps still better known, although his services were not, and could not have been, more splendid. But Admiral Hein had the good fortune to fill the people's purses full of silver just when they had changed their last sixpence, and were looking very hard at the coppers. Indeed, the relief he thereby brought was so great that they made a song about him, and sing it to this very day. I remember the chorus, which I learned at school, 'Piet Hein, His name is small, His deeds are great, He conquered the silver fleet, Hurrah, Hurrah, He con-quer-ed the silver fleet!' And there was not a boy who did not know this chorus, and was ready to join in it at any time. If he could not sing, and the master happened to be out of the way, he waited till we came to the hurrah, and I never met a boy yet who couldn't do that part of the chorus to his own and I dare say to Piet Hein's satisfaction.

Hein was born in the year 1578 in Delfshaven, a small town on the right bank of the Meuse, not far from Rotterdam. His father was a herring-fisher, and poor. But not so very poor as you would imagine. For you must remember that trading was a very risky thing for the Dutch in those days. Flat-bottomed nutshells for ships; compasses, mathematical instruments, charts, and maps of a very faulty kind; unknown currents, savage people, Spanish men-of-war on one hand, pirates on the other, made it quite as probable that a ship would never come back at all as that it would bring home a cargo of treasures. Those who could not afford to lose much, but who were still fond of the sea, invested their money in fishing-boats or coasting-traders, which ran short journeys to the English or Irish coast, or to Dieppe, or to any other place that could be reached in a couple of days. And even that was not without danger. Most of the boats had two or three small cannon, and the crews were all armed to the teeth. They always sailed out in fleets of twelve or twenty, and seldom came back without some long yarn about fights with pirates. Many of the men would return with wounds and great gashes; and sometimes, too, the small fleet would come back with some of the boats missing, and the crews of the rest showing very long faces and solemn mien; and then it was pretty well known that those who had not come back had been made prisoners, and were now in some Spanish ship chained together like dogs.

But at other times the small fleet would come sailing up the river covered with flags, and dragging three or four strange vessels behind them. Then all the people of Delfshaven ran out to the quay, and clapped their hands and waved their handkerchiefs; for they all knew that these had been taken in fair fight. Then the vessels were sold to the highest bidder, and the money was fairly divided amongst the brave fellows; the burgomaster would slap them on the back and shake them by the hand, the Town Council gave them a dinner, the minister on the following Sunday would thank God for their safe return and their good fortuue; and altogether there was so much excitement that these herring-fishers felt themselves quite important, and would not have given up their work for any quiet, peaceable life in the world. I do not know whether old Hein, who was one of these, made much money. Perhaps he liked fighting best; but, at any rate, he earned enough to give his son a good education. But when young Piet grew into his teens, and saw other boys of his age go out with their fathers in the boats, and when he smelt the fresh sea-air, he could not, for the life of him, stop at home; so one fine summer morning, although his mother sobbed and begged him to stay, he was off with his father in the boat, and delighted to dance about on the green waves.

He is supposed to have been thirteen or fourteen at that time, but there is nothing known of him with any certainty in the history of the Netherlands until he was forty-four. He was probably a herring-fisher until he was thirty. Then came the magnificent victory of Heemskerk, and, as a consequence of that victory, a peace of twelve years with Spain. Have you ever seen a young retriever, chained up for a long time and suddenly let loose, bound and jump and race about, and bring his master all sorts of things? The Dutch were very much like this. The war had chained them. They could snarl, and bark, and they could bite too, as you know. But now they were free, and their ships bounded across the seas in all directions, and were soon to be seen in Turkey, Egypt, India, China, Japan, North America, Brazils, and the Cape of Good Hope.

Twenty years of herring-fishing and pirate-fighting had made our Piet Hein a bold and clever seaman, and he had saved some money. He got a larger ship somehow, and sailed to America as soon as the peace was signed. He made money by that, and got a larger ship still. During the twelve years of the peace he was prosperous, cautious, and brave, and he saved a good deal of money. But when the twelve years were over, and the fighting began again as hard as ever, Hein was one of the first to buckle to. He had no mercy for the Spaniards. While there was peace he had left them alone. But he had never forgotten that they had taken him and his father prisoner twice, that they had used them with abominable cruelty, and flogged him till his back was raw. So he was determined to have a fling at the Spaniards on his own hook. He fitted up his ship with the best guns he could buy, and sailed out of the Meuse. He was exceedingly fortunate. Nothing seemed to go wrong with him. One of the oldest books that mentions his name says, 'Time after time he fell into the hands of his enemies, who often pointed their swords and lances at his throat or heart; but, by his good fortune and his cleverness, he escaped all these dangers. Many volumes could be filled with his wonderful adventures, wherein water, wind, fire, and earth seemed to fight for him.' Another says, 'His name was like the drum of Zisca: wherever it was mentioned the Spaniards began to tremble, and it was sufficient to say that Piet Hein was coming to silence the crying children in the cradle.' This you must allow was no common reputation. He never sailed out but he brought home some valuable prize. He was afraid of nobody, and went back for no enemy; and although his courage was as yet only shown in small engagements, in which he engaged as a private trader, he displayed so much judgment and coolness, that people began to say it was a pity that he was not in the country's service.

Two years after the recommencement of the war Piet Hein was offered the post of vice-admiral of the fleet of the West Indian Company, which had been founded previously with a capital of 500,000*l.*, for the purpose of trading with the West Indies and South America. Hein accepted the honour, and sailed under Admiral Willekens from Texel on the 21st of December, 1623, with a fleet of twenty-six vessels. On starting nobody knew what was to be done; for the exact orders were contained in a sealed letter, which was not to be opened until they reached the Brazilian coast. On the 26th of March the following year the island of St. Vincent appeared in sight; but as all the ships had not yet arrived the Admiral determined to keep the letter sealed until the commander of the soldiers should have joined them, employing his time meanwhile in drilling and exercising his troops. After having waited for the commander until the end of April, the Admiral at last sent for all the captains to come on board his ship, and when they had all seated themselves round the table, the Admiral at the head and Hein at his right hand, the letter was solemnly unsealed and read. The orders were to sail as secretly as possible to the town of St. Salvador on the Brazilian coast, take it at any price, leave a strong garrison behind, and inflict as much injury upon the Spanish vessels as they were able. The very same night the plans were made; each captain received his orders, and after having solemnly promised each other to remain true till death, they shook hands all round, and went back to their ships.

St. Salvador, the capital of the Spanish settlement of Bahias, was known to be very strong; it was also known that a large fleet was anchored in the bay, and would help to defend the town. Nevertheless, without hesitation, they sailed on, determined to execute their orders. On the 4th of May, towards the evening, the Dutch fleet dropped anchor about nine miles from shore, so that they could not be perceived by the enemy. There happened to be two men on board who had visited the town before, and who were intimately acquainted with the situation. Like Gibraltar, the city was situated on the shore of a bay, and very powerfully constructed. It was built by the Spanish Governor of Bahias on the summit of a hill, which rose very abruptly to a height of several hundred feet from the sea. It was surrounded by a strong wall, and contained many magnificent houses and palaces. The business offices and warehouses were at the foot of the hill, where a spacious quay had been erected. Three fortresses on the summit commanded the bay, the quay was flanked by two stone redoubts, and within the last years the Governor had built a formidable battery on a rock in front of the quay, which, rising almost perpendicularly out of the water, was all but inaccessible. The council of war having been called together in the admiral's cabin, these things were drawn as correctly as their limited knowledge would permit. Then it was arranged that all the soldiers, about twelve hundred in number, should in the early morning go over to four of the largest vessels, one yacht, and seven sloops. These were to anchor at the entrance of the bay, and hold themselves in readiness to march towards the town at the right moment. The other ships were to sail straight on, and engage the enemy as best they could. Vice-Admiral Hein was to lead the attack.

Next morning at break of day the fleet commenced its movements. The soldiers were all sent over to the four ships, the decks were cleared for action, the guns looked to, the anchors weighed, and Piet Hein, with his ship 'Gelderland,' led the way into the bay. He had no sooner shown his white sails than he was greeted with a shower of bullets and shot from the six forts; but he sailed coolly onward without firing a gun. He saw at once that the fort which had been built on the rock was most strongly manned, and could do him the greatest damage. Round about it on both sides lay fifteen large Spanish vessels, all of them well filled with soldiers from the town. Hein sailed straight at them until he came within musket shot, and then he let them have it as hot as he could. Two other ships, the 'Groningen' and the 'Nassau' had followed him closely and were lying by his side; but the others, for some unexplained reason, remained behind and kept up a distant fire on the town. Against this superior force, then, Hein and his three ships had to contend. The fire was terrifying. From all sides the shot struck their rigging and sails and masts. The decks were covered with blood, but they advanced not an inch. For three long hours they fought, but not one of the enemy's ships had given in, and the captain of the 'Nassau' sent word that his ship was shot through. Hein was frantic with rage. If he received no reinforcement from the rest of the fleet he would be obliged to retire, but rather than retire he determined to risk a last chance.

'Boys,' he exclaimed, drawing his sword, 'we must get at them somehow. Follow me into the boats.' Three small boats were immediately filled with twenty men each, and rowed towards the Spanish galleons. It seemed the madness of despair, thus to advance against the formidable ships of war, amidst smoke and thunder, and a perfect hail of bullets. They reached the first vessels. The Dutchmen climbed up the rigging like cats and flew at the Spanish sailors, sword in one hand and axe in the other. The Spaniards, still with the memory of Gibraltar fresh upon them, were seized with terror. They fall on their knees and cry for mercy. They jump overboard, leaving their ships in the hands of the Dutchmen, and swimming towards the shore, they exclaim that they will all be blown up. In the meantime Piet Hein, with some of his men, had again jumped into his boat and rowed to the next ship. A panic now seized the whole Spanish fleet. Everybody jumped overboard or rowed to shore. Some set fire to their ships, others bored holes in the bottom. In the space of half-an-hour the Spaniards had lost their fifteen ships—seven were in flames, eight in the Vice-Admiral's hands—and the victory had been gained with less than a hundred men.

But now came the real tug of war. The sudden

'BOYS, FOLLOW ME INTO THE BOATS!'   *Page 12.*

defeat had enraged that part of the garrison of St. Salvador whose courage had not as yet given way, and from all sides a murderous fire was directed upon Hein and his small body of men. He had already sent to the admiral for reinforcements, and kept up the fire from his own ships incessantly; but he felt that he could not hold out much longer against the well-directed shots of the rock battery, and would have to retire. At last, through the dense cloud of smoke that surrounded him, he heard the welcome voices of the admiral's men, and fourteen crowded boats came pulling across the bay to his support. Now he felt ready for anything. He jumped into his own boat again, shouted out to the rest to follow, and led straight off to the rock fortress. It was a regular race between the seventeen boats who should get there first. The garrison of the fortress consisted of at least six hundred men. They were all standing on the walls well armed, and firing right and left into the boats; but when they saw the Dutch sailors coming straight at them, their courage sank into their shoes. Most of them climbed down from the walls and jumped into their boats, or began wading towards the shore, it being at that time low water. Piet Hein's boat reached the battery first. There was a strip of rock all round just broad enough for three men to stand side by side. The wall was nine feet high, and built of white and very slippery stone; but the vice-admiral and his men stopped at nothing. They all jumped on to the rock at once; one half of the men stooped with their hands on their knees, and the other half climbed on their backs. The trumpeter was on the top of the wall first, and blew the clear notes of the victory-signal across the water. Piet Hein was second, sword in hand, and then the whole lot followed like a rush of the sea itself across the wall inside the fortress, driving the Spaniards before them into the water, who were exposed to the fire from shore as well as from behind. At eight o'clock the fortress had been taken and the Dutch flag was waving from the wall, but it was open towards the town and afforded no shelter. The guns, it is true, were turned towards the enemy, but the falling dusk made a retreat necessary; the guns were spiked, the ammunition blown up or thrown into the sea, and when the night fell Piet Hein and his men had returned to their fleet, with the intention of following up their conquest in the morning.

It may be imagined that a very sharp watch was kept during the night, for, lying with his fleet close to the quay, and not far from the burning remains of the seven Spanish ships, Hein did not know what tricks the enemy might not play upon him. His situation was rendered more difficult by his receiving no communication from the admiral, who had remained at the entrance of the bay with the rest of the fleet. You may judge his surprise next morning, therefore, when on rowing cautiously to the quay he was challenged in right good Dutch, and found the lower part of the town, with all its warehouses and magazines, quietly occupied by the Admiral and his twelve hundred soldiers. When they had seen the Spanish ships in flames, they had judged it time to do their part of the business, and it was well that they did, for they marched into the place without meeting a soul.

'Well,' said Piet Hein, 'if they have run away from here, perhaps they have left the town too. Suppose we go up and try the gate.'

The admiral was just about to make the same proposition. Led by the two sailors whom I mentioned before, the small army marched up a narrow street without meeting a soldier. They had taken a couple of small cannon to batter the gate; but when they arrived at the ditch a man looked over the wall with a white flag, politely opened the gate, let down the bridge, and requested them to walk in. The Dutch admiral was at first afraid of some treachery and marched in with loaded muskets and ready for action; but the town was deserted. . Every soldier had fled to the woods. Most of the inhabitants were trembling in-doors or had followed the soldiers. The only men left behind were the Spanish Governor de Furtado and his son, who, being ashamed of the cowardly conduct of their fellow-countrymen, met the conquerors in the market-place and were immediately taken prisoners. And now the soldiers and sailors, who were brave men, but rough and fond of riot, could be held no longer. They spread all over the town, entered every house and shop, broke open the churches, stripped the altars, robbed every valuable thing they could lay their hands on, and committed many disgraceful acts of violence. These, however, it is not my business to describe, the more because Admiral Hein had nothing to do with them. He was greatly opposed to them and highly indignant; but the armies and navies were then so constituted that plunder was to the soldier part of his pay, and the Vice-Admiral as well as the Admiral were powerless. Piet Hein, however, managed to return home with his ships almost immediately, after a strong garrison had been left behind in St. Salvador, and many prisoners being taken away to Amsterdam. When it became known that so small a fleet, with not much more than a thousand men on board, had utterly destroyed a Spanish fleet, taken a strong town, the capital of the colony, the private property of the king, the residence of a governor, two judges, and several bishops, and provided with a garrison of nearly two thousand men, and that they had brought home, as tokens of their victory, eight ships laden with several thousand chests and barrels of sugar, wines, oil, and spices, I need not tell you that their reception in the fatherland was uncommonly warm and cordial, and that many a goblet was emptied to the health of the brave Piet Hein, who had done the best part of the work.

But he had not done with St. Salvador yet. That bay was destined to witness a still more extraordinary deed of bravery. For nearly a year the town remained in possession of the Dutch; but the commanding officer dying, and there being no one of sufficient authority to maintain order amongst the garrison, who were the wildest of the wild, they speedily degenerated into a lawless mob, and when, in the following year, Spain sent an overwhelming force and a large fleet, the city was easily retaken after a feeble defence, and the Dutch garrison killed or thrown in prison.

Hein, in the meanwhile, had been raised to the rank of Admiral, and was again out at sea with a fleet of nine large men-of-war and five yachts. He became a veritable terror to the enemy. He had given up trading altogether, and turned warrior; not a chance escaped him, not a Spanish flag passed him that was not pursued and captured. In the year 1626 he received orders to join the fleet of Admiral Boudewyn, who was supposed to be lying somewhere in the neighbourhood of Guadaloupe; and he was expressly told that the West Indian Company expected him to attack the Spanish fleet, which was known to sail about that time every year with a cargo of silver and gold, and was popularly known as 'the silver fleet.' This was exactly the thing Piet Hein wanted, and he sailed out with a joyous heart. But when he reached the appointed latitude no fleet was to be seen or heard of, and, although he lingered about for a considerable time, not another Dutch or Spanish ship did he see, for the very simple reason that, Admiral Boudewyn having died, the Dutch fleet returned home, and the silver fleet, knowing that he was coming one way, had gone home by the other. Then the Admiral lost his temper, and swore. I do not mean that he used bad language, for he was a very pious man; but he swore solemnly that he would not go home until he had destroyed another Spanish fleet.

On the 6th of September, as they were sailing slowly along, the most advanced ship signalled that a Spanish fleet appeared in sight. The Admiral rubbed his hands with delight. That must be the silver fleet; it could be no other. The captains of the other ships were immediately sent for, that no time might be lost; and the Admiral was already going about on his own ship, inspecting every part of it, so that nothing might be wanting. He found for once, however, that his captains were not of the same mind.

'We must attack them to-day,' said the Admiral, when they were all in his cabin. 'They may be gone to-morrow.'

'It is impossible, sir,' said the vice-admiral. 'Do you know how many ships the enemy has?'

'No, I don't know, and I don't care,' answered Hein, who was getting impatient.

'There are forty large ships, sir, and we have only nine that can offer battle; it would be four to one.'

Hein said not a word in reply, for, although he was exceedingly wroth, he would not expose his fleet to so great a risk without the consent of his captains. So he silently bit the points of his moustache, and let the rich prize escape him for the moment.

You may imagine what a bad temper he was in as regards the Spaniards, when he had knocked about the West Indies for seven months without doing anything of importance. But there was a good time coming for him, and, as you will presently see, he made an excellent use of it. The long period of suspense had raised the expectation and anxiety of every man in the fleet to its highest pitch. They were tired of doing nothing, and it had happened on more than one occasion that on going ashore on some island for the purpose of trading, parties of his men —forty, and even sixty, strong—were treacherously surrounded by hundreds of savages and killed. On the 1st of March, 1627, the fleet once more approached the Bay of St. Salvador. Piet Hein knew that it had fallen again into Spanish hands, and his desire to show himself before the city a second time grew upon him. He was informed that a large Spanish fleet lay inside the bay, and he determined to attack it, come what would. He would listen to no sage counsels from his captains this time, but having sternly given the order that they should follow him, he led the way, as before, into the bay, and straight up towards the rock fortress. It was almost a dead calm, and it required all the skill and experience of the navigators to enter the bay and approach the town. The sea had at that moment run out. The bay was extremely shallow, and there was nothing but a narrow channel, through which only one ship at a time could tack about. The array of the enemy's forces, on the other hand, might well have appalled a bolder man than Hein. Taught by their former defeat, the Spaniards had considerably strengthened their works of defence. Thirty large vessels, armed with cannon and manned with troops, lay in front of the quay, protected by the guns of the forts, and drawn up in order of battle. But the Admiral had given the order, and he knew no hesitation. Notwithstanding the calm, notwithstanding the superiority of the enemy, notwithstanding the heavy fire that greeted him once more from all sides, he sailed straight on until he found himself between the Spanish admiral on one side and the vice-admiral on the other. Then he dropped his anchor, and at the same moment every timber in the ship trembled and shook as his thirty-six guns poured their grape-shot and shell into the enemy. Two other ships, the 'Gelderland' and the 'Holland,' had followed him closely, with certain death staring them in the face, and following the example of their Admiral, anchored right in the midst of the enemy's fleet, and pounded away as hard as they could, without pausing to ascertain whether they were supported.

From what follows I can only come to one of two conclusions, that every Spaniard in the fleet or in the town was suddenly struck with a fit, and unable to move, or that they had degenerated into the most contemptible cowards which it is possible to conceive.

Whichever alternative we assume, the result remains sufficiently wonderful. The Admiral, lying right amongst the enemy, had evidently no other prospect than to die in the midst of his foes. He looked at nothing. His ship was surrounded by a dense volume of smoke. Shot after shot from his guns struck the enemy with fearful effect; but he saw it not. They hauled down their flags in token of unconditional surrender; but the smoke made them invisible. The terrific flash of his guns sent death and destruction amongst them. He drifted alongside the Spanish vice-admiral, and immediately gave him a broadside. The Spanish ship rocked violently, the hulk was torn up by the crashing iron, the sea rushed in with uncontrollable violence, and in the midst of the continual thunder she went down so rapidly that three men of the crew could be saved with difficulty. The other ten ships had, in the meantime, managed to come up, and mingled in the fight; but the work of destruction was getting too slow for Piet Hein. He took to his boats, as on the former occasion.

With an audacity which is not altogether commendable, he rowed to the admiral's ship. The agility of the Dutch sailors took the Spaniards by surprise. Before they could arrange their defence, the deck swarmed with Hollanders, who rushed upon them with irresistible force. The Spanish flag was torn down, and amidst a deafening cheer the flag of the Seven Provinces hoisted instead. From ship to ship they flew with an almost incredible fury, and ship after ship was abandoned by the Spaniards. The water between the fleet and the quay was covered with swimming fugitives. The gunners of the different fortresses no longer knew whom to aim at; the Republic's flag was mingled with their own, and guns which had hitherto supported them remained silent. On the quay the people were seized with an extraordinary panic. They saw a terrific vengeance rising before their eyes. The Dutch were irresistible demons whom nothing could oppose, and they already imagined them approaching the city in all directions, to inflict upon it once more the horrors of a sack. But the Admiral was wise. He fought against the fleet, and against the fleet alone. After three hours of the most terrific fighting he gave the order to retire. Then twenty-two Spanish vessels were dragged out of that bay, within sight of the royal governor, while the admiral and his men stood on shore with their wet clothes clinging to their shaking limbs. And yet so difficult was it to get out of the bay that several of the ships ran aground, and had to be got afloat amidst the fire from the town. The Admiral's ship was one of them; but it was no longer a ship. The masts had been shot away; the helm was gone; the water poured in on all sides. All efforts to get it afloat failed. While they were tugging at it, Piet Hein received two bullet-wounds from shore. Another ship received a shot in its powder magazine, and blew up. It was then resolved to abandon the Admiral's ship. The contents were transferred to other vessels, the guns spiked, the hulk set fire to, and thus Piet Hein took his leave of St. Salvador. In triumph he sailed with his twenty-two captured vessels along the whole Brazilian coast. Then the valuable cargo was packed in the four best; the others were burned, and after having waited about in that latitude for some days, lest a second fleet might perhaps come to avenge the first, Piet Hein returned home, and was received with gratitude by the States-General and the people.

I now come to the deed which made him most celebrated, although it was not his greatest.

I told you in the beginning of this article that I remember a song at school of Piet Hein and his silver fleet. This, then, is the story of his capture of that fleet. You must know that, notwithstanding this and other victories, the Seven United Provinces, fighting against Spain, were in a very bad way. They had lost all their money. Disasters at sea, the pirates of Dunkerque and Ostend, and the war together, were more than their pockets could bear. The States-General did not know what to do. The soldiers were clamouring for money, and threatening to run over to the enemy if they did not receive their wage. Two of the provinces had not paid their share of the taxes for more than a year, and said they were beggared. The captains of vessels in the rivers complained that they had not received any money for years. The members of the Amsterdam Board of Admiralty were asked in the public streets why they did not pay their debts. In Rotterdam the members of the Admiralty Board were surrounded by a furious mob, and threatened with violence if they did not pay; but they had nothing, poor men! and they were as sorry as the rest. A body of sailors went from Rotterdam to the Hague, and put themselves in front of the hall where the Dutch Parliament was sitting, and asked each of the members for money. The members shrugged their shoulders, for they had none to give. The country had to borrow money at eighteen per cent.; and yet every town cried out when a new tax was imposed.

One evening, the 16th of November, 1628, when the States-General were again sitting in the Council Chamber of the Hague, in anxious consultation, they heard a strange rumour outside. Several members ran to the windows, and looked out on the court below. A crowd of people were, as usual, awaiting their decision; but now they seemed to be stirred by a strange feeling. Presently the President's servant entered the room with the news that some one had arrived with an important message from the fleet. The messenger was immediately ordered to be admitted, and when he came, it was seen by his face that he was the bringer of good tidings. And indeed he told them that an advice-yacht had just run into Rotterdam with the news that Admiral Hein had captured the whole of the silver fleet without the loss of one man, and that the value of the prizes amounted to more than one million sterling, or twelve million guilders. The councillors could scarcely believe their ears; but when next day the skipper of the yacht appeared before them in person, and they read Hein's writing, they were forced to believe the glorious news, and immediately made it known to the people. What joy there was in every family I need not tell you; for it was a national blessing, just when it was most wanted, and during the five weeks that elapsed before the richly-laden fleet ran into the Dutch ports, the whole country was anxiously looking out for them, and greatly afraid lest the prize should be lost on the way home. We, however, need not wait so long, and may hear all about it at once.

When Hein had returned from Salvador, and received his share of the prizes, he thought it was a pity to let matters rest, and sailed out again almost immediately afterwards, in May, 1628, his fleet having been augmented to thirty-one ships. He was determined to catch the rich Spanish fleet this time, and sailed straight for Havana. Adverse winds, however, compelled him to drift towards the Bay of Matanza, about sixty miles to the east of Havana, not knowing that what he sought was exactly to be found in that direction. Indeed, the silver fleet had also left the port of Havana, and was on its way home, when one of the largest vessels sprung a leak, and the whole fleet had to wait until it was unloaded, overhauled, and repaired. To this circumstance, probably, they owed their loss. The Spanish Governor of Havana, seeing the Dutch fleet, felt at once that the only safety lay in escape. He therefore sent a quick yacht towards evening to apprise the silver fleet of the danger. The yacht never reached its destination. It knocked about the sea for six days, and at last fell into Hein's hands. The Dutch admiral read the letter of advice, and cordially thanked the Governor of Havana for his information. He now knew that the fleet was somewhere in the neighbourhood.

Presently something else happened. On the night of the 8th of September, Captain Janson, of the 'White Lion,' was walking on deck, when he saw a ship coming close to him. Thinking that it was one of his fleet, he cried out through his trumpet that he should take care and port his helm, to avoid collision. Those on the other ship, however, understood not a word, but cried back, *Que quiereis? Que quiereis?* Janson's sailors, on hearing this, clapped their hands with joy. 'They are chaw-bacons,' they exclaimed, this being the vulgar name for the Spaniards; 'for the language they speak is Spanish.' Captain Janson immediately sent a shot into them, the sailors jumped into the boats, and before the poor Spaniards knew what they were at, their ship had been taken, and they were prisoners. There was nothing valuable in the ship; but the papers and the confessions of her crew showed them quite plainly that she belonged to the silver fleet, and had only drifted away in the latter part of the evening. Consequently, the fleet itself could not be many miles distant. This intelligence was sent to Admiral Hein, and you may be sure that he rubbed his hands with delight.

Next morning at break of day every masthead was crowded with sailors on the look-out, as they sailed quietly onwards towards Matanza. 'A sail—two—three—half-a-dozen—ten,' rings in quick succession from one ship to another. Being the swifter sailers, they approached. At the firing of shot, the Spanish flag was hauled down, and nine ships, surrounded by Dutch sloops, surrendered at discretion. But fancy their disappointment when they found their prizes empty, and themselves as far off the expected silver fleet as ever. The masts fill again with sailors; the hunt is continued. Towards noon there was another cry of 'A sail,' and the large hulls of the Spanish galleons appeared on the far horizon. Now commenced the chase. Piet Hein knew that the Bay of Matanza was not far off, and that the enemy was making for it. He therefore spread his fleet out like a fan, and approached his prey. The Spaniards, on the other hand, knew that there was but little chance of escape in open sea, and ran close under shore where they knew the exact soundings, and so tried to creep into the bay. Piet Hein, on seeing this, resolved to cut them off, relying on the swiftness of his ships. Every sail was crowded on to the yards, the fire-pump was brought up, and the sails wetted constantly, but it was of no avail. The Spaniards were too sly for him. They knew their ground too well, and could go where he dared not follow, for fear of running aground. When the dusk fell they had all entered the bay, and the Dutch fleet lay outside, like a pack of hounds that have missed the fox. Several sloops were now sent out to reconnoitre, and they returned with the news that in their hurry and fright the Spaniards had all run aground, and were carrying their valuables and personal property ashore. When Piet Hein heard this he laughed. 'Let them carry,' he said. 'They can't carry it all away in one night, and we'll get the rest to-morrow.'

Scarcely had the rising sun made the objects around dimly visible, when everybody in the Dutch fleet was astir. There was a hard day's work before them. The Spanish ships were splendidly equipped and fully armed; the enormous treasures which they carried on board would not be surrendered without a desperate defence. Every sailor on board had been forced to swear with a great oath that he would defend the cargo with his life, and had taken the sacrament on his promise rather to throw the treasures overboard and burn the ships than allow them to fall into the enemy's hands; and Piet Hein consequently expected a severe battle. Nevertheless, according to his custom, he led the way, followed by the 'Stork,' the 'Falcon,' and the rest of the fleet. At nine o'clock they entered the bay, and beheld the Spanish fleet before them, fixed immovably in the shallow water. This made our Admiral somewhat cautious, for he had no wish to get aground himself, and the complete silence of the Spaniards roused his suspicions whether they had laid some artful snare, which might destroy him unawares. While he signalled his directions to the other ships, the boat of the vice-admiral came alongside of him.

'Come along, Admiral,' he cries from below. 'They haven't got any fight in them. Let us take them with the boats.'

Piet Hein, believing this to be the best plan, jumped into the boat. The example was followed by all the others. The anchors were dropped, and a moment afterwards the surface of the bay swarmed with boats. The first which reached the Spanish admiral was that of Captain Juinbol. The enemy, on his approach, showed fight, and fired off two of their guns, but Juinbol sent them two volleys of musketry in answer, and on summoning them to surrender, he was answered with a 'Yes.' The Admiral's boat at that moment glided alongside. One of the sailors, ambitious to be first, seized a rope, and pulled himself on deck like a cat. The Spanish crew stood by without moving a limb; they did not even attempt to hinder him when with his axe he cut down some of the rigging, and threw it to those below. In a few moments the Dutch were on board, and the Spanish admiral surrendered himself and his fleet. They were treated with but little ceremony; half-an-hour was allowed them to pack their things, they received four days' provisions, and ere another hour was passed, they were all rowed ashore, with permission to go to Havana if they liked.

Thus, without the shedding of one drop of blood, there was captured the richest prize that has ever, perhaps, been known in the history of the world. The wealth was almost uncountable. In one ship, for instance, they found thirty thousand pounds of bar-silver, thirty-one pounds of pure gold, eighty gold chains and cups, a thousand valuable pearls, and an immense number of valuable hides. The silver alone amounted to two hundred thousand pounds in weight, and the value of the metals was correctly estimated at one million sterling. As a curious circumstance I may relate that, while they were counting the money in the cabin, the Spanish admiral's parrot, hearing the chink of the money, flapped his wings, and cried out, *Victoria, victoria! O que bien va!* Which means 'Hurrah, hurrah! How fortunate we are!' which he had probably heard his Spanish master utter very often when he counted over his treasures.

The voyage home was immediately commenced, and executed with all caution. The fleet kept close together, so as to be ready against any enemy. The anxiety at home was tremendous. It was known that the Dunkerque pirates had already sent out a large fleet to waylay Piet Hein. The Dutch Governor of Sluis sent word to the States that Spinola the Spanish governor was fitting out a great number of ships in Antwerp, and it was rumoured that a fleet of sixty large men-of-war had run out of Spain to reconquer the lost treasure. It was even said that the English would take the money away, for you will remember that just at that time the English fleet had come back from the expedition to La Rochelle with bloody heads, and were very angry with everybody all round. But the English behaved admirably on that occasion. Piet Hein, having cleverly eluded all his enemies, was obliged to take shelter from a hurricane in Portsmouth harbour. When it became known what cargo the fleet had on board, there was naturally a great deal of excitement in England. 'The whole of London,' says the Ambassador Joachim, in a letter to the States, 'ran empty of bad people, who wanted to make the Dutchmen's heavy pockets a little lighter.' The Custom-House officers had a great many objections to make, and said something about duty having to be paid. The Government even made some difficulties, and at last offered four men-of-war as a safeguard. But Piet Hein declined all these things politely but firmly, and having sailed away, after many professions of gratitude, ran safely into Goree about the end of December, 1628.

Piet Hein's reception was magnificent. Bonfires were lighted all over the country. Wherever he came he was received as a foreign prince and not as a simple citizen. He would have none of these honours, for he remained the same humble man as of yore; but the honours were thrust upon him. 'See,' he said, when he was received in the Hague with a triumphal procession, and had to dine with the Prince of Orange and the King of Bohemia—'see how the people run mad now, because I bring home such treasures, for which I have done but little. When I fought for them before and risked my life, they never turned round to look at me.' There was a very good reason for this excessive joy on the part of the people, however, for they now felt that poverty was at an end, and that the war could be continued with the enemy's money. Piet Hein found it out too, for he received a goodly share of the booty, and bought himself a nice little house and garden in Delft. He was moreover publicly thanked by the States-General sitting solemnly in council. He and the other heads of the fleet under him were presented with heavy gold chains and medals, which were hung round them by the Secretary, while, by express order, their portraits were beautifully painted on satin and presented to each of the members.

Having now reached the age of fifty, and having saved a very considerable sum of money, Piet Hein was naturally anxious to have done with roving about, and retired to his nice little house at Delft, where he thought to live in comfort with his wife and friends. But it was not to be. The country could not do without him. In April of the following year he was called upon to go out on an expedition against the pirates of Dunkerque. He refused. The States offered him a large salary, but he answered that he had quite enough. Then they pointed to the awful damage which was being done, and the inability of anyone else to subdue the pirates. He hesitated, and said younger men ought to try now. Then they offered to make him admiral-in-chief and lieutenant-general of Holland. The big titles were too much for him, and he accepted. In May, 1629, he sailed out on a reconnoitring expedition all by himself, and on the 20th of the following month was met by three pirate vessels. With his usual impetuosity he went at them, when a cannon-ball cut him in half, and he fell lifeless on the deck of his vessel. The pirates were taken and all thrown overboard in revenge; but Piet Hein had gone for ever. His body was publicly buried in the old church of Amsterdam, not far from that of Heemskerk; but his name lives in the memory of the people to this day.

MARTEN HARPERTS TROMP.

PART I.

NEVER heard his name before? I can scarcely believe that. If you have read any history at all, if you have been passably interested in the doings of our forefathers, if you possess any admiration for those who have made that history something more than the dull record of machine-like labour, you must have heard of Admiral Tromp, or Van Trump, as the English writers of that period delight to call him. He was a man who threw his whole soul into his business, who was brave enough to be prudent, honest enough to be independent, and who so fulfilled each duty that he could afford to bear with patience unmerited rebuke; who gained the highest position without losing his simplicity or candour, and who stood out like the Eddystone rock at sea, a trusty friend and beacon to those whom he served, but a deadly enemy to those who went against him.

Tromp was born of a sea-going family. His grandfather was a coasting trader, and his father, whose house was at Brill, at the mouth of the Meuse, took him to sea in his own ship when he was scarcely nine years old. This was in the year 1606. In the following year, it will be remembered, Van Heemskerk sailed with his expedition to Gibraltar, and destroyed the Spanish fleet. Tromp's father took part in that expedition; and although he must have known that he was running great danger, he resolved to take his boy with him, the more as Marten was very fond of his father, and delighted to go. It is probable that, young though he was, he had already witnessed several small fights at sea, and was therefore somewhat accustomed to the noise. But the terrific uproar of that battle of Gibraltar went beyond him. Before the commencement his father told him to remain in the cabin, and the boy obeyed, although trembling with excitement. But when the cannons began to thunder, when the ship creaked and trembled in every plank, when she rolled and rocked about, and groaned like a living being, when the cabin became full of sulphurous smoke, when the windows broke, the door flew open, the sailors began to shout on deck, and fire as fast as they were able, Marten could stand it no longer in the solitary cabin. He flew on deck towards his father. At that very moment he saw him sink, covered with blood. A bullet had wounded him to death, and Marten came but in time to throw himself on the lifeless body, and cover the pale face with kisses. But it was too late. When Marten saw this, a fierce spirit took possession of him. His face was still wet with tears, but his eyes were flaming with anger, and his voice no longer wept. He ran to the first officer, and, pointing to the Spanish vessel with which they were engaged, he exclaimed, 'Will you not revenge my father's death?' The sailors had been somewhat disheartened by their captain's fall, but these words of the resolute boy revived their courage. They went at it again with a hearty will, boarded the Spanish vessel, and destroyed her.

Having made such a beginning, it will perhaps astonish you that young Tromp remained in the navy. Many men would not have cared to continue in a profession or business the earlier recollections of which had been so melancholy; but for Tromp the very danger had an attraction, and I almost believe that his blood was mixed with sea-water. He was an orphan, and poor. He knew something of the sea, he knew nothing of land business, and therefore he became a sailor. At any rate, we read nothing about his earlier years but that he climbed up gradually from the very lowest post, and it is generally supposed that after the death of his father he began his career on one of the ships as cabin-boy. What happened to him in those days we do not know. That he felt very lonely at times, and often wetted his bread with tears, that he had to work very hard, and was treated with roughness and severity, we may take for granted. But the little fellow stuck to his work, and, although he was not aware of it at the time, he gained a knowledge of every minute detail in the sailor's life that stood him in good stead afterwards.

In 1622, when he was twenty-five, he was promoted to the rank of lieutenant, and two years afterwards the Stadtholder Prince Maurice made him captain of a frigate. He was now to some extent his own master. He was on the road to fame and fortune; it was but seldom that anyone had attained so important a position at so early an age, and it lay with him whether he would imitate the example of those around him and be content to remain a captain, or rise to something higher. For most of his friends had displayed, up to this point of their career, a diligence and industry equal to his own; but to them this position was a limit, to him it was only a beginning. When they had gained the command of a vessel their ambition was satisfied, their studies were abandoned, their books and mathematical instruments were put on the shelf, and they read no more than was sufficient to maintain them in their acquired position.

With Tromp it was different. To him work of any kind came natural. Of a somewhat reserved and modest disposition, exacting in the matter of duty, but kindly withal and cordial, Tromp felt that he had a head upon his shoulders. He felt that where his comrades had done much he could do much more, and he did more. He studied every branch of his profession, he paid the most careful attention to matters that were generally regarded as mere details, and personally convinced himself that his orders were strictly executed. He served at one time under Hein, at another under Willekens, and again under Dorp, and each of these admirals was obliged to confess that young Tromp was a rising man, and that there was something more in him than a mere captain. Indeed, between Hein and Tromp there seems to have been a warm friendship. Tromp never mentioned the admiral's name without expressing great admiration for his genius, and gratitude for his love; while Hein on his part affirmed, shortly before his death, that, although he had known many brave captains, he had always found their virtues modified by faults, but that he could find no fault in Tromp, who possessed all that was required in a naval commander. Their friendship was not of very long duration. In 1629, when Hein set out on his expedition against the Dunkerque pirates, Tromp's ship belonged to the small fleet. As it was the fastest sailer, Hein selected it for the fatal reconnoitre. They were standing side by side on the deck, giving their directions during the fight which followed, when Hein was mortally wounded in the shoulder, and breathed his last in his friend's arms.

It was not long after this painful event that Tromp began to utter the opinion that the organisation of the navy left a great deal to be desired, that the discipline on board the ships was open to much improvement, and that on the whole a thorough change in the management would be desirable and even necessary. He had long been aware of this—he had not studied his profession so thoroughly for nothing—and there had probably been many a long talk on this subject between him and Hein. But, although he was at liberty to think what he liked, the old fogies of the Admiralty at Amsterdam or in Rotterdam were highly indignant when he said anything. They blew out their cheeks, and looked at each other over their spectacles, and shook their heads, and the longer they shook, the angrier they got. Could anything be wrong that was administered by them? Was a young man like this Marten Tromp to pick holes in a coat that had been considered very decent for them and their fathers for the last thirty years? They determined to give Captain Tromp a lesson. They pooh-poohed his suggestions, and when the time came that he should be again appointed to his ship, he found that it had been given to somebody else, and that he was put in a subordinate position. As this, of course, was as much as to say, 'We dont want you,' Captain Tromp quietly sent them back his commission with his compliments, and he would prefer to remain on shore for a few years, saying, at the same time, in a very respectful manner, that they had better take care, for that his words would come true sooner or later, and that they would be forced to do in a hurry what he suggested might be done at leisure. At the same time, being already highly thought of by some of his friends, he accepted a post in some marine office in Flushing, and bided his time.

He had not been on shore many years, when the wisdom of his words could no longer be denied. The Dutch Republic was still at war with Spain, and although that war was now carried on in a very irregular and fitful fashion, it was always the endeavour of each commander to injure, and if possible to destroy, the Spanish forces at sea. But the good fortune of Heemskerk and Hein seemed to have passed away. One undertaking after another failed. Chance after chance was allowed to slip away through mere carelessness. The evils which Tromp had predicted increased. The discipline on board the ships was neglected; the untiring zeal of former days no longer inspired each man. In 1637 a squadron was sent out under Van Dorp to capture a large Spanish fleet which was expected in Dunkerque; but when he was out at sea Van Dorp discovered that he had neither food, nor powder, nor shot. He was forced to return home; but scarcely had he run into the Meuse, when news came overland that the Spanish ships, loaded up to the port-holes with valuable cargo, had just slipped into Dunkerque, and might easily have been captured; that the pirates, seeing him turn tail, had taken and burned half-a-dozen Dutch ships, and were now cruising about for as many more as they could get.

This was more than the people could bear. The admiral and his captains were nearly torn to pieces by the mob. The old fogies of Amsterdam got frightened, and knew not what to do. The States-

General held an inquiry, at which everybody abused everybody else; and all of them blamed the admiral. The admiral requested his dismission, and never went again to sea. Then the Stadtholder, Prince Frederick Henry of Orange, looked round for the best man to occupy the vacant post, and his eye fell on Tromp. Tromp accepted, but not before he had frankly announced his intention to carry out every one of the suggestions which had been so unceremoniously pooh-poohed, and introduce a good many more, which he had pondered deeply during the years of his retirement. A schoolfellow of his, De With, born in the same town, and who had also left the service in disgust, was at the same time appointed vice-admiral, and the two friends now set about reforming the service.

The expectations throughout the country were great, for Tromp and De With were already looked upon as the coming men, and in some verses written about that time they were ordered immediately to sail to Spain and take Madrid, which, that town being a few hundred miles inland, it would have been somewhat difficult for the best of fleets to do. Nor was the popular expectation realised for the first year. The Duke of Marlborough once said that he could better judge the merits of a general by the style of his soldiers than by his order of battle; for that a good general might make a blunder in his battle, but never in his men. The admirals who preceded Tromp had blundered all over the fleet. They were themselves weak and hesitating, and Tromp found the captains careless, unbusinesslike, and unsteady. His first order was to the effect that no captain belonging to a fleet should act independently, but should take his order from the admiral, and fight with one eye on his enemy and the other on the flag. It was no easy task to reform where matters had been allowed to degenerate so far, but personal influence and perseverance triumphed, with the genuine stuff that lay at the bottom. By degrees the old spirit came back, but it came into a new body. The armament of the ships was increased, the guns were made of heavier calibre, the number of each crew was fixed, the duties of each officer and each man were precisely defined, insubordination was punished, and zeal rewarded. Each man was forced to look to his superior for orders instead of to himself, a regular system of flag, lamp, and gun signals was introduced and practised; and without the knowledge of Europe the Dutch fleet became as well organised and perfectly trained as the best army. When this had all been done quietly, and with the greatest patience and good humour, the time came to put it into practice.

It will be remembered that I told you already about the pirates of Dunkerque, who were in partnership with Spain, and seriously damaged the Dutch shipping. In the beginning of 1639 certain good friends in Madrid wrote a private letter to the Stadtholder, warning him that he had better keep a sharp look out, for that there was mischief brewing in Spain. The king, they said, was building a tremendous fleet, and collecting a large army; a formidable armada was expected to sail from Corunna in another month or so, a dozen Dunkerque pirates would meet them half way in the Bay of Biscay, who, with their knowledge of the rivers, and all the ins and outs of the Dutch coast, would easily lead this tremendous fleet into the Meuse, where the army could be landed, marched to Rotterdam and Amsterdam, and then conquer the whole country. Fifty years ago the Dutch would have been greatly frightened at this news, but the war had now lasted nearly seventy years, they had gained ground inch by inch, and they felt that it would have to be a very queer fleet or army that would take them now. Nevertheless measures were taken. To begin with, Tromp, who was always cruising about in that neighbourhood, was ordered to prevent any ships leaving Dunkerque. Tromp wrote back to say that he had only eleven ships, and would require as many more, but before he could receive an answer the Dunkerquers were signalled as leaving the harbour. There were thirteen men of war, three frigates, and seven armed merchantmen. Without a moment's hesitation Tromp attacked them; there was a furious fight for eight hours, Tromp tried repeatedly to sail over the Dunkerque admiral, but in vain. The fight was ended by nightfall and a calm. The two largest pirates were cut off and captured, the vice-admiral was chased ashore and burned, and the remaining seventeen ships had to row back to Dunkerque as fast as they could pull.

This was all very well, and the people in Holland were highly delighted, but even Tromp found that he could not effectually blockade so difficult a port as Dunkerque, and at the same time look after the ships at sea. He was like a nurse with two troublesome babies: as long as he stuck before the harbour the fishermen cried out that they were being neglected, and two hundred of them lay in the mouth of the river not daring to run out; and when he sailed to their assistance those in Holland began to cry that the pirate fleet would slip out. It did slip out, and got clear away before he could sail after it. Of course everybody called him stupid because he could not do two things at one time; but he merely laughed. 'They may get out,' said he, 'but I'll take good care they don't come in again in a hurry.'

The summer wore on, and still Tromp lay with his fleet before Dunkerque. The letters from Spain were full of the new armada. Every port in the kingdom was fitting out ships, every town was sending soldiers. The highest nobles in the land quarrelled with each other to be allowed to go on board and conquer the little republic. Princes, dukes and counts, generals and captains, bishops and priests, asked permission to join the expedition, which was supposed to be great fun. At last it sailed in the beginning of September 1639. Since the year 1588 no such fleet had been on the high seas. It consisted of sixty-seven men of war, fully equipped for service. One of them, the 'Mater Teresa,' of two thousand four hundred tons burden, was the largest vessel that had ever been seen; it carried seventy guns and twelve hundred men; and such names as Sea-monster and Floating-castle, by which it was known among the Dutch sailors, show plainly enough what an impression it had made upon them. The fleet carried in all nearly two thousand guns and twenty-four thousand men. The whole of Europe looked on in amazement, for they thought that with so enormous a force the Dutch could not cope. But somehow the Hollanders do not seem to have been very much afraid. They had pulled through so often, they would pull through again, and they relied implicitly upon Tromp and De With.

But Tromp's force was almost laughable. When he sighted the armada off Beveziers he had only thirteen ships, and not one of these carried more than forty-five guns. Admiral de With was cruising near Dover with six ships, and Banckers blockaded Dunkerque with twelve. Their joint forces therefore amounted to thirty-one ships, they had no more than two thousand five hundred men all told, and they were equally inferior in every other respect.

On the 15th of September, 1639, Tromp sighted the Spanish fleet spreading its white sails over a distance of several miles, and immediately despatched one ship to De With and another to Banckers, with a request to come and help him. At the same time he retired slowly, sailing before the wind, keeping the Spaniards just in sight, and firing a gun every half-hour to let his friends know his whereabouts. It was early morning on the 16th when De With hove in sight. The weather was magnificent, and the delicious sea-breeze invigorated the very sails. As De With jumped on board the admiral's ship, he found all the captains assembled. Tromp began to speak of prudence and waiting, deeming it wiser to let the other side begin. But De With would not hear of this. 'Not a bit of it,' he cried, in his rough, impetuous manner; 'there is room at the bottom for them all, and the sooner we begin to send them there the better.' The plan of battle was then hastily arranged, and after the loving cup had circulated, they rowed each to his own ship. Then, as the armada came drifting down slowly, Tromp ran close up to the Spanish admiral, and let him have a broadside. This was the sign for a general engagement. The Dutch being much lighter took very good care not to come to close quarters, and yet they manœuvred so well and were so smart at their work that the Spaniards, bewildered and confused with their own clumsiness, tacked about, and turned towards the English coast, followed closely by Tromp and De With.

The 17th of September was so foggy and calm that pursuit was impossible. Towards eleven at night, however, the weather cleared. At a council of war it was immediately resolved to renew the attack as soon as the moon had risen, and ebb-tide set in. In order that action might be uniform, and the fleet kept together, Tromp commanded each ship to keep a fire on deck, he engaging to keep two. At about half-past twelve the full moon rose, and the Spanish fleet could be dimly perceived ahead. At one o'clock, at the dead of night, the sea suddenly resounded with a terrific cannonade. The Spanish fleet was attacked with greater fury than before, and retired again. At the break of day, Banckers, who had sailed all night in quest of the shooting, came in with thirteen fresh ships. Thus beset on three sides, the Spanish admiral, D'Oquendo, made all sail for the English coast, and was very glad to get under shelter of the castle of Dover, with the loss of two ships. But he was greatly mistaken if he thought it would end there.

D'Oquendo had certainly chosen a strange place for shelter. On the morning of the 18th he was lying off the Downs, but the Downs in that part resemble nothing so much as a rat-trap. A formidable sand-bank, known as the Goodwin Sands, runs parallel to the English coast for a distance of ten miles, and the channel thus formed, being only four miles broad, is too narrow for the manœuvres of a whole fleet. Tromp saw this at once, and so did the Spanish admiral when it was too late. The moment D'Oquendo dropped his anchors in the Downs, Tromp divided his fleet into two parts; one half, under Banckers, was sent round to the north entrance of the channel, and the other half blocked up the south, and there was the Spanish fleet in a hole. On the right of him the English coast, on the left the Sands, Banckers in front of him, and Tromp in the rear. One sudden blow might have saved him, but that blow he was either too cautious or too cowardly to strike. Tromp, on the other hand, was all activity. He despatched De With, with his nearly sinking ship, to the States, praying them to send him as strong a reinforcement as they could muster. He himself ran over to Calais, and bought forty thousand pounds' of powder, and four thousand cannon balls.

When he returned to his own fleet he found a considerable addition to the happy family. Admiral Sir John Pennington had come with thirty-four English men-of-war to see what was going on. Tromp saluted him, Pennington saluted back, and Tromp rowed to Pennington's ship to pay him a visit.

'What are you doing here with such a large fleet, Admiral Tromp?' says Pennington.

'I am looking after my enemy, who has taken shelter under your guns, Sir John,' says Tromp.

'But you must use no violence in these waters and in sight of these shores,' said the English admiral.

'You need not fear that we shall use any violence to *you*, Sir John.'

'Mind what you are about, Admiral,' said Pennington, 'for I have the king's commands to help whoever is attacked first.'

With this they parted. Tromp felt uncomfortable,

for he had certainly intended to attack the Spaniard. All this was made known to the States-General, and they too felt uncomfortable. They knew that Charles I. was more in favour of Spain than of them, and that he would, if possible, prevent the Spanish fleet being beaten on his own shore. They did not like to get into a war with England, and yet they did not like to let the Spanish fleet escape. One day they sent to Tromp saying that he must wait until he was attacked, the next day that he must attack without waiting, then again that he must ask Pennington's permission, and immediately after that he must not mind Pennington. In fact, they did not know what to do, and no more did Tromp. Day by day the officers from the English fleet called on him to induce him to go. At one time they flattered him, at another they threatened; in the morning they were very cordial, but when they saw in the evening that he was there still they became very haughty. But Tromp laughed at them all round, for he had made up his mind to remain, and he remained.

In the meantime it seemed as if the Dutch had been seized with a ship-building fever. Never before had such a sudden activity been known in the Netherlands. The States ordered all shipowners to give up their ships. They voted large sums of money and raised an army. Every wharf resounded with the shipwright's hammer. The sail-makers, the rope-makers, the outfitters worked day and night. New guns were bought, powder was manufactured, swords, pistols, axes, and all sorts of arms were brought forward by the people. Everybody wanted to go to the new fleet and help to lick the Spaniards. Ship after ship was launched and sent out to the Downs. The soldier who looked for his captain was told to go to Tromp; the burgher who wondered in what manner he would fight was told to go to Tromp who would teach him; the poor man who expressed a wish for money was told to go to Tromp, who would give him plenty of booty. At every court in Europe there was great merriment at the Dutch keeping the Spanish shut up in a corner until they were strong enough to fetch him out of it. It was almost incredible; but day after day wore on, September changed to October, ship after ship sailed out to the Downs, until the small fleet of thirty-one had grown to one hundred and ten. Then Tromp felt himself strong enough to strike his blow, and he struck it with terrific force.

During that month of watching and suspense he had been in a most delicate position. Nothing but his prudence and moderate wisdom could have allowed him to remain. There were intrigues in London and intrigues in the fleet. English sympathy was clearly with the Spaniards; and when some English pilots, under cover of darkness, led thirteen Dunkerque vessels through the Swash safely away, there was manifest pleasure in the English fleet. Tromp said nothing, but closed up that exit with a squadron, and drew closer to the Spaniards. Then Pennington told

Tromp it would be much nobler on his part to run out to sea and wait for his enemy there. Tromp answered that he would like nothing better, if D'Oquendo would do the same. D'Oquendo sent back answer through Pennington that he would have gone long ago but that he had no powder. Tromp sent back to say that he had powder enough for both, and would send him half his.

'Ah,' said D'Oquendo again, 'it is not only powder I want. Many of my ships have no masts and booms, and I must wait until they have arrived from shore.'

'There is no need to wait,' said Tromp. 'I have enough for both. Here is a whole ship-load of my masts, and you are welcome to them if you will only come out and fight.'

D'Oquendo declined with thanks; but he never stirred an inch. Sir John Pennington shrugged his shoulders in disgust; for he could not help thinking D'Oquendo a great coward. But he had received his orders, and he repeated to Tromp that he was bound to fight the man who fired the first shot. There then lay the three fleets, two-hundred men-of-war strong, in sight of each other, and it depended upon Tromp to make them all burst forth in deadly flame and destruction. But Tromp was artful. One day he ordered his sloop to be got ready, and sailed with it right through the Spanish fleet. What he had foreseen happened. Angered by this sight the Spaniards fired at him. The ball only made a hole in the sail;

but it was quite enough. Next day they fired again, and killed a Dutch sailor. Tromp had the body carried to Pennington's ship, with a letter. 'You see,' he said, 'they have begun. They have fired the first shot at us, and by rights you ought to attack them. But if you will keep perfectly neutral I will manage the business all by myself.'

On the night of the 20th of October the wind changed, and blew from the coast. Tromp called a council of war, and settled the plan of attack. Before dawn there arrived other seven ships from Holland, ordering him to engage the enemy in spite of the whole English fleet, and King Charles into the bargain. No sooner had the sun risen than he fired a single shot. At the second shot up flew the sails on the whole Dutch fleet. The anchors were weighed. The battle had come. The Dutch were still far inferior in guns and soldiers; but they were more numerous and lighter in ships, and they made a full use of their advantages. Tromp had brought all his science and experience to bear on the battle. The English, who remained neutral, looked on with amazement. For the first time in the history of naval warfare did they behold a large fleet split up into six independent and compact smaller fleets, each of which manœuvred on his own account. One of the six ran close to the English, and kept a watchful eye on Pennington. The other five squadrons sailed into the Spanish fleet. Attacked on all sides, the heavy, clumsy, unmanageable sea-castles got into confusion. The Admiral of Castillia and twenty-two of his ships deliberately ran ashore, and, under the terrific fire of the impetuous De With, jumped into the sea and swam on shore. The sea-monster 'Mater Teresa,' vainly attacked by three Dutchmen, was at last set fire to by a fire-ship. The thousand men on board yelled and shrieked in their terror, and fell on their knees. Some of the proudest of Spain's nobility begged for mercy. In a few minutes the powder exploded. 'The sight,' says Montanus, 'was awful and horrible. Out of one thousand not two hundred were saved. The others were hurled half-charred into the water, or blown to pieces in the air. Never did the heavens re-echo a more frightful crash. The strand and the sea trembled. The guns were hurled red-hot into the air; and, in the darkness, the flame looked as if hell itself had opened his jaws.'

The rout was complete. It could scarcely be called a battle. Spanish ships ran into each other in the confusion and went down. Eleven of them surrendered without firing a shot. Some stranded on the Goodwin Sands, others ran ashore. D'Oquendo himself got out to sea with twelve ships, and was followed by Tromp, who captured three. Of the sixty-seven men-of-war only eighteen reached Dunkerque in a pitiable condition, the rest were destroyed or taken. Of the twenty-four thousand men five thousand were known to have been killed and wounded, and eighteen hundred were taken prisoners. Hundreds had died of sickness before, hundreds died of their wounds and misfortunes afterwards; and for many and many a day there was cast upon the English and French shores a mass of crushed timbers and shivered beams, chests with treasures, and mangled bodies still clad in the gaily-coloured garments of the Spanish Court, as if the very waves themselves were unwilling to retain the sad records of so awful a catastrophe.

The honours which Tromp received on reaching home would have been amply sufficient to turn the heads of most successful men; but he remained in all things the same. And yet the result of his victory became every day more apparent. The Republic of the Netherlands began to take up a position in Europe equal to that of France and England. Foreign countries either sought her assistance or dreaded her opposition. France concluded an advantageous treaty with her; the Germans sent ambassadors to the States to ask their help; Denmark and Sweden concluded alliances with her; and in so high estimation was she held in London, that two years afterwards a portion of the same fleet, under the same warlike commander, carried across the peaceable Prince William, the Stadtholder's son, who was soon afterwards married to Princess Mary, the eldest daughter of Charles I. It need scarcely be said that when Tromp landed at Dover there were plenty of men to flatter him, and to praise his courage and skill; but he was getting accustomed to this kind of thing. The King of France had already created him Knight of St. Michael, and the King of Denmark had also made him a handsome present. The following year, in 1642, while cruising about in the Channel, he happened to land at Dover just at the time when King Charles and his queen were visiting that city on a royal progress. Tromp immediately went to pay his respects to their Majesties. The king complimented the republican Admiral very graciously, and bestowed upon him the honour of knighthood, which Tromp, who was not so very much of a republican after all, was highly delighted with. I ought after this to call him Sir Marten Tromp, Knt., and perhaps tell you something about Lady Tromp too; but a time was fast approaching when the cordiality and good understanding between the two countries would be torn asunder and utterly destroyed.

At that same ceremony of knighting, King Charles spoke a few words, which became afterwards rather significant. After having praised the Admiral's great skill at sea, he also praised him for having always given due honour to his Majesty by respectfully lowering his flag and firing a salute, whenever he met any of the king's ships, adding, that he had therein fulfilled his duty. Now it was perfectly true that Tromp had lowered his flag and had fired a salute, but he had always done this out of politeness, not out of duty. There lay the difference. The English insisted upon every ship saluting them that sailed in their waters; but they did not consider themselves bound to salute others when they in their turn visited foreign ports. They had taken it into their heads that they were by natural right the rulers of the sea. Charles had built an immense ship, which he called the 'Sovereign of the Seas,' and he told all the world, on the medals struck at the time, that the very ends of the world would be no end to him. Now when the Dutch began to consider that they had entirely defeated Spain, which had hitherto been considered the greatest naval power in the world, they asked themselves why the English had so great a right to call themselves the sovereigns of the seas. They did not like the title, and they began to sneer at it.

There were many other circumstances that caused bad blood between the two nations. To begin with, the English admirals, and those at court, were somewhat offended when Tromp not only attacked and defeated the Spanish fleet upon the English coast, but did so in the presence of the king's fleet, although he knew that the king was against it; and they considered it a great piece of impudence on his part actually to leave one squadron of his fleet out of the fight, to keep watch over Pennington.

Then there was no doubt that the Dutch were very smart in their trading, and frequently cut out the English merchants in their own markets and with their own goods, by consenting to take less profits. They were at that time certainly the most energetic traders in the world, and in this they were assisted by their government, which framed many laws to encourage new enterprises and reward success. In a petition presented to Cromwell the petitioners say:

It is no wonder that these Dutchmen should thrive

before us. Their statesmen are all merchants. They have travelled in foreign countries, they understand the course of trade, and they do everything to further its interests.' In other petitions the fear is expressed that the Dutch would altogether overbalance them. They had already monopolised the trade in the Baltic. The trade of the Mediterranean was falling into their hands, and so adroit were they in negotiating, that when peace was at last concluded with the King of Spain, they got him to promise that he would henceforth use no English cloths, and allow Dutch manufacture only to be sold in the shops. Of course when, after that, an English captain anchored in the harbours of Cadiz or Cartagena, and went on shore with the hope of doing a splendid business, but was told that he had better go back, as he was not wanted, you may imagine that he was not over polite, especially when he saw the Dutchman unloading his vessel before his very nose.

All this created much jealousy and harsh feeling. The English would not give in, the Dutch would not give in, and both began to comprehend that sooner or later the question would have to be decided by arms, when the weaker must go to the wall. This conviction had grown up since the battle of the Downs. Even at that time there are expressions in Tromp's journal showing the dislike in the Dutch fleet towards these haughty redcoats. Matters were not mended when the English began to claim to be saluted as a right. They fired into a whole Swedish fleet off the Isle of

Wight, and brought them into the Downs, because they would not salute. At another time Sir William Penn, when lying in the harbour of Cadiz, wrote in his journal that the Dutch fleet was coming in with flying colours, but he forebore demanding a salute, 'being,' as he says, 'in the king of Spain his port.' Then came the civil war, and the execution of Charles. The Dutch, indignant at the deed, insulted the English ambassador by crying 'King's murderer' behind his carriage in the Hague.

The Roundheads were offended with this Dutch sympathy for the king, and with their friendliness for Prince Rupert's fleet. They were annoyed that the Pretender was allowed to reside in the Hague with his court. They were indignant when some exiled Cavaliers murdered the Parliament's ambassador at the Hague because he had taken part in the king's trial. They would scarcely accept excuses. Matters having gone so far, went further. The question of saluting was revived. Tromp desired to know whether he should treat the Republican flag with the same honour as the king's. The States gave no definite answer, and told him to do what he thought fit. Then there were some squabbles between English and Dutch fishermen; and Cromwell, who considered England aggrieved, issued letters of marque to two ships, allowing them to take away whatever they could, until they had received compensation for their injuries. At the same time it was ordered that every Dutch vessel should be searched to ascertain whether it carried any Cavaliers, or arms and ammunition for them. This, as you may imagine, was an intolerable nuisance, for it was not always done with great prudence or honesty. All efforts to arrange matters failed. The Navigation Act was passed by Parliament, the saluting was ordered to be exacted, and the preparation of a fleet of a hundred and fifty ships was decreed.

As soon as the States heard this, they felt that no time must now be lost. Immediately after the peace with Spain, the fleet had been reduced, and was now in a very pitiable condition. The whole number of ships did not exceed forty, and none of these were very large. Thirty-six new ones were at once ordered, and the Dutch ambassador in London was requested to inform Cromwell of this, but to endeavour to avert a war. An order was sent to Tromp that no searching should be allowed on any account, and that liberties or injuries of any kind should be resisted. Formerly the orders to the Admiral always had been to treat the king's ships with friendliness and courtesy; now he was admonished to exercise his common sense and discretion. He was strictly ordered not to attack, but he was as strictly ordered to suffer no indignities, and as to the flag, for the sake of peace, he was to observe the same customs that had been followed in the king's time.

Such was the condition of affairs when Tromp sailed out with his fleet in April 1652. An otherwise small incident led to the first battle. On the 12th of

May three English men-of-war were lying off Start Point when Captain Young, of the 'President,' descried nine Dutch merchantmen and three men-of-war going home. Captain Young immediately sent the master of his ship to require them to strike their flag. One of the Dutch captains, Zaen, struck his flag, but the second asked Captain Young to come and do it himself. Young sent out his boat, but the boat came back with a curt refusal. Young immediately bore down upon him and gave him a broadside. The Dutchman answered, and for nearly an hour the six ships were engaged in a furious fight. As the Dutch fleet, however, had, amongst other things, half a million of pure gold on board, they thought it wisest to save their cargo, and retired.

Tromp meanwhile was lying off the Flemish coast, between Dunkerque and Newport. He had received orders from home to keep away from the English coast. Unfortunately a terrific hurricane blowing uninterruptedly for four days, threatened to destroy his fleet; and he was compelled to run across to Dover. Knowing that 'Major' Bourne was lying in the Downs with eight men-of-war, he immediately sent two frigates to him to explain his conduct, promising that he would sail for the North Sea when the gale had somewhat abated. Bourne was amiable, accepted the explanation, invited the two captains to take a glass of wine with him, and sent off at the same time for Blake, who was lying in Rye Bay. Blake came up as fast as he could sail, and arrived next day when

Tromp was standing away to the eastward. Suddenly a ship was seen to arrive in the Dutch fleet. Tromp immediately altered his course, and bore down towards Blake. The English explained this by saying that the new vessel brought an order from the States to attack. The fact was that Tromp, as soon as he saw Blake's fleet, and not wishing to begin any quarrel, was turning towards the North Sea, when Captain Zaen came upon him, still excited by his fight with Captain Young off the Start. He implored Tromp not to go away, for that the nine merchantmen, with their valuable cargo, were in great danger of being searched, and might be in English hands at that moment. Tromp's duty was clear. He must protect the Dutch vessels, and he gave the order to tack about, and run towards Blake.

The position was critical; but Tromp took every precaution. As he approached slowly he ordered all sails to be furled, and advanced with reefed top-sails. He sent one sailor aloft to stand by the pendant, and take it in; he sent another to the flag, 'whom,' he says in his letter, 'Mr. Admiral Blake might easily have seen climbing up himself.' But Blake was at that moment in his cabin drinking with some officers. He had conceived the wrong impression that Tromp had a resolution to engage, and had ordered the fleet to lie by in fighting posture. Before Tromp had arrived with the 'Brederode' within the proper distance, and while the sailor was yet climbing up the rigging to the flag, a shot fell from Blake's ship, the 'James,' and a ball passed over Tromp's deck. A second one followed almost immediately. Tromp, who was standing on his quarter-deck, now turned to his captain, and pointing to the sloop that ran behind the 'Brederode,' desired him to draw it alongside, and row with some of the crew to the 'James,' and ask Mr. Admiral Blake for an explanation. The sloop was but half manned, and the sailor had not yet reached the flag, when the 'James,' running forward, fired her third gun. The ball passed right through the 'Brederode,' and smashed one of the sailor's arms. A tremor ran through the whole Dutch fleet. The first blood had been drawn. A peaceable issue was no longer to be thought of.

What now follows is differently related by Blake and Tromp. Blake says: 'After the third shot he (Tromp) let fly a broadside at us;' and the 'Naval Chronicle' adds the somewhat absurd anecdote that he felt very angry and astonished, 'curling his whiskers, as he used to do when he was angry,' when Tromp's shot broke the windows of his ship and shattered the stern. Tromp, on the other hand, says that, after the third shot from the 'James,' he fired one return shot far before her bows. He had, indeed, called back the sailors from the flag and from the sloop, and was undoubtedly prepared for action. Immediately after his shot, the 'James' ran up to him before the wind and discharged a broadside and a volley of musketry, the 'Brederode' returning the greeting without the loss of a moment. The ships, on both sides, now began to discharge single shots at each other ; but for the first half-hour the two admirals' ships alone exchanged broadsides. Tromp had ordered his fleet to act entirely on the defensive, for he would not bear the responsibility of the first attack. He had forty ships, Blake at that moment only thirteen ; but the number of Blake's guns was scarcely inferior. When the firing had lasted about half an hour, Tromp descried Major Bourne coming from the Downs with his squadron. He immediately hoisted out the blood-red flag for a general engagement, and part of the Dutch fleet drew up in line and advanced.

The details of the battle I have been unable to find. It is enough to know that the firing was furious, and that darkness alone separated them. Blake's ship had lost the mizen-mast and was so damaged in rigging and hull as to be almost unmanageable. The other ships of the English fleet had also suffered severely, but Tromp had fared worse. He had lost two ships —one had been sunk and the other taken, while a third could scarcely be kept afloat with the pumps. But he had not struck his flag. On the morning of the 30th of May the two fleets lay in sight of each other for some hours, at a distance of four leagues. Towards mid-day, both turned towards their respective shores to report to their Governments the beginning of the first war between them.

MARTEN HARPERTS TROMP.

PART II.

ALTHOUGH every well-informed person in both countries had foreseen the collision of two equally energetic and jealous powers, Admiral Tromp was received by a portion of the Dutch populace as though he and he alone were the origin of this fray. He bore the imputation with silence. He knew that victory itself would be misconstrued and maligned by the Republican party, for they entertained a fierce hatred towards the Prince of Orange; they viewed all his supporters with jealousy and mistrust, and they would not bear in mind that the admiral had every reason to regard the head of the State with profound admiration and gratitude. But however much public opinion in the Netherlands might be divided against Tromp, it was unanimous against England. Eighty years of war and thirty years of victory had engendered no great spirit of humility amongst the prosperous traders of Amsterdam, and though a peaceful ambassador was immediately despatched to Cromwell, the Dutch men-of-war were actively prepared for service. Within the same week two large fleets ran out to sea, the one under Blake and the other under his great opponent. Tromp was now in command of ninety-six vessels and eleven thousand men. He had again received no special instructions about the flag, but it was understood that he was to allow no indignities whatsoever. He was ordered to hold a general day of prayer on his fleet, and in the event of his meeting the enemy, to use discretion as on previous occasions. Presently the ambassador returned from London with a serious face, and Tromp, seeing that it meant war, sailed straight for the English coast. Blake had run northward, but Sir George Ayscue, newly arrived from Barbadoes with fifteen men-of-war, was lying in the Downs, with orders to remain there until joined by a fleet that was fitting out in the Thames. Tromp, hearing of this, thought it a chance not to be lost. He immediately divided his fleet, closed up each entrance of the Downs with his first and second squadron, and sent the third round to the South Foreland to intercept the coming ships. But those on shore were not asleep either. They stopped the ships in the Medway, and erected such formidable batteries between Deal and Sandown castles for the assistance and protection of Ayscue's fleet, that, what with alternate head-wind and calm, and the smallness of the prize, Tromp resolved to set out in quest of Blake.

No decisive battle had as yet been fought, but it was already plain on both sides of the Channel that the Dutch were fighting under two great disadvantages. Their ships were greatly inferior in size and in guns, and as their commerce was ten times as extensive as that of the English, they offered ten points of attack where the Britons scarcely offered one. Tromp found this out. After leaving Ayscue, a three-fold duty awaited him at home. A fleet of merchantmen lay ready to sail for the Baltic, and another was expected home from the East Indies, and there was considerable anxiety about a number of herring-busses, which it was feared had fallen into Blake's hands. It became Tromp's duty to escort the first to the Sound, which he did in safety; to wait until the second should have arrived and escort it back; and, in the meantime, to afford every protection to the herring-fishers. But Blake had already made short work of the last. He met them, and after a resistance of three hours, the twelve men-of-war that accompanied the fishers were defeated, and the fleet taken or dispersed. On the 6th of August, early in the morning, Tromp hove in sight, but as the two admirals were preparing to engage, a tremendous storm suddenly agitated the ocean. Blake took shelter in the English harbours, Tromp made the best of his way to Texel, but nearly half his fleet and three of the East Indiamen were missing when he arrived, and six of his frigates fell into English hands.

This singular misfortune was a ready weapon for his enemies. A host of pamphlets appeared accusing him of the basest treason, and it was now even said that he had begun the battle with Blake for some private speculation of his own. A court-martial was proposed in the States-General, and all but carried; he was commanded to appear before the High-Mighty Lords in person, a tedious enquiry and discussion took place, and the early autumn had changed to winter before his judges re-appointed him as commander-in-chief of the fleet. Tromp behaved throughout with his usual large-mindedness and honesty. There was not a speck upon his character, and his judges felt that each one might congratulate himself if he came out of so searching an examination so free from blemish. It stands to reason that Tromp was indignant. He held, with justice, that when a man has gained an honourable and illustrious position, want of success and failure of his plans inflict ample punishment in themselves. And the adverse sentence of a court could scarcely have wounded him more than this loss of public confidence. 'To fight the enemy and risk my life, causes no trouble to my mind,' he writes, 'but that, having done all in my power to serve my country, I should come home to be exposed to suspicions, and jealousies, and ill-will—that having done all that a soldier and a sailor can do, with the brains that God has given me, I should be required to give an account of my deeds—this takes away all my pleasure and zeal in the service.'

Nevertheless, for the sake of the country and the service he loved so well, he accepted the post once more. A battle had taken place in the meantime between Ayscue and De Ruyter, in which the latter, although not defeated, had lost very severely. It was also reported that Tromp's absence from the fleet had caused a great amount of dissatisfaction, and that many captains had refused to serve under anyone but their 'Father.' On the 1st of December, 1652, Tromp arrived in the midst of his 'children,' as he called his sailors, and was welcomed with enthusiasm. Amid somewhat boisterous weather the enormous fleet of five hundred merchant ships and ninety-eight men-of-war ran out of the Meuse, but as Blake was reported off the Downs, and Tromp would not risk his fleet, he ordered the merchants and half his men-of-war to put back, and set off himself in quest of his great opponent. When Blake descried him off the Goodwins he felt at once that he would be treated in the same manner as D'Oquendo, unless he managed to quit the Downs and fight in open sea. It was in the afternoon of December 9, when he ran out with forty-six ships, carrying Tromp in full cry after him. It was Blake's plan to reach Rye Bay, where he might receive some assistance. It was Tromp's plan to cut him off. The chase lasted till dark, Tromp anchoring two miles N.W. of Dover. Next day Tromp hoisted the blue flag for general pursuit. The wind was violent. All sails were crowded, the masts bent, and the waves washed over the deck in the eager chase. At one o'clock the faster Dutch ships reach the slower English, and shots were exchanged. At three o'clock Tromp had reached Dungeness Head,

BATTLE BETWEEN TROMP AND BLAKE OFF DOVER.

and Blake saw himself forced to engage. Running with his ship the 'Triumph' before the wind, he passed Tromp and exchanged a volley. The English 'Garland,' Captain Battin, of forty-eight guns, followed at his heels, and would also have passed had not Tromp bored a hole into her stern with his bowsprit and ran alongside of her. Almost immediately afterwards the English Captain Ackson, with his 'Adventure' of forty guns, settled on Tromp's other side. A terrific cannonade now commenced. The Dutch Vice-Admiral Evertsen, who was always following his chief like a dog, ran alongside the 'Adventure,' and there lay the four ships, tossed by the waves, and invisible in a dense cloud of smoke. The fight lasted over an hour. Tromp's secretary was shot by his side, but his men, inspired by the Admiral's words, jumped over on to the 'Garland's' deck. They found that nearly all the officers had fallen, the dead bodies numbered over sixty and covered the deck. The crew surrendered and the Orange flag was nailed to the mast. Evertsen in the meantime had captured the 'Adventure' in the same manner, while that part of the fleet which had been able to keep up the pace was busily engaged against the rest of the English. Blake fought gallantly but was forced to give in. Had the day lasted a few hours longer the whole British fleet would have been destroyed, but as Blake himself says in his letter, 'by occasion of the night coming on we were saved, being then left almost alone.' He reached Dover in a sadly disabled condition; two of his ships had been captured, one was burned, three were sunk, and his loss in dead and wounded was very considerable. Blake was naturally much cast down. He accused many of his captains with baseness of spirit, prayed that their Honours of the Admiralty might be pleased to send down some gentlemen to make an impartial and strict examination of the deportment of several commanders, and hoped that they might give him, their unworthy servant, a discharge from this employment, so far too great for him.

Tromp, on the other hand, was elated by his success, and proposed to his captains to sail up the Thames, since the rest of the English fleet had gone there for shelter; but although the scheme was enthusiastically received, the dangers of the navigation, and the want of pilots, proved insurmountable objections. It was after this battle that he is reported to have sailed for some days up and down the Channel with a broom fixed to his mainmast, as if he were resolved to sweep the sea of the English, but I am much inclined to doubt this story. Not only must it have been a broom of immense size to be distinguished at such a distance, but there is not the least mention of it in any of the books kept on the Dutch fleet at that time, and Dutch tradition is equally silent on the subject. The only authority that I have been able to find is an absurd little news-pamphlet published about that time in London, and which has been copied word for word by everybody afterwards as if it were the New Testament. Against this testimony we may put the serene temperament, the moderation and modesty of a great man, who never before and never afterwards performed any deed out of mere show, and who had as high an opinion of Blake as Blake had of him.

It was during this battle, too, that while the Dutch admiral stood on his own deck watching the battle, one of his sailors hurried past him with a bag of powder, and not recognising him, told him to get out of his way, dealing him at the same time a box on the ear that nearly knocked him down. Tromp said not a word, but walked to a less busy part of the vessel. When the battle was over, he called the man before him. The sailor remembered having given somebody a blow, but was terrified to find that it was the admiral himself. 'You need not be afraid, my son,' said Tromp, 'for you did your duty. Never allow any man to interfere in the execution of your orders. But next time you hit, don't hit so hard.' The man was thereupon promoted.

There can be no doubt that the Dutch felt very proud of their victory. It was given out by the States that everyone who cared for the risk might fit out a privateer and make war on his own account. There was an immediate activity in all the ports. The restless spirit which had been somewhat checked by the war, became stronger than ever. There was a regular rush. Over a hundred letters of marque were issued in one week. Hundreds of English coasting ships and fisher boats were captured. Two

Zealand privateers, who had got up a sort of partnership, brought thirteen prizes into port in eleven days, and so fierce was the mutual hatred thereby developed, that an Englishman and Dutchman could meet nowhere without coming to blows. Two fishing-smacks met near the Dogger Bank. One was from Vlieland, the other from Harwich. Neither was armed. The English began the battle by a volley of stones, the Dutch answered by a broadside of wood-blocks. The English then took to their boat-hooks, the Dutch to their oars; and having thus belaboured each other for some time, the latter got on board the Harwich boat, forced the crew into their own hold among their fish, fastened down the hatches, and brought the prize into the Zuyder Zee.

During this time, however, the Dutch government committed a sad blunder. Tromp warned them in vain that the English were a harder enemy to deal with than the Spanish. The States foolishly declined to make any improvements, although they must have known that a second contest was inevitable. Their slowness in giving and executing orders prevented a new fleet being built or the old one being repaired. Not a grain of powder, not a round of ammunition, not a new ship was sent to Tromp after his victory, but he was packed off to the Bay of Biscay in escort of one hundred and fifty merchantmen, with the order to bring back another fleet that lay waiting for him there. He went, but he had scarcely arrived, in the middle of February, when an express yacht from the

States ordered him to make all haste home, as they had reason to believe that another English fleet had run out and was blocking up the mouth of the river. It was true enough. Great preparations had been made in England to wipe out the disgrace, while the Dutch sat with their hands in their pockets. When Tromp arrived off Portland on the 28th February, he looked at his captain and his captain looked at him, and nodded.

'There they are, sir,' said he, pointing to eighty English men-of-war that were lying right in his way, 'and there is little doubt what they want.'

'There they are, indeed,' said Tromp; 'they want fighting, methinks, and they'll have plenty of it.'

His dispositions were soon made. The wind was in his favour, and Tromp could therefore begin the battle when he liked. The merchantmen and a sufficient number of men-of-war were ordered to the rear, and the fleet was divided into three squadrons: Florisz had the van, Evertsen the centre, and De Ruyter the rear. The English were divided into two squadrons; Blake and Deane had the one, and General Monk, newly arrived from Scotland, commanded the other. It was eight o'clock in the morning when Tromp's ship, the 'Brederode,' met the English admiral's ship, the 'Triumph,' with Blake and Deane standing side by side on the quarter-deck. The fight lasted till darkness, and was carried on with great fury. For miles the sea was covered with ships that lay together in threes or fours, and broke out into flame and smoke. De Ruyter was surrounded by a whole cluster of his enemies until he was rescued by Evertsen and his squadron. The Dutch Captain Poort sailed into the English frigate 'Sampson,' but so damaged her that on jumping over with his crew, friend and foe went down together. The Dutch Captain Cleydeyck, beset on each side by an enemy, was already on his way to the powder stores to blow up his vessel, when his friend Regemorter came to his assistance. Cleydeyck's ship was sinking, but in the moment of despair he led his men to board the English 'Prosperous.' Captain Barker was killed and the ship taken, when suddenly Captain Veysey, of the English frigate 'Merlin,' came up, forced him to abandon the 'Prosperous' and take refuge, with all his men, on his friend's ship, while his own went to the bottom. While the fight was at its hottest, Tromp, whose eye was everywhere, descried with alarm that Blake was quietly trying to outflank him, and that some of the swiftest English ships were sailing past him at several miles' distance in order to reach the merchantmen. It was in moments like this that his marvellous organisation appeared to its best advantage. In the fiercest heat of battle, when to the unaccustomed eye the scene must have been one of hopeless confusion, and when friend and foe seemed so intermingled as to defy detection, the admiral's signals flew up the mainmast. Instantly the tactics were changed. De Ruyter withdrew his squadron from the battle, and gave chase to the flanking ships; the rest of the fleet gathered, slowly retreating, round their admiral, and while stoutly maintaining the contest, drew, in the form of a half-moon, like a protecting shepherd and his dogs, round the flock of merchantmen entrusted to their care. The manœuvre was successful. The night fell —but not a ship had been lost.

A council of war was now called on the Dutch fleet. The losses had been heavy, and everyone was hard at work to repair the damages and leaks. The question was put whether it would not be wiser to let the merchantmen go home alone and take their chance, whereby the movements of the Dutch fleet would be rendered free. But Tromp would not hear of it. He had been ordered to see them home, and bring them home he would, whatever came of it. At the break of day on the 1st of March all the captains were called on board the Admiral's ship, acquainted with the resolution, and exhorted by the Admiral himself to uphold the honour of the flag. It was ten o'clock, six leagues off Dungeness, when the fight commenced; but the fury of the previous day had somewhat abated. Tromp, with admirable self-command, kept on the defensive. His position was changed somewhat to his advantage. On the previous day Blake lay between him and the Dutch coast; on this morning he had gained a free road to the Meuze, but he had lost the wind. He formed once more into a gigantic half circle, spreading out for many miles. Florisz lay at one flank, De Ruyter at the other, and he himself in the middle, and enclosed in this hedge, the merchant fleet drifted slowly towards the harbour of safety. Try what they would, the English could not break this barrier. They first charged one flank, and then the other: Florisz and De Ruyter were both rendered helpless; two frigates and a few merchantmen, who were too clumsy or too ignorant to remain within the protected circle, were captured, but the fleet itself was untouched. Six times did Blake try furiously to break through this half-moon, and six times he was compelled to withdraw. The second night fell, and still the Dutch fleet continued its way homeward.

The day had been one of fearful excitement, and the night brought no relief. No sooner had the firing ceased than captain after captain came on board the Admiral's ship and reported his losses. One had so suffered in his rigging that he could scarcely follow, another could only keep afloat by pumping, and nearly all complained loudly that they had very little powder or shot left. The one man in all this commotion and excitement who remained calm and collected was the Admiral himself. He assured his 'children' that their country required them to do, no more than their duty, and that they did very well if they fulfilled that. He sent them away much comforted; but it was doubtless an hour of bitter trouble to him, alone in his cabin, when he thought that after such exertions and so much danger, the miserable carelessness of the Admiralty at home might perhaps cause every advantage to be lost. And there is but little doubt that, with a less intrepid warrior, the whole, or nearly the whole fleet, would have fallen into English hands.

On the morning of the 2nd of March the two enemies sighted each other off Beveziers. The wind was again in Blake's favour, but again there lay before him that unbreakable half circle that barred his way to the rich merchant fleet. The attack began at nine, and for two hours each side compelled the other's admiration by the fury of its charges or its gallant resistance. But at eleven Tromp beheld the disaster which he had anticipated. Half his captains had lost every particle of ammunition. Beset by the enemy, unable to answer, and fearful lest some greater calamity than defeat might befall them, their spirits drooped, and several made all sail towards their own coasts. Quick as lightning Tromp crossed their path, for instant resolve alone could counteract such disgraceful behaviour. It might have been easy for him to follow their flight, and throw the blame on his want of ammunition and the culpable neglect of his government. But he clenched his teeth, and resolved to fight to the last. A broadside soon arrested the fugitives, and they were asked in the sharpest manner whether they preferred to act as villains and be shot afterwards, or to return to their places, show the enemy neither their weakness nor their fear, and leave the defence to him. Cowed by this determined language they returned. Happily Blake had drawn off. There was a lull in the fight, and Tromp, without disturbing his circle, ordered all sail to the French shallows, where he knew that Blake could not follow him. But the lull was only for a moment. At three o'clock in the afternoon the English Admiral, having gathered his ships together, gave the sign for a final attack. Tromp met him boldly. Only thirty ships of his fleet were by this time able to return fire; but as he saw Blake advancing, he signalled all sails to be stowed. The fleet, thus arrested in its homeward course, calmly awaited the attack. The shock was terrific, and many a Dutchman, beset by superior numbers, went down to his grave in the troubled waters. But for the last time the half-moon remained unbroken. A number of merchantmen, venturing in their clumsiness too near the French coast, were captured by the English, but the bulk of the fleet was saved. Between four and five o'clock the British fire ceased. Blake, acknowledging that further attack was useless, stood out to sea, and left fourteen of his frigates to harass the enemy by a fitful fire. Then Tromp's captains came swarming on board. There was scarcely a shot left, and the greater number of the ships had to be kept afloat by pumping. De Ruyter and Florisz, who had guarded the flanks, had to be tugged. Five men-of-war were burned, four had been captured, twenty-four merchant-men were missing, there were nearly two thousand killed and wounded, and as many prisoners. But Tromp kept to the fore. He was at any moment ready to fire his last shot, and hoisting a lamp in his mast, he continued his way with his sail half mast high. At midnight the British fires disappeared, and next morning the Admiral looked for his enemy in vain. But he was three days in making his way from Calais to the Meuze, a distance which he would have otherwise completed in little more than a day.

Whichever way this battle is looked upon, it must alway be considered a masterpiece of prudence and courage. Not only was the English fleet superior in mere numbers, but its movements were perfectly free, whereas Tromp had to take care, not only for himself, but for his convoy. Blake had not been out of port more than a week : his men were fresh, his ships were stronger and larger, his guns more numerous. Tromp, on the other hand, had suffered severely, not only in his battle off Dungeness, but by more than one severe storm. His men were exhausted by three months of cold and fatigue; ammunition and provisions alike were wanting ; and notwithstanding this, he managed to cut his way through the enemy, and bring all those who were wise enough to obey his orders safely into port.

But do you think that the old fogies of Amsterdam or Zealand listened to him when he told them how nearly all had been lost by their carelessness? Not a bit of it. They were much too wise to listen to advice. You can look at some of their portraits in the Amsterdam National Gallery—worthy old fellows, with white hair and gold spectacles and double chins, and looking as if they were very fond of a good dinner, and could not possibly make a mistake.

'We are much indebted to you, Mr. Tromp,' said they; 'you have behaved nobly, and with heroic courage. We are proud to have you as our Admiral, and so on; but we do not think that our fleet is so bad as you say. It has done pretty well, considering. As for the ammunition, you will not fight another three days' battle in a hurry; and we are building a new fleet that will be good enough for anything.'

But Tromp shook his head warningly. 'You will find out your mistake too late, my lords,' he said. 'England is a large country, and if we desire to fight her, we must put forth our utmost strength. Our ships are too small, our guns are too few; some of our captains are shamefully ignorant, and have no business to be captains at all; our sailors are wretchedly paid, and our soldiers look like a pack of robbers.'

There was a slight change for the better after that, but it was only slight, and it was not for Tromp to refuse obedience to orders, however slow and foolish his masters might be. He was out again in the middle of May with ninety-eight men-of-war and six fireships; but before taking the command, he wrote a letter to the States, imploring them to make his fleet stronger, as he must otherwise inevitably suffer a defeat. This letter produced no effect; he sailed with a convoy of two hundred merchantmen to the Shetland Islands, and lingered in that latitude for another of the same size, which he was to bring into port.

The second fleet, however, had not yet arrived at the place of appointment, when an advice-yacht of the States reached him with a pressing order to return at once, as the English fleet was out again, and cruising in the Channel. The meeting took place near the village of Newport, on the Flemish coast, at eleven o'clock of June 12, 1653. On the one side there were Tromp, De Ruyter, De With, and Evertsen; on the other, Monk, Deane, Penn, and Lawson. The number of ships was exactly equal, but the wind was in favour of the English. Monk had profited by Tromp's tactics, and now ranged his fleet in the form of a half-moon, with which, having the wind, he came bearing down on the Dutch. His heavier weight and calibre soon gave him the superiority. Slowly but unmistakeably the Dutch were forced to retire. Most of them fought bravely; but the ignorance and cowardice of the rest thereby became so much the more conspicuous. It was nine o'clock before the fighting ceased, and the night was passed by the Dutch in anxious expectation of an attack. At break of day a council of war revealed the danger of their position. There was the old story of want of provisions, want of ammunition, want of men, want of everything. Tromp nearly lost his courage; but to turn his back on the enemy while he had a shot left was not in his nature. The English meanwhile, reinforced by Blake with eighteen fresh ships, were again ranged in their half-moon. Tromp saw that his only chance lay in a daring and skilful attempt to take the wind out of their sails ; but the very elements seemed to be against him. He was on the point of success, when a sudden calm disturbed his whole plan, and rendered half his fleet useless. The English meanwhile advanced slowly, led by Vice-Admiral Penn. Tromp had abandoned all hope of victory ; but he was resolved to die hard. As Penn approached, he deliberately ran alongside of him, and the two vessels poured their broadsides and volleys of musketry into each other. After a frightful struggle, Tromp carried Penn's quarter-deck ; but immediately thirteen British men-of-war came to the rescue of their Vice-Admiral. Tromp was surrounded and overwhelmed. From all sides the English rushed on to his deck, and foot by foot his men were obliged to retire below. Then there was a terrific cheer amongst the English ; but it came to a sudden end. Determined not to surrender, the Admiral, while some of his men were fighting on the stairs, had dragged two small barrels of gunpowder to the centre of the middle-deck, and set fire to them. They exploded with an awful crash. Half the upper deck, filled with English sailors, was blown away ; the other half was burning. At this moment De With and De Ruyter, seeing their leader in such danger, rushed up with part of their squadrons and crashed into the dense group. A cluster of thirty vessels lay almost board-a-board. It was scarcely possible to distinguish one's neighbour, for the very light of day was obscured by the volumes of smoke they sent forth. At this critical moment the ignorance and cowardice of some of the Dutch captains decided the day against them. Seeing their leaders thus engaged, they became confused, and fled. Some ran against each other, and were either taken or sunk; some were cut off or surprised. Then Tromp saw that his sun of victory had set, and ordered a retreat towards Flushing. The pursuit was hot. The fighting lasted with unabated fury till one o'clock in the morning; nor would the English have abandoned the chase at that hour had they not been afraid to get on to the shoals. They carried thirteen Dutch vessels and thirteen hundred prisoners in triumph behind them. Six Dutch ships had been sunk, two were blown up, and the number of dead and wounded was larger than at any former period. The defeat was complete and unmistakeable; and when the four Admirals landed in Flushing, their mien and behaviour was so cast down and dejected that the worst was at once known. The people were crowded on the quay in eager expectation, and the States had sent down special commissioners to learn the issue of the contest. When the rough and impetuous De With had gained the shore, he told the ambassadors, with a great oath, that they might sell all their navy, for that the English were henceforth masters of the seas. Evertsen solemnly declared that a disgrace had fallen upon the country as a just punishment of heaven. De Ruyter swore with solemnity that he would never go to sea again, unless a total change took place. And when 'Father' Tromp himself stepped out of the boat, with a face that had lost all its wonted cheerfulness and good-humour, the people were not slow to believe the truth of his words, 'that the navy had been shamefully neglected, and that there were fifty ships in the English fleet better than his best.'

This plain language was repeated in a full sitting of the States at the Hague, and some of the men whose duty it had been to supply the fleet, were forced to blush at the shortcomings there revealed. Meanwhile, the English were in the highest spirits, and chuckling with delight over their victory. In London they sung such verses as these in the streets :—

I.
The moody Dutch are tame and cool—
  They pray and wish for peace ;
Our gallant navy in the pool
  Has melted all their grease.

II.
Brave Blake and Ayscue are the men,
  Have squeezed their spunge of riches.
When they have conquered Holland, then
  The Dutch may sell their breeches.

III.
When they are drunk awhile they fight ;
  But after run, swear, mutter,
Their buns are all too cold and light
  To melt our English butter.

IV.
Turk, Pope, or Devil we defy :
  Courage, brave English venter,
Since Fate crowns you with victory,
  The world lies open—enter.

But worse than this, the English fleet remained in the Channel, and blockaded the ports. Not a herring-fisher could run out, not a merchantman could come in. In the busiest season of the year, trade was at a complete standstill, and the Dutch might as well go to bed, unless they intended to make a supreme effort and regain what they had lost. When they felt their reputation, their prosperity, and their very safety thus endangered, the High-Mighty Lords at the Hague, who had been taking things too easily, began to wake up out of their drowsiness, and rub their eyes. Messengers were now despatched to all ports and wharves to fit out as many old ships, and build as many new, as there were hands to do the work. Whatever happened to be in the stocks for other nations was bought. The Admiralty, the trading companies, the private merchants, were ordered to make a return of all the ships serviceable for war. The most strenuous efforts were made to attract able men to the service. Wages were nearly doubled. A pension after a term of service, or a sum of money to the relatives in case of death, was promised. Compensation for wounds and the loss of limbs was fixed at a liberal scale. He who captured an English man-of-war, would be rewarded by promotion; he who seized an admiral's ship, or even a flag, would receive a considerable sum of money in addition. On the other hand, desertion from the ranks and culpable ignorance were to be punished with death. The States were in earnest, and so determined to muster a large number of men, that by a decree all the beggars who were not physically incapable, were sent to the fleet to undergo a year's service. A proclamation called upon the people to assist in chasing the enemy from their shores, nor was the appeal made in vain. The number of volunteers became embarrassing. Many men of the highest position willingly took the lowest posts. More than one rich merchant went himself on one of the ships, while he undertook the equipment, clothing, and pay of a certain number of sailors. Ministers of the gospel volunteered to accompany the fleet, and remind the officers and men of their duty towards God and their country. A wave of that enthusiasm which had all but disappeared in the universal welfare, ran from one corner of the land to the other, for was not the British fleet swaggering up and down the Channel with unbearable insolence, with a broom fixed to the Admiral's mainmast?

For six weeks Tromp, to whom every one looked, and who directed all efforts, worked with the energy of a giant. In the first week of August, a new fleet of more than one hundred sail was ready to battle with the enemy. But under the immense pressure, Tromp lost his wonted hopefulness and elasticity of temper. He saw that it was a last and desperate effort, the reckless throw of the dice on which the ruin of the country was staked. Gloomy thoughts and anxious forebodings filled his mind; he saw clearly that with so many new ships, and new commanders, so many willing but uninstructed men, so much that was crude and disjointed, so much that was superficial and pretended, they were not in a position to cope with a powerful and victorious enemy. The very fact that he had to give advice in every difficulty, and that a whole nation in its hour of tribulation confided its destiny to him, whose brain and whose hands were after all liable to commit an irreparable mistake, filled him with sadness. For he loved them. His large and manly heart, the beating of which was not quickened by one throb in the supreme hour of his own danger, trembled for that of others, and seemed glad of an opportunity to lay down his life for them.

'Your lordships,' he wrote in the latter days of July, 'are putting more upon my shoulders than I can bear. One man cannot do all this in these times. And if I be shot, or fall ill, or some other mishap deprive your lordships of your commander, what is to be done? In any case,' he adds, 'you may be confident of this, that I shall die as I have lived, an honest man, and to the welfare of my beloved country.' With this, he sailed on the 6th of August. The new fleet had been built in three ports, Wielingen, Goeree, and Texel, of which the two former are situated in the south, and the latter in the north of the Netherlands. Tromp's portion of the fleet, eighty-two men-of-war strong, ran out of the Meuze with a very boisterous sea, but favourable wind. His aged mother had accompanied him on board the 'Brederode' to give him a last farewell. When on the point of leaving the ship, she turned towards the sailors, and in her simplicity admonished them to support her son with all courage, and never to abandon him to the enemy.

Their answer was, 'We would rather set fire to the ship, than surrender him.' And when the worthy old lady expressed herself somewhat doubtful of so much devotion, she was answered by so hearty and unanimous a cheer of the men for 'Father Tromp,' that she left the ship and her son much comforted.

On the 8th of August, the English fleet under Monk was discovered about four o'clock in the afternoon, lying in front of Texel, plainly with the object of preventing Admiral de With and his fleet from running out and joining Tromp. The latter, although perfectly well aware that he was much inferior in strength to Monk, resolved to engage him, and draw him away to the open sea, so as to give De With an opportunity to run out. The fight commenced within sight of the Dutch coast. Thousands of inhabitants had flocked to the sand-hills to witness the awful spectacle, and for five hours their ears were filled, and their senses bewildered by the terrific clangour of battle. Long after the sun had set, and the deepening dusk obscured the fleets as they drifted seaward, the echoes of the hills were awakened by the simultaneous reports of thousands of guns. The noise had been great, but the actual result of that day's battle amounted to nothing positive. Neither Monk nor Tromp had gained any advantages, neither had captured an enemy's ship or lost one of his own; but Tromp had accomplished his object. He had remained sufficiently far from his enemy not to be touched by his musket-fire, and still had drawn him away to sea.

De With was now free, and ran out that same night in the most extraordinary fashion, following the sound of the cannon, and coming up with Tromp about five o'clock in the afternoon of the next day effected his juncture within sight of the enemy. The wind had been so violent during that day, and the sea so boisterous, that neither Admiral deemed it wise to begin an engagement in which the fury of either party was violent enough, without adding the rage of heaven. Penn says it was 'blowing so hard in gusts, we could scarcely keep our top-sails half-mast high; sometimes down as low as they could stand.'

On Sunday morning the 10th of August, the wind had changed to the north-west, in favour of the English, and Monk prudently resolved to delay no longer, but take his chance. There seems to have been a stern determination in both fleets to let this battle decide the issue between them. Tromp had somewhat more solemnly than usual admonished his captains, while he divided his fleet into five squadrons. Monk, who was becoming weary of sea-fighting, ordered his captains to give or take no quarter. 'The taking of ships in a fight,' he says, 'always weakens the fleet, by sending of other ships with them; wherefore to make short work of it, ye must rather send an enemy to the bottom, than take him.' Between the villages of Scheveningen and ter Heide, the battle commenced. Never before had the sea witnessed such a collision. The English sternly determined to keep the victory they had won, to remain sovereigns of the sea, to give no quarter, and allow no escape; and the Dutch, wrought up to a high pitch of excitement by their previous defeats, by the knowledge that they were fighting for their existence, and within sight of the shores which they had wrung from the ocean, and snatched out of Spanish hands; both Protestant in religion, and devout in spirit; having but lately suffered and fought against the same enemy, and for the same sacred purpose, were now fully fixed in their bloody purpose to destroy each other. All brotherly love, all esteem, all goodwill had passed away. The flaming sulphur that spurted out of ten thousand cannon supplanted the light of heaven. 'In a few hours,' says Burchett, 'the air was filled with fragments of ships blown up, and human bodies, and the sea dyed with the blood of the slain and wounded.'

Once already Tromp had broken through the English line of battle, and forced Monk to change front. At about midday he hoisted the signal for a repetition of the manœuvre, hoping thereby to divide and scatter the English fleet. Cool and collected as ever, he gave his instructions with admirable precision. At one moment on the quarter-deck, watching the different squadrons through his telescope, singling out with rare judgment the best men for each order, and giving the most befitting duty to each captain, he was the pivot on which the whole action turned. At this moment, Rear-Admiral Goodson was in front of him and eager to engage. For some unexplained reason, Tromp's signal at that moment was not understood by the fleet, and the advance was not made as uniformly as he desired. He saw himself and part of his squadron in the danger of being surrounded by Goodson. Roused to momentary displeasure by what he considered want of skill or courage on the part of De Ruyter and the other Admirals, he exclaimed, 'If anything has to be done, there is nobody to do it but myself. Nobody comes to relieve me until I have opened a way for them.' While saying these words, Goodson had advanced, and was running past him, followed by his squadron in line, under a terrific fire from both sides. Tromp's ship was soon enveloped in smoke and invisible. The other Admirals, who had watched and waited the hoisting of the red flag, lost sight of her for a time. When she reappeared at last out of the obscuring cloud, there waved instead of the red flag, another, which carried consternation into the hearts of every captain. They were summoned to the Admiral's ship. Their worst fears were realised. On a few pillows in his cabin, they found the lifeless body of their great commander weltering in blood. From the second ship that followed Goodson a musket-ball had pierced his heart as he was descending the steps to the maindeck, and he had scarcely breath enough to say a few words of encouragement and affection to the sailors who came grouping around him, and he had not time to finish the prayer to the Great Judge before whom he was about to appear, when he gave up his life, as his father and many of his friends had done before him, at his post on the deck of his ship. It is my intention to describe the end of this fearful battle when I shall speak to you of De With and De Ruyter. The grief of these commanders was profound; but it was unanimously resolved to keep the disaster secret, that no man might become disheartened. The red flag was hoisted, Evertsen was entrusted with the command, the others returned to their vessels, and the battle was continued. Thus round about his body there waged one of the most furious battles that had ever been seen ; and what more befitting end could there be for a man who had been nursed by the winds of the Atlantic, whose school had been a man-of-war, whose love had been for his sailors, and in whom the quality of soldier was not more admired than that of justice? Those who have the opportunity should visit his magnificent tomb in Delft, where he was buried with great pomp and remember part of what is written on that tomb by the nation, that 'He left to posterity a grand example of mastery in naval warfare, of fidelity to the State, of prudence, of courage, of intrepidity and of immovable firmness.'

WITTE CORNELIS DE WITH.

ADMIRAL DE WITH was a man whose life I find it very difficult to describe without saying either too little or too much. You have come across his name already more than once in the Life of Admiral Tromp, but you may be very thankful that you did not come across himself; for if you had been in his way, or if he thought you were going to be in his way, he would probably have taken you by the collar, and sent you rolling to the other side of his deck, with very little politeness or ceremony. I have asked myself the question whether he ought to be included in the list of Great Dutch Admirals, and at one moment I have answered yes, and at another no. I will, therefore, let you judge for yourselves, and tell you with impartiality what he did, and how he did it. Whatever else he may have been, he was one of the most prominent men of his day; and no boy who has studied the history of the Netherlands can be ignorant of his name. For forty-two long years he displayed, in the service of his country, an amount of courage and perseverance under difficulties, in which none of the other Admirals excelled him. He was engaged in no less than fifty sea-fights, and commanded a large fleet, or part of a large fleet, in fifteen great battles. His body was covered with wounds; he was frequently indisposed, and twice dangerously ill, in consequence of exposing himself too much; and yet when he died on the deck of his ship, and with the enemy in front of him, he did not leave much wealth or property behind, and amidst the crowd of mourners who followed his body to the grave, he scarcely numbered a friend. With many admirable qualities, he was totally without self-control. He deliberately spoiled his own life, and marred his own happiness, because he would not curb his temper. He was so savage, so jealous, so overbearing, that he made enemies of all his friends, and at the same time so harsh and stern, and even cruel, that he made no friends amongst his enemies.

He began life in very humble circumstances in the neighbourhood of Briel. His father, who was a small farmer, and poor, died within three years of his son's birth, and although the mother's work and the income of the farm seemed to have brought in enough for them to live on, this sad accident compelled De With to look out for himself at an age when other boys are guided and helped by their father's love. He saw when he could scarcely crawl—and he tumbled out of his cradle as soon as he could—that whatever was to be his in this world, he must fight for; and as he wanted a good deal, and did not dislike the fighting, there was plenty for him to do.

His mother had managed to send him to school, where he learned a little, and did a great deal of mischief. But one day, when he was eleven years old, she heard of this, and calling him into her room, gave him a sound lecture. Old Farmer De With had belonged to the Baptist congregation of Briel, and the Baptists in those days were very much like the Quakers; they strictly forbade any one to return blow for blow; they would not even defend themselves, and held it a great sin to go fighting and quarrelling all over the place. Now when Mother De With heard that her son was such a good hand at this she felt deeply shocked. The boy was fond of his mother, and no doubt somewhat afraid of her; so, having listened to the lecture, he promised that as a Baptist boy he would not fight again. I need not tell you, however, that this very soon became unbearable for him. When the boys at school heard of it, they roared with laughter, and the poor fellow was teased most unmercifully. They played all sorts of tricks on him, and when he wanted to find out and punish them, they all came up to him and held up their fingers, and said, 'Now, mind, you must not fight.'

One day, when this had been going on for some time, and when he had been more than usually teased, Cornelis said to himself that he would stand it no longer. He dare not break his promise, and yet there was Walter, his neighbour, who had put a dead cat in his desk—he must give him a drubbing. So what did he do? He went quietly to the Protestant minister, without anybody knowing of it, and had himself baptized; and as he went home, he said to himself, I may do what I like now, for I am no longer a Baptist boy. And they found it out next day at school. There was no more teasing, no more dead cats, and Walter's back felt sore for many a day afterwards. His mother, of course, was deeply grieved; but what was to be done? As the boy grew older, he grew worse instead of better; and while others settled down to some quiet business or trade, Cornelis continued to display the same pugnacious and restless spirit. Whenever there was a row in the town he was sure to be in it, and his work, of course, suffered in consequence. They tried him at everything, but nothing would succeed. He was, in plain words, a wicked boy. He went rope-making, but was sent away. Then he went to a button-factory, then to a tannery, but in neither of these employments could he keep peace with the rest of the men. As he had a great liking for the sea, they thought sail-making might suit him, but even this was of no use; and when he was at last apprenticed to a tailor, he fairly ran away. 'It is no use, mother,' he said, 'I was born for the sea. When I stand on the bank and see the ships sailing in and out of the Meuze, I feel that I must go to sea, and that I shall never do any good for myself on shore.' So in 1616, when he was seventeen years old, he took service as cabin-boy in an East India merchantman, and sailed for Java.

When he returned from his first voyage he had

certainly shown that he was better fitted for the sea than for anything else. He had led a queer kind of life. In Java his sharpness and cleverness attracted the attention of the Governor of Fort Jacatra—at that time the only Dutch settlement; and as De With felt himself fitted for something higher than a cabin-attendant, he accepted the governor's offer and entered his service. Partly personal companion, partly steward of the castle, and partly corporal over a detachment of the garrison; getting into rows with the governor, and with the garrison, and with the natives; he, nevertheless, did some very useful work, and so distinguished himself in storming the town of Jacatra, and establishing the present Batavia that when he returned to the Netherlands in 1620 he was able to leave the East India Company, and become lieutenant on one of the States' ships. The expeditions in which he took part were numerous, but not very interesting. He got a ship of his own at last, and when Admiral Piet Hein set out on his memorable expedition to capture the silver fleet, De With was chosen as the captain of the flag-ship. As this expedition has already been described in a former paper, I will only say that De With chased the yacht, which had been sent off to warn the Spanish fleet, and captured it, whereupon he loudly claimed having done more than all the rest together in capturing the fleet itself. The Admiral, as you may imagine, was disgusted at this, and so were the States. He never received one penny reward for this deed, and used to complain to the end of his days about the shocking ingratitude of his country.

I have already told you that after Hein's death, Tromp, who was then only a captain, felt disgusted with the service and left it, and that his friend and school-fellow, De With, did the same thing. The latter, however, had another reason why he left the service—namely, the ill-feeling which had already arisen between him and other captains. The harshness of temper which had shown itself so violently at school had not been softened either by his subsequent life or by himself. He would have been a truly great man had he, with the knowledge of this defect, striven to conquer it, as he strove to conquer Spaniards or Peruvians. It was doubtless a fine thing to rise from a cabin-boy to a captain, and continue his studies unaided by any one, and to fight single-handed against half-a-dozen enemies, and come off victorious; but it would have been a much finer thing had he shown some sympathy with the weak, some mercy for those who were in his power, and forgiveness for those who had offended him. But of these qualities he knew nothing. Always anxious to let everybody about him know who and what he was, what he thought on such and such matters, what he had seen, he would also try to prove why the opinion of every other person was absurd and wrong. As a natural consequence he quarrelled with all the other captains, as I have said, and left the service in disgust.

At that time Tromp and he were still good friends.

They were both on land, and both considered the cleverest captains in the service. In the meanwhile he had married, and accumulated a sufficient amount of property to become sheriff of the town of Briel. But life ashore suited him no more than it suited Tromp, and so when, in 1637, the post of Admiral became vacant, De With declared loudly that he and Tromp were the only men who could fill the post, and that he being, of course, the best man would get it. The States and the Stadtholder, however, seemed to take a different view of the matter, and called upon Tromp. De With was dreadfully disappointed, and looked upon Tromp as having done him a personal injury. It is true he was somewhat appeased when, in acknowledgment of his great merit, they made him Vice-Admiral of Holland; but he never forgave Tromp, and from that moment a coolness sprang up between them, which poor Tromp, who had done nothing to cause it, exerted all his power to clear up.

As far as the service was concerned they worked well enough together, but the unreasonable jealousy of De With could not fail to produce a very unpleasant impression on Tromp. One day while De With was cruising in front of Dunkerque, a considerable pirate fleet hove in sight. Although the number of his ships was only five, and two of his captains earnestly counselled him not to attack the enemy, who had nearly double that number, De With would hear of nothing but attack. The pirates made for the open sea, and De With went after them. For four days he followed them about everywhere; he tried all he could to begin a battle, but the pirates knew better. After having led him about for all that time without firing a shot, a storm arose, and the pirates slipped away. De With sailed home in disgust. Two of his captains, who were either afraid of fighting or offended at him, had sailed home before him, and told Admiral Tromp that the Vice-Admiral had knocked about the sea for four days in sight of a pirate fleet, without daring to engage it.

Tromp foolishly believed the story, and when De With came ashore you may imagine how he stared with astonishment and rage at being severely reprimanded by the Admiral. He broke out into the most furious passion, and insisted upon having a court-martial. Tromp advised him to be moderate, admit his fault, and ask the Stadtholder to pardon it; but this only increased his fury. A court-martial was held, with Tromp as president; but its progress was uncommonly slow; the evidence was scarcely to be got at, for every man in the fleet seemed to have taken a dislike to De With, and it was many months before the verdict was pronounced. De With had already threatened several times to take the law into his own hands if matters did not move on more quickly. He was honourably acquitted, as he really deserved to be, and his conduct as a faithful servant of the State and a bold seaman was praised; but it would seem that very few, beside himself, were glad of this honourable acquittal.

No accusation could have been more unfair, and more directly opposed to his character. There was nothing he liked so much as fighting. If they had accused him of cruelty to his men, of ungodly language, of risking the lives of his men to very little purpose, he would probably have been condemned on any one or all of these charges; but unshrinking courage was perhaps the only virtue which he possessed. Tromp is usually praised for the defeat of D'Oquendo in the Downs in 1639, but there is no doubt that this battle would never have taken place but for De With. It came about in this wise. You will remember that the great Armada was expected. Tromp with his squadron was cruising in front of Dunkerque; De With was over on the English coast, when Captain de Groot came to him at midnight with an order from Tromp to join him immediately, as the Spanish fleet was in sight. De With asked what the Admiral was doing.

'I do not think he means to fight,' said the Captain. 'He held a council of war this afternoon; but he would give no advice, left the chair, and told the captains that they must make it out amongst themselves, adding that if we fight the enemy we are sure to be destroyed, and if we go away we will be received at home as scoundrels.'

When De With heard this he got into a fury. The idea of retiring when the enemy was in sight seemed to him something impossible. He made all sail at once, and came up with Tromp's fleet early in the morning. No sooner had he got on board than he began blowing up the Admiral for his hesitation. Tromp shrugged his shoulders and looked miserable, for, being a cautious man, he never forgot that if he were defeated there was no other fleet to protect the coasts. But De With would have nothing to do with these scruples. He only knew two things—that the enemy was in front of him, and that he must fight him. 'We are in for it now,' he said; 'we can do nothing else but live and die as faithful servants of the State. Let us fly no longer, but attack the enemy.' 'But we can't,' said Tromp. 'Look at them; they are ten times as strong as we are,' and so saying he pointed to D'Oquendo's fleet, which covered the sea for miles. But De With didn't care. He knew only one thing a man-of-war should do, and that was to fight. 'I had rather get my neck broken by these Spaniards,' he added, 'than by the mob when we come back, without firing a shot.' Having spoken in this fashion for some time, Tromp at last gave in. At that solemn hour all differences were forgotten; they shook hands, and drank a glass of wine together in the cabin, while they settled the plan of battle. De With having gone back to his ship, singled out that part of the Spanish fleet which was densest, and where the largest number of great ships were lying close together. Thither he steered with his squadron of small vessels, and ran right into the midst of them. More than once he was surrounded by five large galleons, who directed their fire upon him from all sides, he sailing in be-

TROMP AND DE WITT SETTLING THE PLAN OF BATTLE.
Page 128.

tween them, and returning shot for shot with wonderful precision and coolness. His sails were reduced to mere rags, half his tackle was torn away, his mainmast was cut through, no less than a dozen shots had entered one side of the ship and gone out at the other, his stern was in flames, and the sea was rushing into the hold through more than one leak; but he stood on his deck grinning with delight, and cheering his men. The Spaniards, not accustomed to such violence, withdrew towards the English coast, and De With steered towards Tromp. When he stepped on to the Admiral's deck, he was 'besmeared, begrimed, limping, and an unsightly object to look at;' and he asked Tromp, with a sort of grim humour, whether he had any desire to hold another court-martial on him.

There can be no doubt, that this splendid bravery of his was the main cause why D'Oquendo retired to the Downs; for had Tromp been allowed to go his own way, he would certainly have remained on the defensive, and hesitated with his attack so long that the Spaniards might at last have summoned courage enough to beat him. Strange to say, when the great battle was afterwards fought in the Downs, De With remained inactive. His vessels being in a totally helpless condition, he was towed to Zealand, and returned a week later with another ship. When the morning of the battle came, he naturally expected to take a foremost part; but a serious difficulty presented itself. There was the English fleet, and somebody must keep out of the fight to look after it. Tromp could not; Evertsen had received distinct orders from his own Admiralty-board to refuse anything of the kind; nobody else cared for the post, when De With, with an admirable solicitude to further the common interests, offered to remain on the watch, although he too burned with desire to cover himself with glory. For this disinterested conduct he was justly praised; but he would certainly have been more amply rewarded had he not boasted about what he would have done, and spoken so much about what others did not do. Had the conduct of this affair been entrusted to him, it is certain that he would not have accomplished anything like the victory Tromp afterwards gained. He had no conception of patience. He did not understand the wisdom of biding his time. As commander-in-chief he would probably have attacked the Spanish fleet again and again, until his small force had been exhausted, and at least part of the Spanish fleet saved. Tromp, on the other hand, showed his wisdom. Knowing the energy of his former schoolfellow, he sent him off to Holland to hurry on the States, and kept D'Oquendo in that rat-trap until he was strong enough not only to defeat, but to destroy him.

During the thirteen years which elapsed between this battle and the first English war, De With went through all sorts of adventures and misfortunes. He lost his second wife while away with the fleet on the Brazilian coast, and although she left him eleven young children, he was not allowed to come home.

A man can do a good deal of quarrelling in thirteen years' time, if he only sets about it in the right way, as our Admiral did. The whole fleet, from the highest officer to the lowest cabin-boy, detested him heartily for his selfishness, his cruelty, his overbearing and imperious behaviour. And the authorities of the South American colony detested him equally for his insolence and his intolerable rudeness, and did all they could to make his life unpleasant.

This would have been hard to bear for the meekest and most patient of men, especially when he knew that a motherless family was much in need of him at home. He stormed and swore and raged, but all to no purpose. He was certainly most shockingly treated, but it was his own fault. Nobody cared to have him in the Netherlands, and orders were sent over to keep him in South America as long as possible. But those in Brazil did not care for him either, and thwarted all his projects. Some of his letters are almost ludicrous in their passion. He complained of having nothing but old and musty bread, dried fish which was rotten and worm-eaten; the rice and peas were uneatable, the pork and meat had turned to pure salt, and those on shore refused him the commonest things, because they said they had not enough for themselves. The worm was eating into his ships, but the colonial government would listen to nothing. 'The meanest slave,' he writes, 'nay a dog, would receive more care from these men than an Admiral.' 'I vow to Heaven,' he wrote again, 'an honest man is too good to end his life in this abominable place; and if I am to die in this starvation-hole, I would much rather go and serve the Great Turk, if he would only allow me to worship my God after my own fashion.'

All this, however, had not the slightest effect on the colonial government, which, to tell the truth, was composed of the most small-minded, pettifogging, and hateful creatures in the world. De With's patience was at last exhausted. For the sixth time he asked permission to go, but was again refused. He had made up his mind all the same, and sailed, two of his ships arriving in the Meuze with starved, shivering, and nearly naked sailors, in the midsummer of 1650. Intelligence of this serious act of insubordination had been sent to the Netherlands before him. He was received coldly. He was admitted to a full sitting of the States at the Hague, where he gave an account of his journey; but on the same afternoon he was arrested in his hotel, put in prison, and sentries posted at his door. The Solicitor-General of the Netherlands prepared an accusation against him, and the States were called upon to condemn him to death, and forfeit his worldly possessions to the country. Such was the condition to which he had been brought, principally by his own fault; and so determined a spirit was there in the country against him, that the idea of his being put to death seems to have excited no great amount of indignation or pity. But he had been too good a servant of his country to be thus rewarded. After a good deal of haggling and useless discussion whether he could be tried at all, he was acquitted of the graver charges, and merely condemned to pay the cost of the trial and of his own imprisonment, and to forfeit his salary during that time. The fact was, the judges thought that he had suffered quite enough out there, and as he was a violent opponent of the Stadtholder, the republican party in the Netherlands thought it wiser not to make an enemy of him altogether.

Indeed, although he was so very unpopular, nobody could deny that he was a very brave and able commander; and as there were a great many people who looked upon Tromp with jealousy and envy, they thought it wise to support De With, not because he was Tromp's superior, but because he was his enemy. Now you will remember that in August of the year 1652, Tromp was very unfortunate, in so far that he ran out with a very large fleet, failed to meet with Blake, was attacked by a violent storm, and had to return home with the loss of a good many ships. Immediately all his enemies cried out that it was a shame he had ever been allowed to command the fleet, and that there was a much better man ashore, who would be sure to sweep the English off the seas. De With of course came forward at once, with little modesty, but plenty of confidence; and with the new fleet that was given to him, he loudly promised to do great things. He knew that the whole nation was watching him, and that now or never was the time to make himself a great name by some bold stroke. He ran out of the harbours with forty-five men-of-war, and was joined by De Ruyter; but the winds and the sea would favour neither Admiral, and a terrific storm well-nigh stranded his entire fleet on the coast, and so damaged many of the vessels, that eleven out of the seventy ships had to be sent home. Nevertheless De With had made up his mind to do something wonderful, and now resolved to run to the Downs and attack Blake in his own waters.

But he had not been more than a few days in command when he began to see that although the fleet was bound to obey him, it was not bound to love him as it loved Tromp, and that his presence created a spirit of aversion and hatred which had the most disastrous consequences. His ship being one of the smallest, he rowed to that formerly occupied by Tromp. But the sailors, who adored their late Admiral, and grieved for his loss, would have nothing to do with him. They refused to throw him a rope, they would not even let down a ladder for him to come on board, and threatened, that if he attempted anything of the kind they would fire into his boat and drown him. Time was pressing. De With rowed to another ship, and took command of it. He found the captain an old and incapable dotard of seventy, the officers totally inexperienced and stupid, the sailors drunken and insolent. Any other man would have been disgusted, but it just suited his character. He wrote with some humour, 'I have to take upon me the duties of captain, lieutenant, mate, gunner, gunner's-mate, even including the provost.' But he was equal to it all. In very little time he had arranged everything; the signals were hoisted, and the fleet set out in quest of Blake. Unfortunately for him, Blake had heard of his plan, and determined to anticipate him.

On the morning of the 8th of October, 1652, Blake ran out of the Downs, and came upon De With with so unexpected a rush that the Dutch Admiral had no time to call a council of war, but sent word to the captains by an advice-yacht to keep close together. He himself behaved with his usual splendid bravery. At three o'clock the battle commenced, and it lasted till long after sunset. The fleets were very unequal. Blake had sixty-eight ships; De With only sixty-four. Blake's ship, the 'Resolution,' had sixty-eight guns, and eight hundred men; the largest ship in the Dutch fleet had only fifty guns and two hundred and fifty to three hundred men. Nevertheless, although he was advised to retire, De With gave the signal to engage. With his own ship he singled out the 'Resolution,' and was the first to return the English fire. Long before the close of the fight he was in a shocking condition, but he fought on. Twenty of the captains, who hated him, and were perhaps too cowardly to do their duty, kept out of the fight; but the rest fought with marvellous determination. 'I fought from three till sunset,' said De With, 'and during that time I saw nothing but smoke, fire, and English.'

Blake says he gained the victory, and pursued the Dutch fleet; and the English historians of that time describe the whole action rather as a flight than as a battle. The Dutch, on the other hand, say that they anchored with burning fires during the night in their own position, and only discovered their great losses next morning at daybreak. Half the fleet turned out to be in a helpless condition, and most captains counselled that retreat was the only thing left to them. But De With would not hear of it. He had come out to do something great, and he would rather sacrifice the whole fleet and every man in it to his ambition, than return to his country defeated. His reproaches to those who had remained inactive were violent and bitter. He threatened them that there was wood enough in the country to make gibbets for them all, and implored them with folded hands to be cowards no longer. But the council of war remained cold to his entreaties. He was too much disliked for anyone of them willingly to contribute to his success; and besides the fleet was too weak to be able to resist Blake for a moment. De With flew into an uncontrollable fury, and blamed them all round for cowardice; but De Ruyter, who was his Vice-Admiral, calmly reminded him that the fleet had been entrusted to their care, not to lose it, but to use it, and that however hard it might be to retire, it was the only thing they could do. The retreat was resolved on, and although Blake harassed the Dutch rear during the whole of the afternoon, no great damage was done, and De With anchored in the Meuze on the 10th of October.

His rage and disappointment were, as you may imagine, excessive. He loudly protested against the cowardice of the captains, nor did he rest until they had been brought to trial and severely punished. But this could not alter the fact that he had been defeated. The storm of reproach and insult that overwhelmed him on his return was far greater than that which had greeted Tromp. He had moreover the intense mortification of seeing his great rival once more appointed commander-in-chief of the fleet, while he was again reduced to the rank of Vice-Admiral. Spite, disappointment, and envy, which he could vent upon no one, undermined his health, which had already seriously suffered. He attempted to take his post on the fleet, but became so alarmingly ill that he was forced to return home, where, for many a day, his life was despaired of.

I now come to the battle in which Tromp lost his life. It will be remembered that the fitting out of this fleet, after the thorough defeat in June 1653, was the last and desperate effort of the Dutch to maintain themselves at sea. The whole country felt it. Every man worked with a will, and the youngest child awaited the result with anxiety. It will also be remembered that De With with his fleet of thirty-one ships lay in the northern port of Texel, where he was blockaded by Monk. On the 6th of August, Tromp ran out of the southern ports, attacked the English fleet and drew it away to sea, in order to give De With room to run out and join him. Nothing could more fully illustrate the Vice-Admiral's splendid qualities than his behaviour on this occasion. He had constantly hurried on the building of the fleet in those quarters; but when he heard Tromp's cannon out at sea, a number of the heaviest ships were not ready. Indeed, nothing had been prepared for this hurried departure. Nevertheless he gave the order to make ready. Everybody exclaimed that it was impossible. The wind out at sea howled with furious violence right on to the coast, and sent the foaming waves rushing into the harbour. Every beacon had been taken away for the sake of the enemy; there was not a pilot in the Texel, there was not a captain or sailor in the Helder who would take charge of the fleet. They could scarcely keep on their legs, and how could they prevent the big ships from drifting on to the sandbanks? But De With knew that there was fighting going on, and he could not, for the life of him, remain in port. He ordered all fishermen of the town to run out with their boats and flaming torches, and anchor on every dangerous shoal, on both sides of the narrow mouth of the Zuyder Zee. It was nearly midnight before the tide ran out. The fleet of fishing smacks, with their flaming lights dancing on the waves, had already sailed, and were lining the channel on both sides with strange fantastic spots. Sombre and gloomy clouds chased with rapidity across the moon. A small but dense rain made every object indistinct. The pilots ashore shook their heads gravely, and an anxious crowd braved the inclemency of the weather to witness this extraordinary feat. Under those circumstances, and nerved by the very magnitude of the danger, De With went on board with a light heart, and led the way. A few hours' tacking against the wind proved that his idea was by no means impossible. He got to sea without a single accident, and effected his juncture with Tromp in the course of the following morning.

I have already partly described to you that furious battle of Texel which now took place, and in which the great Admiral lost his life. It will, I think, interest you to read an account written by a French gentleman, who embarked on board a sloop of war to be an eye-witness of the battle. 'On the 10th,' he says, 'they came to a decisive battle. The English had endeavoured to gain the wind; but Admiral Tromp having always kept that advantage, and having drawn his own fleet in a line parallel to that of the English, bore down upon them, and began the battle with so much fury, that many ships were very soon dismasted, others sunk, and others on fire. The two fleets were afterwards enveloped in a cloud of smoke so dense, that it was impossible to form a judgment of the fierceness of the battle otherwise than by the horrible noise of the cannon with which the air resounded, and by mountains of fire which every now and then were seen rising out of the smoke, with a crash which gave sufficient notice that whole ships were blowing up. In fact, many ships were blown up; and in particular, it is said, that Admiral Tromp, having perceived three English ships which had run foul of each other, immediately sent a fire ship, which arrived so precisely in time, that they all took fire at the same instant, and blew up with a report capable of striking terror into the breast of the most intrepid. Nevertheless, the English encountered with incredible valour all the efforts of the Dutch, and were seen to perish rather than to give way. The death of Tromp having damped the courage of the Dutch, the action was no longer so violent; and the smoke dispersing, the two fleets were seen in a condition which showed the horrible fury of the conflict. The whole sea was covered with dead bodies, with fragments, and with hulls of ships still smoking or burning. Throughout the remainder of the two fleets were seen only dismasted vessels, and sails perforated throughout by cannon-balls. Nearly thirty ships perished between the two parties; and the English, having pursued the enemy as far as the Texel, had the honour of the victory, which cost them as dear as it did the vanquished.'

Indeed, the defeat of the Dutch was complete. After the death of the Admiral, the fighting was renewed with the same fury. Three times the fleets sailed past each other in full line of battle, and at last as by common resolution dashed into the conflict. Ship after ship was riddled with shot and went down, burying its dead or dying in the depth of the ocean.

John Evertsen signalled that somebody must tow him to Goree. He himself was all but insensible through loss of blood, having been severely wounded; his own son, who commanded his ship as captain, lay dying in the cabin; there were over fifty dead and wounded; his masts, bulwarks, and tackle were entirely destroyed, and the water entered the ship through no less than two holes below water mark. De Ruyter was in as sad a plight. His ship, the 'Lamb,' having only thirty-six guns and one hundred and fifty men, had lost one mast, its rudder, all sails, while eighty-one of his men were either killed or wounded. Ship after ship left the battle and came running into the Meuze disabled and nearly sinking; but amongst them De With was not. He had now assumed the command, and the blood-red flag still waved from his mast. He would hear of no retreat, and lay in the most dangerous position, thundering away as though he had resolved not again to return to the Netherlands defeated. But fortune was against him. Towards the evening a dozen captains retreated, making all sail homeward, although still perfectly able to fight. De With, furious at this cowardice, fired several shots after them, but in vain. They disappeared, and there was nothing left but to follow them. He signalled the fifteen ships which were still left, to keep close together and retreat slowly. Hedged in on nearly every side by the overwhelming squadrons of Monk, Penn, and Lawson, De With kept up a resolute face towards the enemy, and when the night fell only one sinking vessel had been abandoned to them.

The Dutch deny that they were defeated, for, say they, De With remained with his part of the fleet at sea all night and the greater part of next day, whereas the English disappeared at night and were seen no more upon the Dutch coast, having abandoned, in consequence of this battle, the blockade of eight weeks which had been so destructive to Dutch commerce. Nevertheless the Dutch had been obliged to retreat, and could not possibly have sustained an engagement upon the second day; and what is more to the purpose, they hastened to conclude a peace in which all the advantages were on the side of the English; and nothing could more clearly show that they began to feel that England's power was greater than they could resist.

De With of course was furious against those captains who had treacherously abandoned their duty and left the battle. He railed against them wherever he was, and a court-martial was called. There were more than a dozen; their influence was powerful in the States, and their relations with the highest people in the land made it a matter of difficulty; but they were all condemned to more or less punishment, and disgraced. This, you may imagine, did not render our De With a bit more popular. Indeed, although his conduct during the battle had been beyond criticism there was neither enthusiasm for him amongst his inferiors, nor cordiality amongst his equals. After

Tromp's death it was generally expected that, as oldest Vice-Admiral, he would have been appointed in his stead; but the States-General dared not give him the command. It was only lately that six vessels of the fleet had one after another deliberately refused to receive him on board as Admiral, and he had come to the States with the somewhat original request to allow him to have the worst of these put in between two others and bombarded for a couple of hours. A man who inspired such feelings as these could not be put at the head of the country's fleet, and Tromp's place was therefore filled by Wassenaer van Obdam, a nobleman of distinguished reputation and of considerable wealth, and a cavalry officer of great courage and experience, but as ignorant of the management of ships as De With was of the art of pleasing others and controlling himself.

But as he was no sailor, and therefore no rival, Wassenaer was no object of hatred to De With. Indeed, the new Admiral seems to have been the only man in the fleet with whom De With had never had a quarrel, and in the various expeditions which he undertook under his command there seems to have been less contention and jealousy than hitherto. For a short period the arms of the Republic were at rest, and thankfully was that rest accepted and enjoyed by men who, like De With, had scarcely been out of harness for years. It would have been thought, indeed, that after so many struggles and dangers the little mannie in his tub would have been content to end his days in peace, so long as he was not meddled with. But the clever statesmen who managed the thinking part of his business saw, with admirable clearness, that sitting still was the most dangerous thing he could do. Money and all the good things of this earth were flowing in upon him, and they very justly feared that if he were allowed quietly to sit down and eat and drink as much as he liked, he would begin to grow dangerously stout, sleep a great deal, work less and less, until at last some one would come on tiptoe behind him while he was dozing, upset his tub, send him rolling on the ground, and do with him pretty much what he pleased. This the statesmen would allow on no account, so in a few years' time they had begun a war with Portugal, and a part of the fleet was sent off to bombard Lisbon.

In 1658, Charles, the King of Sweden, happened to take it into his head, for reasons which I cannot very well explain here, that he should very much like to have Denmark added to his kingdom. He collected a large army and navy, sailed from the Swedish coast across to the island of Seeland, landed his troops, enclosed the town of Copenhagen on land by his army and at sea by his fleet, and swore that he would not go away until he had taken the town. The King of Denmark sent in a hurry to the Hague, and the States immediately promised help, for they had already a bone to pick with the Swedish king. Wassenaer and De With were summoned at once, a fleet was got ready, and in the beginning of November it appeared at that narrow entrance of the Baltic which is known as the Sound. On each side of the channel the Swedes had a formidable fortress, and a large fleet, under the celebrated Admiral Wrangel, lay behind it to dispute the passage of the Dutch.

On the morning of the 8th, when the sun had risen, Wassenaer signalled the fleet to advance. De With had begged to be allowed to lead the van, and with his ship, the 'Brederode,' which had carried his old rival Tromp so long, he sailed into the Channel. Under a heavy fire from the forts on each shore, to which he returned not a shot, he sailed straight up to the Swedish Admiral and gave him a broadside. The Swedish Vice-Admiral thereupon approaching, De With rushed about the deck frantically exclaiming, 'I must board him, I must board him; he shall not escape.' Engaged in close conflict with this opponent, he was beset by two others; but his fire was so well aimed that one of them received a shot in the powder stores and was blown up, while the other was obliged to withdraw. Even the Vice-Admiral was constrained to slacken his fire, when unfortunately De With's ship was carried away by some capricious current and fixed on a shoal. He signalled, but no one could come to his assistance. Meanwhile a second vessel attacked him in the rear, while the Swedish Vice-Admiral still threatened him in front. For two hours he returned this cross fire with coolness and intrepidity, signalling at intervals for assistance which came not, for the battle was raging hotly in the Sound. At this hour a bullet wounded him in the leg, and he fell, but being supported by some of his officers, he refused to leave the deck, and continued to issue his commands. Not long afterwards a second bullet wounded him in a vital part. He had barely strength enough to exclaim, 'Fear not the face of your enemies, but remember the great Lord, and fight for your wives and children.' But the greatness of the calamity overwhelmed his men with terror. The enemy perceived it, and rushed on to the deck of the vessel. When the dying Admiral beheld this outrage to a ship which had never seen an enemy, the fierce, indomitable spirit blazed up once more. He crawled to his knees and seized the sword which he would not surrender. Feebly, for he was exhausted with loss of blood and approaching death, he strove with many a gasp against the overwhelming host. Overpowered, and gently seized, he was led with faltering steps across a plank to the enemy's vessel. His spirit still lingered as he listened to the sounds of battle around him. There was an evident trouble on his mind, and he asked frequently what had become of his ship. When he was at last informed that she had sunk without having surrendered to the enemy, he laid his head down contentedly and died.

The Swedish king, who had watched the engagement from shore, was moved to tears when he beheld the body, and for three days it was exposed in state to the populace. Wrapped in white satin, and conducted by one of the bravest Swedish captains, in a frigate draped with black crape, the body was then sent to the Netherlands, as a tribute from the enemy to so much valour. He was buried with much pomp, and at the country's expense, in Rotterdam. The procession that followed the hearse was almost endless; but although everyone admitted his great qualities, and could not deny the eminent services which he had rendered to the Republic, it was sad to reflect that he had produced a spirit of dissatisfaction in the fleet, which on more than one occasion had seriously endangered the welfare of the country.

MICHIEL ADRIANSZOON DE RUYTER.

PART I.

THERE was not, in the whole of that busy little Holland, a busier or more prosperous little town than Flushing. Even at present, although the steamboat and railway have drawn much of its trade to other parts, it has maintained so comfortable a footing that it remains the envy of many a neighbouring town. But two hundred and fifty years ago it was a sight worth seeing, when from the quay of the city you gazed on a thick forest of masts and spars, while whole fleets, consisting at times of hundreds of ships, sailed away for the Baltic, or arrived from America, or lay at anchor in the stream waiting for cargo. There was a rowing of little boats backwards and forwards, and an eager bustling of merchants and captains, brawny porters almost doubled under heavy burdens, sailors hurrying ashore to get their pay, and soldiers hastening aboard their new ship. There was a hubbub of voices in many a foreign tongue, buying, selling, or haggling over a few groats, laughing at some old joke, or giving a hearty welcome to an old friend; while the stout burgomaster, panting with the heat, blew up a clumsy fellow for treading on his toes, and the sailors in the river were a-hoying their chorus, as they weighed the anchor with a long pull, a strong pull, and a pull altogether.

There was not much laziness in Flushing in the early part of 1600, I warrant you. Times were too good for that, and money was coming too fast to let it slip by. The twelve years' truce, as I stated in a former article, had done the Hollanders much good. Their trade had increased to a fabulous extent, and the shipbuilders and ropemakers had more orders than they could execute; for let them offer as high and comfortable wages as they liked, there was generally some captain who would offer more, and draw the strongest and most active fellows away to sea. It was a time of wonderful activity, in which labour and wealth seemed to increase fourfold with every succeeding year.

It was in the summer of the year 1617 that those inhabitants of Flushing who happened to be on the market-place suddenly stopped their business, collected in groups, stared up into the sky, and pointed with outstretched hands at the church spire. There had arisen quite a bustle amongst the apple-women; the farmers' wives left their stalls to have a better look, the old dames told the young ones that it was a disgrace to God's house, and the young women answered that they were very glad *their* sons never did such things. Elderly men shook their sticks, and promised the young rascal a good whacking if he came down without breaking his neck. The fat farmers could not even comprehend how he had ever got there. The very pigs caught the excitement, and began to grunt and squeal with a new vigour. What was it? The church steeple was being repaired; but that surely could not cause the astonishment, for it had been going on during the last week, and besides, at this very moment the slaters had gone to dinner, and the work was at a standstill until it pleased them to return. And yet there was somebody up there who seemed to take things very coolly. It was a boy of about ten or eleven, who had somehow succeeded in reaching the very pinnacle of the church tower, had seated himself astride on the ball, and was now waving his cap frantically at the people below, and bawling with all the power of his little lungs, to show them that he was really there. The more those below stared and shouted to him to come down the more he waved his cap; and he even became so bold as to perform several gymnastic feats while holding on to the weather-cock with one hand. Those below, however, could see what the foolish boy could not—namely, that the workmen had taken away the ladders by which he had got up, and that he could not get down again.

By this time he had been recognised as the ne'er-do-well young rascal, the son of Michiel the brewer, and some began to say, that it would not matter much if he did break his neck in coming down; but

THE FLUSHING PEOPLE STARING AT DE RUYTER ON THE TOP OF THE CHURCH TOWER. *Page 180*

it was very evident that the adventurous lad was not put out by a trifle. When he thought it time to go down, he began to look for the ladder, but found it gone. The crowd below looked up in silence, and with bated breath. Young Michiel stood for a moment with a puzzled smile on his lips. To slide down would have been certain death, for the parapet of the tower would not have stopped his course. There was apparently nothing for it but to wait until the ladders came; but for this young Michiel had no patience. He soon found a way down. In a trice his heel had kicked in half-a-dozen of the slates. The wooden framework on which they rested formed a sort of ladder, by which he climbed down, kicked in some more, climbed further down, and repeated this process until he landed safely on the parapet of the tower, where, with another wave of his cap, he disappeared down the stair, and having got into the church, began to play such mischief with the organ, that the beadle, who had been chasing him all over the building, had to run for his father in despair.

That he was soundly whipped I need scarcely tell you. His father, who carried heavy beer-barrels on his shoulders all day long, could make himself felt quickly enough; but young Michiel got in for a thrashing so often that he was by this time almost accustomed to it. There was, indeed, not a naughtier boy than Michiel in all Flushing. Scarcely a day went past that his mother did not shed hot tears over him, or that his father did not take down the birch rod from the nail in the chimney corner. He was sent to one school after another, but instead of working, he played the most outrageous tricks upon the masters, and set up quite a revolution among the boys, by whom he was idolised. At last his father—he was but a poor man himself, and did not see the fun of paying for a son who would not learn—managed to get him into the rope-yard of Messrs. Lampsens, where our Michiel had to turn the wheel for sixpence a week. But he behaved no better in business than he had done in the school. In a very short time he was unanimously elected commander-in-chief of all the boys in the yard. With his little army of followers he used to make raids upon his enemies, and deal out the most summary punishment and revenge. Instead of turning his wheel, he used to get up regular pitched battles outside the town, where you might see him in all his glory, hammering away at some sturdy opponent. More than once he was sent about his business by Mr. Lampsens, his employer; and it was only owing to his father's entreaties that he was again admitted to the yard. But it was no good. Michiel would not do for business, that was plain enough. He became more unmanageable than ever. Always at the water-side, or in the boats, or up the mast of some ship, or going about with young sailors just returned from a long voyage, to whose yarns he listened with eagerness, he no sooner got to his wheel, or in the ropeyard, than he showed signs of laziness and unwillingness to act the drudge.

'Look here, Michielson,' Mr. Lampsens at last said to the boy's father, 'that son of yours will come to grief if you are not very careful. He is a bad lot, all over, and I'll have nothing more to do with him.'

'I am afraid he is, sir,' said the brewer, shaking his head dolefully; 'he seems to be no good on shore, sir, and I would have sent him away to sea long ago, but that his mother is afraid he will get drowned.'

'Better drowned than hung,' said Lampsens; 'besides, he is sure to break his neck if he climbs up any more church towers. Send him to sea. There is a ship of mine just going out to the West Indies; he can go in that if you like, and if he tries on any of his pranks there——' Mr. Lampsens did not finish the sentence, but twirled a stout piece of rope through the air by way of elucidation, and left the honest brewer to make up his perplexed mind.

Young Michiel received the news with a shout of joy, and bounded with burning cheeks out of the house to talk about the matter with some of his friends. The mother's objections were overcome, and within a few days the lad was at sea as boatswain's boy. A remarkable change immediately came over him. He seemed to have left all his vices ashore with his old clothes.

It was on the 26th of December 1618, that Michiel went to sea. He was then eleven years old: he was, therefore, born in the year 1607, about a month before Jacob van Heemskerk gained that splendid victory in the bay of Gibraltar. I have hitherto called him Michiel alone, although De Ruyter stands at the head of the page; and before I go on, I may as well explain how our hero came by his name. The poor people in those days had very often no regular family name. If a man happened to be baptised John, and his father's name was William, he was generally called John, William's son, which in course of conversation, became John Williamson. Then if this John in his turn had sons, he generally called the first one William after his grandfather; and the people round about called him William, John's son, or William Johnson, and this went on, turn and turn about, for ever so long. Now our hero's grandfather was called Michiel, Adrian's son, or Adrianszon, and this man's son, of course, was called Adrian Michielson. It was also the fashion to call people after their employment or business, or after some peculiar habit or quality they or their houses or their families possessed. One of the ancestors of the great Dean of St. Patrick, for instance, was a quick runner, and therefore he was called Swift. Now it would have been quite in the order of things if his friends had called our hero's father Adrian Michielson Brewer, and then, of course, I would have to write about Admiral Brewer; or if he had been very stout, they might have called him Potbelly. But it so happened that the brewer's wife, whose name was Jane, had married him without her family knowing anything about it. He arranged to fetch her with a horse, and ride with her to a neighbouring town; and when Jane said that she could not ride, her lover assured her that did not matter in the least, as she would sit behind him on the same horse, and could catch hold of him. Next morning came, and with it Michielson and his horse. They rode to church, were married, and lived very happily ever afterwards; but when her friends heard in what manner she had gone to her wedding, there was no end to the teasing and fun about her ride, and she got the nickname of *the Cavalier*, or, as they would say in Dutch, 'De Ruyter.' Now every boy at school knew about this, as a matter of course, and whenever they wanted to make young Michiel angry, they used to call him 'De Ruyter' after his mother's nickname. But the lad had too much common sense to be angry at that: he did not mind it a bit, and as there were at least half-a-dozen sailors on the ship in which he went out of the name of Michiel, he was very soon known by no other name than De Ruyter, and kept it to his dying day.

I have already said that his conduct changed altogether the moment he set foot on board the ship. In later years, when he had earned for himself a great reputation, he very often spake about his youth, and always frankly confessed that he had been a very naughty lad, but as long as he was ashore he felt that he was good for nothing but the sea, and that he would remain a trouble to himself and all those around him unless be became a sailor. Young Michiel was now in his element, and he had as much of the sea as he liked. On the same ship where he served his apprenticeship as boatswain's boy, there happened to be a negro lad who served as sailor. Some years ago he had been taken by the Spaniards from his native island, on the African coast, and sold as a slave. After being passed from hand to hand, he was taken by a Dutch skipper and brought to Flushing, where of course he was at once a free man. This negro seemed to have taken a great fancy for young Michiel, and as he could tell the most wonderful stories of his African home—the lions, and tigers, and elephants they had to fight with, and the way in which they lived, in small huts and in the trees—you may imagine that Michiel listened to him as long and as often as he could. When the negro lad had been in Flushing for some time, he was converted to the Christian religion, and baptised in one of the churches; and as they were puzzled what to call him, they gave him the name by which the sailors of the East and West India Companies were generally known, and he was baptised as 'John Company.' With this John Company, then, our Michiel was very friendly, and whenever the poor lad was teased about his black skin or thick curly hair, De Ruyter was always ready to defend him. Many, many years afterwards they met again under very different circumstances, in very different positions—which I will relate to you presently.

The hard work and the sea air made our Michiel a strong, well-grown lad for his age; for after he had returned from his second journey, when he was scarcely fifteen years old, he was enrolled with the other sailors of the merchant navy, to serve in the army as arquebusier. Although so young, he did his duty better than most of the soldiers, and having bought a horse, gained considerable reputation in several sorties from the city of Bergen, where he and his regiment were at one time besieged by the Spaniards. He was already earning a soldier's full pay, and when the sailors were no longer wanted in the army, he was at once promoted, on board a man-of-war, to boatswain's mate, a post of some trust, which would have been too much for most lads of sixteen. Many were the adventures which he now encountered, and the only thing we must constantly regret is, the great modesty and reluctance to talk and write about his own person, which kept De Ruyter from ever telling to others, or describing himself, what happened either then or afterwards.

The manner in which he frequently escaped the greatest dangers is sufficiently wonderful, but if you follow the lives of most great and brave soldiers, you will find that those who fear nothing suffer least, whereas those who are always thinking about the greatness of the danger, and what splendid fellows they must be to remain so near death without running away, are very often overcome and crushed at the outset. Now De Ruyter feared nothing. It is not likely that he knew what great things were in store for him, but he was always amongst the first in any fight, and constantly exposed himself to all sorts of dangers. One day, while jumping, sword in hand, from the ship in which he served to a Spanish man-of-war, he was wounded in the head by a lance; but although the wound was exceedingly painful, and might have turned out dangerous, he quickly recovered. He was afterwards concerned in nearly a hundred fights; and, as you will presently hear, some of them were no matter for joking, but in not one of them did he receive a scratch, or as much as a blow, although he was generally in the very midst of the fray, and hundreds of friends and foes were killed around him.

Not long afterwards, while still a sailor, his ship was captured by some pirates, the crew were robbed of all they had, and sent ashore, in Spain, as prisoners. With two other sailors he was so fortunate as to escape. Destitute of everything except an old suit of clothes, he found himself obliged to walk through Spain, France, and Belgium, with his two companions, each in his turn begging his bread at the doors of the houses. He afterwards frequently said he could never forget the events of that pilgrimage, and we may safely assume that it was owing to these and similar experiences of suffering, privation, and poverty that he displayed so much kindness and thoughtfulness to those whom the chance of war put into his power.

He was now about twenty-one years old. Not a

trace was left of his former wickedness. He was healthy and honest-looking, and strong in mind as well as body, and so good a seaman had he become that Messrs. Lampsens, his former employers, engaged him as boatswain on one of their ships. Gradually rising, from step to step, we see him on a ship of his own in the year 1640, when he was thirty-three years old. He deserved it. He had gained no honours except by hard work and conscientious application to his duty. He was a great genius, no doubt, and even though he had not studied much, he might still have risen to a considerable height in those days of warfare. But we shall see him presently occupying the highest position, simply because he was the ablest man in the fleet. During the time that he was boatswain, mate, and captain, whenever he found anything in his journeys that was interesting, and that nobody had noticed before, he made a careful note of it, and remembered it faithfully.

As he was very fond of mathematics, he employed his spare time in making new maps of the places he visited, and notwithstanding his rude instruments, he drew them with so much correctness that some of them are in use now, and have received but little alteration. It need scarcely be said that, in consequence of all this, his name became known to the authorities. Mr. Lampsens, his employer, who was burgomaster and member of the States-General, knew very well what a good fellow he had in his service, and so one day, in 1641, when the republic was preparing a fleet to assist the Portuguese, in the Mediterranean, De Ruyter was suddenly called to the camp of Prince Maurice, the Stadtholder, and to his surprise and delight, he was there and then not only made captain of a man-of-war, but rear-admiral of the fleet, the commissions being handed to him on two sheets of parchment, with large seals of red wax, and a whole string of signatures attached to them.

When the first flush of satisfaction had passed away, De Ruyter felt dissatisfied. War seems to have been altogether a distasteful occupation to him. Till the end of his days he always professed a dislike to it. He was of a homely disposition. In the height of his fame, there was more attraction for him in a quiet chat with a few friends at his own fireside than in all the pomp and show of the Hague, the splendid carriages, the rich uniforms, the brilliant reviews, balls, and parties, that were given by others, and that others said should be given by him. And at sea he very much preferred sailing about as his own master, and earning an honest livelihood by trade. He was not ambitious like De With, nor was he a born warrior like Tromp, and he would have been content if he had never outshone the brilliant courage of the one, or the prudence and sagacity of the other. But just as gold only exists in certain countries, which, when discovered, must yield of their substance to the whole of mankind, so a great man who has golden qualities, and finds many honours thrust upon him, would not be a great man if he refused to bear his honourable burden, that others may profit by his strength. It was impossible now to get rid of so honourable a post, and as long as the war lasted, the new rear-admiral performed his duty with all his might. In one battle off Cape St. Vincent, the fight was so hot that when his sinking ship was afterwards examined, he found several holes under water, one of which measured three feet by two, through which the sea came rushing in. He got into Flushing in a pitiable condition. Many sails and some of his rigging had been torn away by the violent storms, the ship had to be abandoned, the sailors were all but exhausted, and De Ruyter himself had quite enough of it. He made all haste to get into his own ship again, and sail away to the West Indies, before the States had time to send him on another expedition with the fleet, nor could the repeated offers that were made by the Admiralty, induce him to go in for another war.

The fact was that he led a much pleasanter life as captain for Messrs. Lampsens, than as rear-admiral for the States. He had a large share in the cargo of the ship, and part of the profits was his. He was at the same time entirely independent, could go wherever he thought fit without consulting admirals or officers, and was not exposed to the constant risk and danger of a man-of-war. After having been thus employed for nine successive years, he could already boast of having anchored in every important harbour of the world; but there were a good many snug, out-of-the-way places that other captains had not the pluck or the cleverness to sail to, and when he got there he had it very nearly all his own way. The poor, good-for-nothing lad of Flushing had actually become rich, and his old father and mother were now comfortably settled in a nice little cottage outside the town. You will no doubt think that Captain Michiel was uncommonly fortunate, and so he was; but a great deal of his success was simply owing to his unswerving honesty. Men never make a greater mistake than when they think that because a well-known person is great in some things, he must necessarily be foolish or wicked in others. We see in De Ruyter a decided proof to the contrary. To those around him and to himself he was as simple and guileless as the dove, but when occasion required it, he displayed a cunning and sagacity far above that of the serpent, while the fulfilling of his duties remained his first object.

One day, arriving with his ship on some part of the African coast, he called upon the prince of that region, and showed him some specimens of his cargo. Amongst other things he had a very fine piece of brown cloth, which took the prince's fancy amazingly. He threw it over one shoulder and then over the other, and admired the effect in the looking-glass with a pleased smile, but when he heard the price that smile was changed in an instant. He was a rich man, but liked to buy things cheap, and offered half the money. De Ruyter refused, and began to pack up at once. The prince stopped him.

'I have made up my mind to have that piece,' he said, 'and you *must* give it me.'

De Ruyter refused again, saying that his masters had given that price, and that he would cheat them if he sold it for less. The prince tried all he could, but in vain. Then he threatened, and pointed to his sword, saying that there were dark cellars in his palace into which he could thrust him without anyone knowing anything about it. Instead of frightening De Ruyter, it made him wild.

'Excuse me, prince,' said he boldly, while all the officers of the court were standing by, 'this is very cowardly. You would not dare to say such a thing if I were on board my ship. If you want the piece particularly I will give it you, but I shall never sell it under price.'

The prince left him in a great rage, and for two hours De Ruyter was in uncertainty whether he was to be killed or not. At last the prince returned, calmed down, but still desirous to have the piece at the low price; but again the resolute captain refused, and offered it as a present. Then turning to his courtiers, the prince exclaimed—

'Behold how faithfully and bravely this Christian works for his masters. Take heed that ye work in the same way for me.'

Whereupon, baring the captain's breast, he laid his hand upon his heart, as a token of friendship, endowed him with rich presents, spread a great feast in his honour, and made a solemn covenant with him whereby he and he alone was allowed to trade, at great profit, with that nation. De Ruyter of course was delighted.

It now became instantly the fashion at that court to wear brown cloth. Not only was that sold at a great profit, but everything else in the ship was equally well disposed of, and he returned home laden with a whole host of precious things which he got for a mere bargain.

As a curious instance of the manner in which his life was preserved, it may be mentioned that, meeting an English man-of-war on his homeward journey, in the Channel, he ordered a salute of half-a-dozen guns. While he stood behind one of the pieces it suddenly exploded. Everybody round about was hurt, one man was killed, another lost both his legs, half-a-dozen were seriously wounded, but he alone escaped without a hurt. Not long afterwards one of the sailors came running up to him with the unwelcome news that a Dunkerque pirate was in sight, towing a prize behind her. Now De Ruyter had a very valuable cargo, which it would be a pity to lose. Being heavily laden, it was no use attempting to escape, but he knew that his ship was largely built and looked in the distance like a man-of-war, so, though he had scarcely half-a-dozen guns on board, he hoisted the Admiral's colours, made all sail, and bore down upon the pirate. The Dunkerque, afraid to have an encounter with so large and determined an adversary, let go his prize and fled, whereupon De Ruyter coolly turned homeward and dragged another man's prize with him into port.

On another occasion his cunning was equally for-

tunate in saving his ship. He was returning from
Ireland with a cargo principally consisting of butter,
and had anchored not far from the Isle of Wight.
A large number of other merchantmen were already
riding at anchor in the same place. A few of these
were waiting for a favourable wind, but the greater
part, terrified by the pirates that were cruising up and
down the Channel in great numbers, dared not go
out. The November storms were raging, winter was
at hand, and every day became precious. Moreover
butter was scarce in Zealand at that moment, and
so, though his ship was small and badly armed,
De Ruyter determined to risk it. He had not been
out very long when a pirate was descried bearing
down on him. In vain all sails were spread to the
rushing winds—every gust, every wave brought the
pirate nearer. The men were at their wits' end, but
our captain knew a trick or two. He ordered his
men to take off their boots and stockings, and a score
or so of butter barrels were brought on deck. In a
very few minutes these had been knocked to pieces,
and the butter was thickly spread all over the deck
and outside the ship. Not a rope or a spar that was
not glib and slippery. Even without their boots and
stockings the sailors could scarcely keep on their
legs. On came the pirate, not knowing what was in
store for him. De Ruyter assumed an air of penitent
submission, and allowed them to come alongside
quietly. But lo! when they jumped over, fully
armed, with pistol in one hand and sword in the other,

they slipped about and tumbled over each other on the buttery deck like so many rats. One fellow shot head foremost down into the cabin, where he was immediately sat upon by the boy; another slid all across the deck, and shot out into the sea by an opposite porthole. Not one of them could stand on his legs, and, as these bad men are generally superstitious, an idea seized them that the ship was possessed of the devil; they hurried back into their own ship, cast loose, and De Ruyter got safely into port at the expense of a few pounds of butter.

Coupled with such marvellous cleverness, he possessed a generosity and largeness of heart that endeared him to every sailor. On one of his journeys, while the war with Spain was still going on, and he was commander of a small frigate, misfortune sent a large Spanish galleon in his way. Fearing that he would be overcome in a contest, De Ruyter wisely sought to escape, was chased, overtaken, and compelled to fight. Then he went at it with all his might. Their positions were quickly changed. The venturous Spaniard was too slow and heavy to follow the quick Dutchman in all his movements, and ere an hour had gone by he would gladly have retired. But De Ruyter was now master of the situation, and poured volley after volley into his big enemy until he began to sink. The Spaniard hoisted a white flag and begged for mercy. The Dutch sailors were against this, but De Ruyter ordered the boats to be put out and the Spanish crew was brought on board. Instead of being grateful for their lives, however, they remained sulky. De Ruyter went up to the captain,—

'Would you have treated us with equal generosity, if you had sunk this ship?' asked he, in a stern voice.

The haughty Spaniard shook his head.

'It was my intention,' he answered, 'to drown every one of you.'

'Then you'll go overboard,' said De Ruyter, indignant at this answer; and, turning to his sailors, ordered them to tie each prisoner hand and foot, with a cannon-ball round his neck, and throw him into the sea. The men began to lament, the captain remained stern; but when he too was being tied his savage haughtiness forsook him, and, falling on his knees, he begged for mercy. As De Ruyter wanted no more, it was readily given, and the subdued captain and his men were put ashore at the first opportunity, with a severe reprimand to be more just and generous in future.

All these adventures, however exciting and glorious they may have been, at last satisfied De Ruyter's desire for a roaming life. The energy and restlessness of youth had been changed, and when he arrived home in the latter end of 1651, he had made up his mind that nothing would induce him to go to sea again. He was now forty-five years old, and during his successful and enterprising life he had managed to save a considerable fortune. He married, for the third time, the widow of one of his friends; thanked his late employers very cordially for their kindness, but declined all offers, and retired to his native town, fully intending henceforth to enjoy in the bosom of his family that repose to which he was already justly entitled. So pleasant a prospect did not, however, last much longer than the winter with which it had commenced. The happy days of Spring had scarcely commenced, and we may picture De Ruyter working in his little garden in the most peaceful manner possible, when the war with England broke out. Now De Ruyter had never been regularly trained to the navy, and a naval war did not, therefore, concern him much. Many of his friends immediately applied for posts, and sailed to the fleet with their ships; but he stopped at home, for the mere love of adventure was no longer powerful in him. But he was too well known to remain long unemployed.

While Tromp had sailed away with one fleet to tackle Blake, another had been got ready and was only waiting for a commander; and De Ruyter was requested to come to the Hague and get his commission. Then all his good resolutions went to the wind. When he looked at his nice little house, at his young wife and his children, he hesitated it is true; and when he thought of the strength of the great English Republic, and their endless resources, he doubted whether there would be any use in fighting. But his country wanted him, all his friends were already in service, and so he rode to the Hague, where the High Mighty Lords handed him a piece of parchment, in which their 'earnest, manly, pious, well-beloved and faithful Captain De Ruyter' was appointed Vice-Admiral of the second fleet.

On the 26th of August he was opposed by Sir Geo. Ayscue, and a fierce battle which lasted the greater part of the day was the consequence. De Ruyter was in command of about thirty men-of-war and sixty merchantmen, which he had been instructed to see safely beyond the reach of the enemy. The result of this battle was not decisive. Neither Ayscue nor De Ruyter gained a victory, and when night fell both admirals drifted away in opposite directions, while De Ruyter could at any rate say that he had not lost one of the merchantmen entrusted to his charge.

It would be tedious to relate once more the details of those battles that took place in the first war between the two countries. In nearly each of these De Ruyter took part, as commander of one of the squadrons. But there was no pleasure for him in the service even now. His sudden promotion was a source of continual envy to others and annoyance to himself. Soon after the battle with Ayscue, he served under De With as Vice-Admiral in another battle against Blake, where both were defeated. De With as usual quarrelled with him and wounded him deeply —while several captains, who had entered the service before him, and who were now bursting with jealousy at his promotion, maligned and libelled him in every way, and so disgusted him that he finally resolved to put up with it no longer, and retire to his quiet house once more. But the States-General had already discovered, in the few engagements in which he had taken part, that De Ruyter, above all others, was the coming man, and much pains were taken to keep him. He had been challenged to a duel, but the States, in a public letter, rebuked this proceeding, thanked him for his services, and maintained him in his authority, honour, and office. He was appointed to the squadron which De With's illness had left without a commander. Somewhat later, when he had again given the most brilliant proof of his ability and courage, in the battle off Dover, he was presented with a sum of 125*l.* and a yearly salary of 200*l.* in recognition of his services. Indeed, from all sides rewards and honours came flowing in upon him, without his seeking ; and it would be difficult to point to another instance of so great disinterestedness and humility—seeing that at every new mark of honour, and every step of promotion, he discovered an earnest wish to retire from the scene of action and leave these things to men more worthy.

While he was at sea, battling with a furious storm, the Admiralty of Holland unanimously appointed him Vice-Admiral. The commission was put into his hand as he stepped ashore, but he would not accept it, and begged leave to consult his friends in Flushing. After some anxious consultation he made up his mind to refuse, and presently wrote :

'I have beaten about the seas from my very childhood, and braved so many dangers that I would fain end my days in rest, for I fear that, by accepting this post, I would be tempted to become ambitious for still higher things and more glory, which would ill become me.'

But it was of no use; they could not do without him at the Hague, and he was sent for. The Great Pensionary—or Prime Minister—John de Wit, invited him to a quiet dinner, and had a long talk with him. John de Wit was a clever talker, and there were not many men whom he could not wind round his finger. Simple De Ruyter had but little to say against his arguments, and, before half an hour had elapsed, all the resolutions which he had taken in Flushing had gone back to Flushing through the air, and De Ruyter was Vice-Admiral of Holland—the second leader of the Fleet. He sold his little house, bought another one in Amsterdam, and went to Middleburgh to thank the Admiralty of Zealand, his former masters, for their kindness and confidence—informing them at the same time that he was now resolved to devote the whole of his life, and all his strength, to the service of his country. In truth, Pensionary de Wit had made another man of him. Hitherto he had only thought of his duties towards himself, his wife, and his family; but the Pensionary, who remained unmarried and lived in a small house with one servant, that he might with the greater zeal work for the greatness and welfare of his country, showed him that it is as much a man's duty to work for his fellow-creatures as to work for himself.

There was now an end to his retirement, and he was sent all over the world to uphold the honour of the Dutch flag, and protect the interests of its trade. Peace with England having been concluded, pirates were again the great obstacles with which he had to deal. Dunkerque had been taken by the French king, and the Channel was therefore comparatively safe, but the Mediterranean Sea swarmed with them. The cities on the African coast inhabited by Moors, and all sorts of runaway scapegraces who were obliged to fly from their native countries, throve amazingly on this kind of business. Algiers, Tunis, Tripoli, Morocco, and a good many others, belonged to nobody but themselves, maintained quite a fleet of pirate vessels fitted up as men-of-war, with which they chased every unlucky merchantman that fell in their way; but whenever a man-of-war hove in sight they made all sail and escaped into their own harbours. The only way to suppress this traffic and protect the Dutch merchantmen was to act with firmness, but not with too much harshness. They were a difficult set of people to deal with, for they often had a number of sailors from the Netherlands or from England whom they had bought or sold as slaves and could murder at any moment if rage and desire for revenge impelled them. Moreover they were always at war with each other, and De Ruyter saw that it was only by keeping friends with the one that he could punish the second, and by clever negotiation to buy all the prisoners and European slaves that were pining in their cellars, or doing hard work in their galleys. A man with less sagacity could not have got on with them at all, for he would probably have bombarded them all round, whereupon they would probably have combined against him, done him a great deal of harm, killed the prisoners, and remained as strong and as hurtful as ever.

So profitable, although dishonest, an employment as that of pirate, attracted many adventurers. Men who did not belong to these African States, bought a large and armed vessel, and aggravated their crime by sailing under the colours of a respectable and neutral State.

Connected with this is another interesting incident of his life, which I may as well relate. It had happened one day when De Ruyter had just commenced sailing with a ship of his own, that he was seized by a French man-of-war on the coast of Africa, under the pretence that he came from a port with which France was at war. It was pretty well known that the French captain, Lalande, was a great rogue, and that although he carried the French flag he was nothing better than a cruel pirate. Nothing daunted, De Ruyter rowed on board the Frenchman and tried what he could to get away. He spoke of himself, his wife and family, his master, and even threatened the captain with the vengeance of the States-General, but all to no purpose. Lalande laughed and told him since he had a good prize he would stick to it. Exhausted and vexed, De Ruyter rose to leave, when Lalande, perhaps with some pity, offered him something to drink, and gave him the choice of wine or water. De Ruyter, looking the French captain full in the face, said, in a calm and haughty tone, 'Why do you give me this choice? Give me what becomes my position. If I am a prisoner, let me have water; but if I am a free man, as I should be, I will accept a glass of wine.' Lalande was greatly struck, and smilingly ordered a bottle of his best wine, having drunk which with his guest he allowed him to depart with his ship unharmed.

But a time came when the tables were turned. Towards the end of February, 1657, while he was still with his fleet in the Mediterranean, a Hamburg captain complained to Admiral De Ruyter that he had been chased by a French pirate. De Ruyter immediately resolved to give chase, and came up with two pirates early next morning. The moment the latter perceived what enemy they had to deal with, they endeavoured to escape, but De Ruyter had his fire hose turned against the sails, and after an exciting chase of some hours, his cannon brought the fugitives to a halt. The captain of the largest vessel was instantly summoned on board the Admiral's ship. The first lieutenant of the pirate returned with a polite explanation that he had no right to make this demand, as the vessels were French property. De Ruyter winked his eye, sent the lieutenant downstairs, and sent for the captain again. Another lieutenant returned with more explanations and apologies. De Ruyter got rather angry at this, for he was not a man to be trifled with, and some of his other ships having in the meantime come up, he ordered them to lie by the pirate's side. Then he sent for the last time to the captain, warning him that if he did not come at once he would be sent to the bottom. This brought him out of his hole, but fancy their mutual surprise when, on gaining the deck, the old French captain Lalande and De Ruyter confronted each other. What a striking contrast between the hesitating, stealthy, and skulking conduct of the one, and the bold, honest, and dauntless behaviour of the other! Lalande had been going downwards ever since, and now his fall had come. De Ruyter had been steadily rising, and was now his master in every respect. A certain feeling of gratitude prompted him to treat Lalande with every consideration, but release him he neither could nor would. It was true the ship belonged to the king nominally, and had been fitted out by rich but dishonest French nobles, who received in return one-third of the spoil. But Lalande was a notorious pirate. There were twenty sentences out against him, and the amount of the Dutch ships alone which he had seized amounted to over 100,000*l.* The two ships were seized, the 400 men put in the stocks, and when the Dutch fleet arrived at Barcelona, the prisoners were landed and the vessels sold for about ten thousand pounds. Deaf to all appeals except those of duty, De Ruyter detained the captains, and sent them in a man-of-war to Holland. They were tried, convicted, and hanged; and although the French Government made a terrific noise and threatened war and destruction, the States-General held their ground manfully, and De Ruyter was cordially thanked for his determined and judicious conduct. We now approach the time when the little Republic was again involved in a terrible war at sea, and the safety of its fleet, the existence of its commerce, and its reputation abroad, depended almost entirely upon De Ruyter.

MICHIEL ADRIANSZOON DE RUYTER.

PART II.

WHEN I described to you the battle of the Sound between the Dutch and Swedish fleets, I stopped short at the death of Admiral De With, who so bravely commenced it. That the fighting was desperate on both sides the description must have shown you, but after the Vice-Admiral's death the fury of the combat seemed to increase tenfold and lasted for many hours. The Dutch were at length victorious. That is to say, the passage through the Sound to the Baltic and Copenhagen, which had been disputed by the Swedes, was thrown open, and the Swedes had lost eight men-of-war, three of which Admiral Van Opdam carried in triumph behind him. The Swedish fleet retired to the harbour of Landscron, and was there blockaded; while that very same night the siege of Copenhagen was raised, and the Dutch Admiral received with every expression of enthusiasm.

This victory, which made a great sensation throughout Europe, roused the jealousy and anger of England and France, for they began to feel the absurdity of being overshadowed in political importance by so small a country. When they heard, therefore, that the Dutch intended to send a small army to the assistance of Denmark, the English and French Ambassadors in the Hague protested in the strongest possible terms. But the Grand Pensionary De Witt knew his business; he laughed in his sleeve, and equipped his little army all the same. As it was on the point of leaving, however, a letter suddenly arrived from the ambassador in London, with a warning that Young Richard Cromwell was determined not to allow the Dutch to have it all their own way in the North, and had prepared a large fleet to assist the Swedes if the Dutch assisted the Danes. By this time the autumn was far advanced; ice began to block up the rivers, and Admiral Opdam having returned with part of his fleet in consequence of a serious illness, the expedition was postponed till the following year.

As another collision with England was now in prospect, the Dutch Government during the winter hurried on the building of a good fleet. On the 20th of May, 1659, forty men-of-war ran out of the Meuze. The Dutch naval architects had profited by the late war; they had adopted the latest improvements, and had spared no trouble and expense to render this fleet worthy of its fame. Most of the ships were new and of elegant shape, the sailors had been carefully picked, the little army of 4,000 men was well disciplined and compact, and the nation viewed the departure of this expedition with evident pride and satisfaction.

A sharp contest had taken place in the States General as to the appointment of the Admiral. Some were for Evertsen—some for De Ruyter. The former, it would seem, had much in his favour, for he had served in the fleet during the whole of his life, and was the older of the two by many years; but the city of Amsterdam and the province of Holland were all-powerful, the Grand Pensionary himself spoke in favour of De Ruyter, and he was appointed Commander-in-Chief. When the fleet had run out to sea, it will be easily imagined that when old Evertsen was compelled to send for orders to the ship of a much younger, and as he thought far less experienced man, he showed his indignation in his behaviour. When he met De Ruyter on his own deck he treated him with rudeness and ill-concealed spite. But De Ruyter was large-minded enough to forgive what he had a perfect right to punish, and treated the veteran with a kindness and consideration that completely won the old man's heart. The fleet, however, was for several months doomed to inaction, for both England and France, and at their request the Dutch Ambassadors also, endeavoured with much talking and writing, holding of conferences and drawing up of treaties, to move the King of Sweden to other resolutions. Charles Gustavus, however, was obstinate—he held the island of Funen, and try what they would, he was resolved to keep it, although it really belonged to Denmark. Then the King of Denmark resolved to take more determined steps, and requested De Ruyter to assist him.

On the 9th of November the Dutch fleet—then consisting of 75 men-of-war—appeared before Nyborg, the fortified city. A landing had already been attempted, but failed. De Ruyter now executed a clever stratagem. When the night had fallen, all the boats were sent out with but a few men in each, and these were ordered to raise a confusion, fire their guns, and row about with lights, making as much noise as they could. The trick succeeded. The Swedes, thinking that a landing would be attempted at this particular spot, assembled the whole of their army to resist the invasion. But early next morning, before sunrise, De Ruyter quietly weighed anchor, and sailed away unperceived to Kartemunde, about thirty miles higher up the coast, where he knew the shore seemed almost cut out for a landing. The garrison of Kartemunde, as had been expected, was not sufficient to oppose the hostile army. Foremost in one of the boats to cheer his men, De Ruyter witnessed the attack, saw his men jump out of the boats into the water, scramble ashore under a heavy fire, and remained exposed to that fire himself until the Swedish soldiery, which had earned a splendid reputation under Gustavus Adolphus, was defeated and obliged to retreat inside the town. The guns of the fleet greatly assisted the movement, Kartemunde itself was for some hours bombarded, and at last abandoned by the Swedes, who retreated in confusion. The whole of the land forces were now sent ashore. About a week later, when the army had enjoyed plenty of rest, it was joined by the Danish forces, and the march towards Nyborg was commenced.

This city was one of the most important fortresses in the North of Europe. Bordered on one side by the sea, and situated on a gentle and well-fortified height towards the land, the King of Sweden had laughed haughtily when he heard that Nyborg was going to be attacked. The Swedish soldiers still enjoyed with perfect justice a reputation for unequalled bravery, and the King imagined that they were not only brave, but unconquerable. On the 24th of November the Swedish forces had taken up a position on the inclined ground in front of the town, and thrown up earthworks for their own protection. At eleven o'clock the Danish-Dutch army advanced to the attack, the Danish cavalry opening the battle with great bravery. The Swedes, however, fought with the courage of despair, for they knew that their only hope lay in a vigorous defence and a defeat of the invader. Again and again they obliged the allies to retreat; they even issued from behind their entrenchments to pursue their advantage; both flanks of the attacking forces were put to flight, although obstinately resisting, but the centre by a clever manœuvre suddenly turned upon the Swedes in the midst of their hot pursuit—attacked them in the rear, threw them into hopeless confusion, and chased them into the town, the two wings joining in the rout. The two Swedish commanders, seeing that the game was lost, escaped in a fishing boat to the neighbouring island of Seelandt, but the unfortunate army, seized with a panic, crushed itself with a frenzied desire for safety through the narrow gates into the town. This was De Ruyter's moment. He had sailed along the shore keeping pace with the army, and had so arranged the fleet round about the town, that it was exposed on three sides to his fire. Half his ships lay in the harbour within pistol shot of the Quay. As the stream of trembling and exhausted soldiers poured into streets so narrow that they could not hold one-tenth the number, the fleet began a furious cannonade. Every gun did service until it glowed. The shells crashed into the dense mass of infantry and cavalry. A shower of tiles and bricks was mixed with the iron missiles. The terrific noise of the incessant explosions, the smoke and flames, the heart-rending cries of the wounded, the shrieks of women and children, caused many a veteran soldier on that fleet to turn pale with horror. There was no escape, no safety anywhere. Danger and death filled the air, and penetrated to the more sheltered corners. A trumpeter was despatched from inside to the commander of the land forces, and another to De Ruyter. The latter promised to cease firing for an hour, until they should have conferred with the General. Exactly at the hour the fire commenced again with one terrific burst of hundreds of cannon. The Swedes were

CAPTURE OF NYBORG. (*From an Old Dutch Engraving.*)

terrified beyond control. They had endeavoured to make objections, but at the renewal of the bombardment they signed an unconditional surrender. The whole of the Swedish army, about 7,000 men and 3,000 horse, went into captivity, and Denmark had regained its liberty. The Swedes were completely overcome—the King was so dejected that he died in February of the following year—and the presence of De Ruyter in those waters, during the whole of the winter and the following summer, forced the Swedes much against their will to conclude and carry out a disadvantageous peace.

A victory so signal was calculated to render the influence of the Dutch Republic, both with Sweden and Denmark, a matter of great attention to England. It had been very well understood by both peoples, that when they concluded peace in 1654, it was not likely to be a very long one. The English looked upon their large country, the hundreds of miles of sea-coast, their excellent harbours, and their great wealth, and they asked themselves why they should not be the very first sea-power in the world, and why the greater part of the trade should not be in their hands. But then the Dutch, on the other hand, asked themselves why in the world they should not be allowed to continue their trade in their own way as long as they did not interfere with England. Since the peace, however, it was too clearly seen that there was interfering and interfering. When the Dutch made a settlement on some island and stirred up the natives not to trade with the English on any account, they had a perfect right to do so, but the English of course did not like it. When the English wanted to have a dispute settled one way in the North, and the Dutch fleet came sailing up to the capital and said, 'Nothing of the kind—it must be settled the other way, just as we like it,' the friendship between the two nations was not thereby increased. When Charles the Second ascended the English throne, it was thought that so amiable a monarch would be moved, alike by gratitude and interest, to preserve a good understanding. The first shouts of enthusiastic welcome had stirred his soul in the midst of the Dutch people, and when he was in misfortune, and his person in danger, it was the Dutch who had sheltered and honoured him with more respect and affection than any other nation in Europe had ever cared to display, and the Dutch now reasonably expected that some pleasant recollections would linger in his memory when he had regained the brilliant eminence of his father's throne. But they were disappointed. The King's recollections of Holland were not altogether pleasant. The peace in 1654 had been contracted with the usurper Cromwell, notwithstanding his protests, and by one of the clauses it had been settled that his full cousin, the young heir to the Stadtholdership, should never attain that dignity in his life. It is probable, for these and similar reasons, that the King had for some time cherished the idea of a war, and was rather glad of an opportunity to let it come on with some show of decency.

Had there been no public opinion in the matter, the King's private feelings and those prevalent at Court would not have brought about a war, but popular sentiment had again risen high. Jealousy about the Dutch successes in the Baltic, and a host of complaints too small and trivial to be mentioned, fanned the flame, and the House of Commons moved an address to the King, promising to assist him with their lives and fortunes in asserting the rights of his crown against the wrongs, dishonours, and indignities offered by the Dutch.

It is always interesting to trace the actual beginning and progress of a war, for it will generally be found that the greatest events are preceded by trivial and even laughable occurrences. Charles, who seemed to be rather in a hurry to revenge himself on his former hosts, secretly sent Sir Robert Holmes with a fleet to the South African coast, where that Admiral attacked the Dutch Settlements right and left, took castle after castle, and carried off a large quantity of goods with him. The Dutch had not been prepared for this in the least, and loudly complained. The king entered into long explanations, sent Sir Robert Holmes to the Tower for a little while, but pay for damages, or give back what he had taken, he would not. When Grand Pensionary De Witt saw this, he said to himself, 'Very well, your Majesty; two can play at that game.' Now De Witt knew that no war with a foreign Power, nor any hostile act, could be begun by the fleet unless the authorisation were read in full council of the States General; and he also knew that if any such document were read out in the ordinary manner, the English Ambassador at the Hague, Downing, would be sure to hear of it, and warn them in London. This was exactly what he did not want. So what did he do? On Saturday, the 9th of August, he called together seven of the members whom he trusted, and said to them, 'Admiral De Ruyter is at this moment with English Admiral Lawson in the Mediterranean. Lawson dreams of nothing, and if we can tell De Ruyter quietly to go to the African coast and take back those forts, he will have it all his own way.' This clever plan was applauded and discussed, and the instructions to De Ruyter were drawn up. When Monday, the 11th, came, these seven gentlemen had each agreed to play his own part. The States General assembled; the president took his seat, and the secretary began to read a number of documents of a dry and formal character, to which, if no one objected, the president signed his name for the whole of the assembly. At that moment each of the seven gentlemen began a discussion with his neighbours, some of them walked up and down the room, others took a couple of their colleagues outside to tell them something very secret, and one or two got their friends to the windows on the pretence of showing them a very extraordinary scene in the court-yard, where a curious crowd was always gaping at the windows, While all this was going on, and nobody listening to what they considered to be dry and formal documents, the secretary came to De Ruyter's instructions, which he read so quickly that even the president, with whom somebody had begun a conversation, did not know what it contained, and signed it in perfect good faith. When the reading and signing were done, the members all took their seats, never thinking that their silence had given consent to so important a document, while the authorisation was speedily despatched by special messenger through Belgium, France, and Spain, to the admiral, a copy of the letter being sent to Cadiz, another to Malaga, and a third to Alicante.

De Ruyter had been in the Mediterranean since the beginning of May, and it was certainly a very fortunate thing for the fleet which he commanded that no rupture, either with England or with the pirates, took place during that time, as he was attacked by a severe, and what at one moment threatened to become a fatal, illness. A slight difference between him and Lawson about striking the flag had passed over, but both Admirals knew that affairs at home did not look very cheerful, and consequently they narrowly watched each other's movements. Every dispatch which he received from home contained the warning, 'Keep your eye on Lawson, follow his fleet, and take care that he does not slip away.' And he himself had written back that he was sure Lawson had some mischievous intention, and would outwit him. On the 1st of September he arrived at Malaga. One of the officers, who was sent ashore in a sloop, heard, on passing some merchants and citizens on the beach, that a special messenger had arrived for De Ruyter with important letters, that some English men-of-war had taken three Dutch merchantmen, and that war was already declared. The town was in considerable excitement at the news, and the other captains of the fleet, having heard the same intelligence, immediately rowed on board the 'Spiegel' to ascertain how far the letters confirmed the news. De Ruyter had very carefully opened his dispatches, and, being a very truthful man, was somewhat puzzled to give an answer, for the captains and the people ashore were too wide-awake to believe that the States General would send a special messenger for a mere trifle. He answered very coolly that his letters mentioned nothing about war, and that it was hoped the mutual differences might yet be settled in a friendly manner, but that it was necessary to sail at once for Alicante. Lawson had heard of this messenger too, and was thereby rendered doubly suspicious. It was altogether a ticklish affair. For three weeks De Ruyter sailed up and down through the Straits of Gibraltar, touching either one or the other of the three ports, on the pretence of cleaning his ships, recruiting his men, and preparing for a voyage to Greece and Turkey. Lawson met him once or twice, and the utmost civility was exchanged between them. So perfectly did De Ruyter keep his plans to himself that Lawson was completely misled, and not one of the Dutch captains had the slightest idea what was going to be done. In the meantime De Ruyter filled his ships with bread, salted meat, fresh water, and war stores, but in such small quantities, or in so roundabout a fashion, that no suspicion was aroused.

It was not, however, until the 5th of October, and therefore five weeks after the receipt of his instructions, that he found himself in a position to set out on his voyage. He had passed Lawson in the morning lying at anchor in Cadiz Bay, and the English captain, who had paid a polite visit to De Ruyter, had been given to understand that the Dutch fleet was going home. When they had sailed for two days, the Admiral hoisted the white flag, and all the captains came on board. 'You have probably been wondering where we were going to, gentlemen,' said he, 'for, instead of going home, we are going straight on towards the Cape of Good Hope. I will now tell you what my instructions are, but as I myself was requested not to mention the matter even to my wife, you will not feel hurt by my silence.' The instructions were then read, and the plan unfolded in all its simplicity, and I dare say there was many a laugh at the expense of good old Lawson, who was lying at Cadiz. On the 22nd October, early in the morning, the fleet anchored at the island Goeree, about a thousand yards in front of Cape Verde, and found nine English merchantmen and one man-of-war in front of the fortress, which had been lately taken from the English. As resistance was useless, the English garrison and the ships saw themselves compelled to surrender, while all the booty and valuable property which had been accumulated was carried into the Dutch ships. A very curious incident took place on this island, which strangely illustrates the truth that, after all, this world is not so very large. Three or four men-of-war had sailed round to the other side of the island to keep a watchful eye on the native negroes and obtain some fresh water. The boats having landed, Rear-Admiral Zaen was greatly astonished to find among the natives one man who understood and spoke Dutch. The negro asked them who commanded the fleet, and upon hearing the Admiral's name, he said pensively, 'Michiel, Michiel De Ruyter? I remember that some five or six and forty years ago there was a cabin-boy in Flushing of that name;' whereupon Zaen assured him that the same man now commanded the fleet. 'I cannot believe it,' repeated the old negro; 'it is impossible that a man should have been a cabin-boy and now an Admiral.' But when he was again and again assured of the fact, he requested to be taken on board the 'Spiegel;' having reached which, he immediately recognised, and was recognised by, the Admiral, his former play-fellow. They were both equally astonished and pleased at so extraordinary a meeting, after so many years and such varied events, and when they began to speak about old times, the Admiral more than once burst out in a hearty laugh when the negro, whose memory was wonderfully accurate, recounted some prank of their youth which he himself had forgotten. So retentive was the man's memory, that he could name without the slightest hesitation the streets, bridges, and various quarters of the town, where they had played together, and the names and nicknames of their comrades. De Ruyter treated him with the greatest kindness and courtesy, and was glad to hear that Fortune had also favoured him by making him Viceroy over what the biographer contemptuously calls 'a few niggers.' Having been baptised in Flushing, he told the Admiral that he still remembered the catechism and the Lord's Prayer, and that he had tried to civilise and instruct his children, but whenever he mentioned the Bible they laughed in his face and made fun of him. Nevertheless, he preferred his little island to any other, and refused, with evident horror, the offer to be taken back to Zeeland and his old house. He very much preferred smoking his pipe in front of his hut, and seeing half the village crawling about him in the mud; and when the Admiral presented him with a couple of old uniforms, and some other trifles which are held in much esteem in that country, and gave him a salute of honour as he stepped into the boat, the old fellow was in the seventh heaven of pride and contentment, and talked about nothing else to his dusky and naked companions for the rest of his life.

The fort of Goeree having been recaptured, the fleet sailed along the Western Coast of Africa, and visited the Dutch possessions one after the other, restoring what had been taken, reinforcing garrisons, taking the English vessels that seemed armed for the purpose of resistance, and dealing out everywhere the most summary punishment. At length the fleet arrived at Fort Cormantin, a castle built upon a rock, and considered inaccessible. There was an English garrison in the castle, and a small army of native negroes to assist them. But De Ruyter meeting with another and friendly tribe of natives, was able to land his men in a jungle. The English had erected a battery on the top of the neighbouring hill, and it was not until pressed by superior numbers that they retreated within the walls of the castle. That very same night De Ruyter ordered the castle itself to be stormed. The negroes were commanded by their king, a bloodthirsty ruffian of the name of Kabess; and it was his cruelty, and the fearful hatred against the Dutch, which urged him on to commit, during the desperate storming of the fort, some of the most revolting atrocities, which he ended at last by committing suicide. The fort was taken, and the garrison made prisoners and transferred to some of the ships. The fleet then turned towards America. On the 30th of April he sailed somewhat foolishly into the Bay of Barbadoes, where a fire from the forts and about 36 vessels that had anchored along the quay gave him so warm a reception that he was obliged to retire, with great damage. By this time he encountered more than one vessel newly arrived from the Netherlands with the intelligence that war had been declared between the two countries, and that he might safely hurry home to get his share of the fighting.

After so extraordinary an expedition, peace was of course out of the question. The feeling in England was very bitter, and the preparations for war were carried on with great resolution. King Charles smelt a rat very soon. Lawson had returned from the Mediterranean with the discovery that De Ruyter's fleet had been equipped for several months, and was away on some mischief. Two or three other matters equally aroused suspicion. The King wrote to Ambassador Downing in the Hague to ascertain the truth of the matter, but Downing wrote back that such was impossible, as he had heard nothing of it. Downing was a foolish man, and so conceited of his own cleverness and influence that he boasted to be the real governor of Holland. When he was therefore again requested to make some inquiries he got angry, went to Pensionary De Witt, and asked him in the coolest manner possible whether this was true about De Ruyter. John De Witt smiled. 'I can assure your Excellency,' he answered, in a very open manner, 'that the province of Holland has given the Admiral no orders about which his Majesty King Charles need trouble himself; and as for the States General, it would be useless for me to say anything about their resolutions, as nothing happens in their sittings which you do not find out somehow.' Downing was perfectly content, and wrote back to the king that there was no truth in the report, and that De Ruyter was still sailing somewhere about in the Mediterranean. But when ships actually arrived from the African coast, and there could be no more doubt about the affair, it was resolved in England to fit out a large fleet immediately. Downing complained loudly that he had been disgracefully treated, but when he was presently recalled to London, few even at St. James's did not much blame De Witt for so cleverly hocussing a man who was distinguished by no better qualities than overbearing insolence and fawning servility.

When De Ruyter arrived in the Netherlands with his fleet he found the condition of affairs in Holland vastly different from what he had left them. During his journey home he had been disturbed by serious misgivings as to the danger which he might incur in sailing straight for Texel, seeing that he carried half-a-dozen English prizes in his fleet. He therefore thought it best to steer his course by Iceland and Norway, and came down very cautiously. In one of the northern ports he received a letter from the States informing him that a terrific battle had taken place on the 13th of June, in which Wassenaer and his Vice-Admiral had both been killed, and the fleet defeated. He was also warned by other vessels that the English fleet, having heard of his coming, was cruising for him, and that those in Holland were looking out for him eagerly, as there was no one else now to command the fleet. It is needless to describe how during a fortnight he advanced with the greatest caution, having posted advice-yachts several miles in front to warn him. The two fleets must have been uncommonly close to each other more than once, but, fortunately for De Ruyter, a thick fog hung over the sea during the greater part of that time, so that he was enabled to run into the West Ems on the 6th of August without the loss of a single vessel. The news of his arrival spread through the Netherlands with the rapidity of lightning, and a joyous shout of welcome went up from all sides. 'Men and women came in thousands on to the fleet and De Ruyter's ships, from which there dangled many English flags as trophies and signs of victory. From early morning till late at night, for many days, people came from town, village, and the country to see him. Noblemen vied with commoners to show their joy at his safe arrival, and many a genteel and honest woman fell on his neck and kissed him, as if she had received her own father or brother from death.'

The popular spirit, which had been very depressed in consequence of the late defeat and the death of two Admirals, rebounded with hope. Within a few hours after his arrival De Ruyter had despatched letters to the States General and to the Councils of the most important provinces. Pensionary De Witt, who received his letter in the middle of the night, got out of bed and sent back an answer immediately, to the effect that about ninety men-of-war were lying in Texel for him, and asking him when he would be ready with his fleet to join them and take the command. De Ruyter answered immediately that his ships were very dirty, the sails and tackle all but useless, and the greater part of his men so exhausted that it would be necessary to allow them to go ashore for some time to restore their former vigour. As for himself and the greater part of his captains, they were ready to serve their country at once. By a unanimous vote he was thereupon appointed to the post of Lieutenant-Admiral General of the fleet, which had become vacant by the death of Wassenaer; and without going to visit his wife or family, he landed at Delfzyl, was received in every city through which he passed with military honours and a salute, and, crossing the Zuyder Zee in a small yacht, made his appearance in Texel on the 16th of August. He was here met by deputies from the States, who handed him his commission, and received his oath of fidelity as commander-in-chief of the whole fleet. Shortly after sunrise on the morning of the 18th of August, and thus not a fortnight after his return from a voyage of more than a year's duration, he reached the fleet, and was solemnly received by the authorised Commissioners of the States General, and by them formally presented to all the captains as 'the first person on the fleet' under the Commissioners from the Hague.

The scene must have been impressive, for it was invested with a portion of that dignified gravity which belonged to the States General. It will not be uninteresting to explain how it was that De Ruyter was so suddenly raised to the highest post. The last defeat had shown everybody too plainly that they were playing a dangerous and losing game, and that England was not to be trifled with. While De Ruyter was away on his secret expedition, that great and untiring genius, John de Witt, had thrown all his energy into the reconstruction and improvement of the fleet, and he had effected great changes. But there was a spirit of dissatisfaction throughout the whole country, and therefore also on the fleet. There were two parties, one in favour of the young Prince William of Orange, and the other the stern Republican party, which had resolved that the Prince should never become Stadtholder. Now you must know that the Stadtholder was in virtue of his office head of the fleet, so that when any captain or sailor had anything to complain of, the Prince's friends used to tell him that it would be quite different if only the Prince were allowed to become Stadtholder. That this spirit was very strong on the fleet nobody could deny, and it was feared that at some moment the sailors might refuse to work, except for the Prince. There was another difficulty. The only two men who were fit to be Admirals, except De Ruyter, were John Evertsen and Cornelis Tromp, the son of our old friend Martin. But both these men were strong friends of the Stadtholder. One of them must be appointed Admiral, but either of them was almost certain to increase the dissatisfaction on the fleet. Pensionary De Witt alone was not puzzled by the situation. He managed to get Tromp appointed, but he also induced the States General to appoint a commission of three members, who were to represent the States on board the fleet, and under whose direct orders the Admiral was to hold office. This was done with the two-fold object of inspiring greater zeal and obedience amongst the captains, and to prevent any political plot from being carried out. But it was really De Witt's plan, to enable him to be on the fleet himself. So he not only got himself appointed as Chief Commissioner, but so influenced the States that one of his colleagues was a harmless old man of eighty, and the other one of his private friends. Now, although they were obliged to get on together, you may easily imagine that there was a good deal of embarrassment in their mutual relations, Evertsen being jealous of Tromp, Tromp suspicious of De Witt, and De Witt being determined to keep a sharp eye on both these gentlemen.

Such was the state of affairs when suddenly De Ruyter landed. De Witt felt at once that he would be out of the difficulty if he could only get De Ruyter appointed as Admiral-in-Chief, for he knew that De Ruyter's sole aim and ambition was the furtherance of the country's good. Through his great influence the appointment was made, and everybody on the fleet received the news with joy except Tromp. He stoutly refused to serve under anyone; and as his jealous temperament was unreasonable, it required a very sharp letter from the States to remind him of his duty. When De Ruyter arrived on the fleet at last he was heartily welcomed by all. Tromp, who was a jolly good fellow at heart, shook his hand cordially, and grey-headed Evertsen nobly confessed that he was the only fit man for the command. So enthusiastic a reception had never yet been given to anyone; and De Ruyter, who was a singularly humble man, felt great surprise. He could not conceive the reason, but others who had followed his career knew that he had never yet undertaken anything which he had not accomplished with perfect satisfaction to everyone. Whatever his hand had found to do he had done with all his might; and in this supreme hour the people felt instinctively that he was their man. But the high expectations which had been raised throughout the country were doomed to a sad disappointment. The fleet steered its course northward, in the hope of finding the English. From later accounts it appears that on the 24th and 25th of August the two fleets must have passed within a few miles of each other, but without meeting. De Ruyter arrived in the port of Bergen, in Norway, and after having remained there for some days, he determined to conduct a fleet of about fifty merchantmen, which had assembled there, back to the Dutch ports.

Between the 8th and 9th of September the great fleet of nearly two hundred ships was attacked by a terrific storm. In vain De Ruyter tried every art which his vast experience could suggest to keep the fleet together. Pensionary De Witt, who had never been at sea before, braved the fury of the storm, and stood on the quarter-deck by his side for three hours, drenched by the rain and the beating waves, to assist him in looking out. For three days the fury of the elements frustrated all their efforts, and the mighty flock of sea-monsters was hurled away in all directions. Most of them were greatly damaged; two fire-ships went down with all hands; while two merchantmen and eight of the finest men-of-war got amongst the English, and were captured after a sufficiently courageous resistance. You will probably remember that this was not the first storm that had scattered and severely damaged the fleet. Tromp had suffered from it; De Witt had been nearly ruined, and it would probably have fared but little better with De Ruyter, however popular he might be, but for the fortunate circumstance that the Commissioners were on board while it happened. The opinion of the working classes in any country is generally unreasonable; it is their tendency to run into violent extremes, and their praise is often as groundless as their blame is unjust. When the large fleet was out at sea the whole country was of course in a state of intense excitement. Nobody did any business. Every little fishing-smack that ran into port was assailed by a crowd of eager questioners. If it thundered, the people a hundred miles inland fancied they heard the guns of battle, and every flash of lightning was foolishly taken for the fire of the cannon. When, therefore, the fleet returned, not as it had left, decked with flags, and spreading a thousand white and glittering sails majestically before the wind, but shattered and broken, with half-destroyed rigging, tattered sails, and exhausted seamen, and ship after ship dropped its anchor in a sneaking fashion, looking still more wretched than the others, it was not so very unnatural that the poor and hard-working people who were paying for all this, should feel disgusted, and cry that it was the fault of the Admiral.

The Admiral, however, pointed with a serene smile to Pensionary De Witt and his two fellow-commissioners, and then these gentlemen, in whom the people felt the profoundest confidence, smiled gently, and said, 'It is quite right. We have done all we could, and the Admiral has done nothing that we did not approve of. Nevertheless, here we are. We have not seen the enemy, and the storm has been too strong for us. But never mind; we'll have better luck next time.' Whereupon the people saw very plainly that matters could not be helped, shrugged their shoulders, and walked away, hoping that the English might catch it next time the fleet went out. But the popular wish was doomed to disappointment for that year at least. There was no catching on either side, although De Ruyter tried hard enough. In the beginning of October he had sufficiently recovered to run across to Harwich with another fleet of ninety men-of-war, but the few English ships that could be seen wisely ran up the Thames. On every hill there flamed a fire; the long line of coast was marked at night by a chain of flames, and crowds of armed men gathered on the beach wherever the fleet appeared to oppose an attempted invasion. As it was found useless to begin anything so late in the season, and with such rough weather, the Council of War resolved, on the 2nd of November, to return to Holland and put up for the winter. This second failure of the expedition occasioned a vast amount of unpleasant criticism, and all sorts of rumours were flying about concerning the violent quarrels between De Ruyter and the Pensionary De Witt. Both men were deeply grieved at these reports, and in order to show the people that they were absolutely unfounded, De Ruyter accepted De Witt's invitation to his own house in the Hague.

His stay in the political capital was marked by the greatest honours. He was introduced into the midst of the best society, and received with the respect due to his great reputation. It must have been strangely pleasant to be visited by the rich nobles, to be invited to dinner by ambassadors of foreign Courts, and, simple and artless as he was, to converse with those delicate and haughty ladies who were courted by princes. He was ordered to attend a full sitting of the States General. When he entered they all rose and saluted him. The usher led him to an arm-chair by the side of the president; he was allowed to keep on his hat, and when the narrative of his various exploits had been listened to attentively, the legislators, with courteous gravity, unanimously resolved that he had admirably performed his duty, and deserved well of his country. The provincial States of Holland paid him the same compliment, and presented him with a silver vase to the value of 150*l.*, while the different Admiralty Boards actually quarrelled who should have the honour of his services. It is pleasant to find that with such honours he remained unchanged in all those fine qualities that so endeared him to the people. His simplicity and honesty were certainly not less than before; and, instead of imitating the lavish display of the wealthy men around him, he was always dressed in the simplest and least expensive uniform. Nor did his piety forsake him in this prosperity. A traveller one day happening to be busy in his room in a certain hotel in Rotterdam, heard a man's voice in the next room imploring God to give him simplicity of spirit; that he might not become proud; to give him strength in the execution of his great duty; to give him the heart and courage of a hero, and spare him for the service of his country. Greatly moved with what he had heard, the traveller went down-stairs and asked of the landlord who it was that occupied the room next to his own. It was De Ruyter. He had just returned from the Rotterdam Admiralty Board, laden with new honours, for which he was thus pouring out his soul.

During the winter the Admiral worked very hard at the reconstruction of the old, and the building of a new fleet. Seventy new vessels had been voted by the States, and every wharf was busy. When the soft spring threw the rivers and seas open to navigation, the little Republic was fully prepared for a war with its great rival. The Bishop of Munster and the other small States, that had been tempted by England to worry the Republic on land, were all pacified. The Kings of Denmark and Sweden had solemnly pledged themselves to remain neutral. The King of France had, on the other hand, promised to assist, and a fleet under the Duke de Beaufort had already been equipped and sent out to join the Dutch against the English. On the 11th of April De Ruyter ran out to sea on his splendid and afterwards celebrated ship, the 'Seven Provinces,' which has become inseparably connected with his name. It carried eighty guns and five hundred men, and it was unanimously pronounced one of the most graceful and swiftest ships that had ever breasted the waves. Eleven others of the same kind were launched about the same time, and sent to Texel, where the fleet was to assemble. On the 16th of May the young Prince of Orange, the husband of Princess Mary of England, accompanied by the Elector of Brandenburg and a whole host of princes and nobles, paid a visit to the Admiral. The sailors had manned the yards, and the whole fleet thundered a welcome as the young descendant of the great William stepped on board. An enthusiastic cheer went up amongst the sailors at the sight of him, and from every other ship the cry of 'Long live the Prince!' was repeated again and again. For two days the illustrious party went the round of the fleet visiting the finest ships; they were treated to a splendid dinner on board the 'Seven Provinces,' whereupon the young Prince showed the kindness of his heart by distributing a goodly sum of money and several tuns of beer among the sailors. After dinner two frigates entertained the party with a sham fight, but one of De Ruyter's sailors, who had probably taken too much of the beer, conceived the remarkable resolution of showing the noble visitors that a Dutch sailor was not afraid of anything. He secretly climbed to the main topgallant masthead, and when he saw the attention of all fixed upon him, began a series of antics, which ended by his standing on his head, and sticking his feet up in the air. Contrary to the poor fellow's ambition, the Prince was greatly disgusted at this act of bravado, and De Ruyter, who was naturally indignant, would have put the man in irons at once, but for the kind interposition of the Brandenburg Elector, who interceded for him.

At last in the beginning of June the fleet was ready. There were eighty-five men-of-war, carrying nearly five thousand cannon and twenty-two thousand men. The fleet was accompanied by sixteen fireships and other non-combatant vessels. The number of hulls was over a hundred. At the same time that the States General sent the Admiral the order to sail, he received a list of the English fleet, which had just left the

Thames in search of the Dutch. There were eighty-one men-of-war, and about an equal number of guns and men, under the command of Prince Rupert, Monk, Ayscue, and Sir Thomas Allen. At this news De Ruyter hoisted the signal to make all sail, and set out to fight that famous battle of four days that has never in the history of this world been surpassed for the splendid bravery and resolute perseverance displayed by each antagonist.

MICHIEL ADRIANSZOON DE RUYTER.

PART III.

ENGLAND was determined to punish the little republican fellow for his insolence, and so confident was she of her power to drive him off the seas for ever, that she rejected the offer of the French king to arrange matters between them. Now Louis the Fourteenth happened to be an exceedingly proud king, who never liked being snubbed, and so to revenge himself for this refusal he declared war at once, and sent out his fleet. The King of Denmark followed suit, and the Elector of Brandenburg, whose land lay in the heart of Germany, and could not therefore lose much, also promised to help. England, however, cared but little. Her fleet was ready, and she was determined to show the whole world what she could do with it. It was divided into two portions. Monk commanded the greater, about sixty large men-of-war; while Prince Rupert, with five-and-twenty, was to go against the French fleet and prevent it from joining the Dutch. Monk started on his expedition quite confident of success. He had no idea of the enemy's strength, and he seems to have had very little opinion of their courage, for his only fear was that they should run away and not give him the chance to beat them. I have already told you that De Ruyter's fleet was composed of eighty-five men-of-war, none of which could compare with the largest of Monk's. On the 9th of June, the Admiral having divided his fleet into three squadrons, under himself, young Evertsen, and C. Tromp, sailed for the Downs, where he anchored on the evening of the 10th. In the early morning of the 11th Monk appeared in sight, eight miles E.S.E. of the North Foreland. A pretty stiff breeze blew from the south-west in his favour, and he might therefore easily have evaded the engagement as soon as he saw that De Ruyter was stronger, but he was ambitious to gain his great victory with an inferior number of ships and without the assistance of Rupert, of whom he was somewhat jealous.

De Ruyter immediately saw that Monk was about to commit a blunder, and signalled an order to Evertsen on his right and Tromp on his left to allow the English to keep the weathergage. On they came full sail, in three squadrons, Monk having the red flag, Sir George Ayscue the white, and Sir Thomas Tiddyman the blue. It was shortly after one o'clock when Ayscue's advance-guard under Sir William Berkeley met Cornelis Tromp, who headed his squadron with his own ship. The meeting of those two, in sight of the fleets that were fast approaching each other, was terrible. The squadrons mingled at once in fierce combat, and became enveloped in a dense cloud. Tromp's ship, which had stood the first charge, was rendered so helpless that it answered neither to rudder nor sails, and had to be towed away, while Sir William Berkeley, after a cannonade of an hour, drew off to repair somewhat, and leave Tromp to get another ship. Before the battle was yet general a terrific explosion, almost immediately followed by another, with large columns of flame shooting up towards heaven, struck a momentary terror into the hearts of the combatants, and showed them what they had to expect. Two Dutch men-of-war had received a shot in their powder stores, and had blown up.

Monk and Tiddyman, having advanced far enough towards De Ruyter with Evertsen on his right, opened fire. With an obstinacy and a dogged courage that would have been admirable in a young captain, but was astonishing in a man who could not add one grain to his reputation, though he endangered an honourable old age, Monk fiercely attacked his great enemy again and again; but De Ruyter met him to the full, and forced him back into his former position. For now as the wind freshened and the sea ran very hollow, the great advantage of the Dutch became apparent. The English ships were slenderly built, like frigates, and high-rigged. They were too heavily loaded with guns; they rolled so unsteadily on the waves, that the water threatened to rush into the port-holes, and the lowest tier had to be closed, while a great part of their shot fell short of the enemy and splashed harmlessly in the sea. The Dutch ships, on the other hand, were more heavily built, and as they lurched on the lee-side were much more able to take a steady aim. From half-past one till five the two fleets sailed past each other in squadrons, approaching and drawing back in obedience to the waves and tide while they exchanged broadside after broadside. At five o'clock Monk signalled for a tack towards the English coast, as he was afraid to fall on to the Flemish sands. While the fleet executed this order, Sir William Berkeley's squadron, which had done wonders of daring and had already suffered terribly, happened to bring up the rear. The Vice-Admiral's own ship, the 'Swiftsure,' with the 'George' and the 'Sevenwold,' being the last, were almost helpless, but the 'Swiftsure's' seventy guns were flaming away in defiance of the enemy, when Dutch Captain Adriansen made his way to her and jumped on board at the head of his men. A fearful struggle took place on the deck; every inch was contested. From mast to mast the English crew were pressed back, some of them jumped overboard and swam to other ships, others surrendered, but Sir William Berkeley himself sternly refused to yield. He stood with his back against the companion ladder and fought with despair. Adriansen summoned him to cease resistance, but one of the Dutch firing a pistol at him wounded him in the throat. The sword dropped out of the hero's hand, and he ran wounded and bleeding into his cabin. When the Dutch sailors rushed after him they found him stretched upon the table dead, and with his arms thrown out wildly. So much determination and courage compelled the admiration of his enemies, and Captain Adriansen gave orders that the body should be treated with the greatest respect and conveyed with the captured ship to the harbour of Goeree.

Monk having now tacked about and directed his course northward, was observed to cast his anchor, probably deeming that he would have time to somewhat gather his fleet together and repair his injuries. But De Ruyter would give him no rest. He immediately hoisted the signal for a general attack, and advanced; whereupon Monk, not wishing to be behindhand, cut his cables, and rushed once more into the fight. Till eight o'clock at night the combat was kept up with undiminished fury. Monk himself lost all sails. One of his ships passing by De Ruyter received so well-aimed a broadside, that she reeled over like a wounded deer and sank slowly in the waves. At the same time, towards the fall of night, Sir John Harman, the Rear-Admiral of the white flag, found his ship, the 'Injury,' so dangerously damaged, that he attempted to withdraw towards the rear. The Dutch perceived it, and bore down upon him. Harman summoned his men to stand by, for at this moment a fire-ship already enveloped in a vicious cloud of black and sulphurous smoke, came up against them with a crash. Every moment was precious, but the smoke was so dense and so blinding, that although the two vessels were fixed, no grappling irons could be seen. The boatswain boldly jumped over, and the flame breaking out at that moment, he cut the irons with his axe and parted the two ships. Vice-Admiral Evertsen, at this, sent off a second fire-ship, already in flames. Harman's men, exhausted by the fight, lost courage at the approach of so terrible a danger, and fifty men jumped overboard. The rigging was already partly in flames, but Harman, although scorched, stood his ground. With his own sword he cut down two of the flying cowards, and summoned them to save the ship. They turned and once more went to work with despair. Buckets flew from hand to hand, the axes cut away the spars and rigging that were already burning, the fire-ship was cast loose a second time, and although a falling spar crushed Harman's leg, he congratulated himself on having escaped the greater danger.

But Evertsen, determined to destroy so dangerous a foe, sent off a third fire-ship, and began to cannonade him. In the midst of his agony, Sir John calmly gave his directions. His bearing inspired the men with new courage, and so neatly did the gunners take their aim at the approaching enemy that she sank midway between them pierced by four shots. Then Sir John turned round and stood away for Harwich, feeling that he had fully performed his share of the work. But before leaving he had made up his mind to give his antagonist Evertsen a final adieu, and as he veered slowly round he fired his last broadside.

Evertsen, standing on his deck, watched with curious admiration the other's splendid bravery, when one of the cannon-balls struck him in the chest, and stretched him lifeless on his own deck. The destroyer was himself destroyed, while Harman, having had his wound looked to in Harwich, lived to fight many another battle.

The evening had now fallen, and the sea was illumined with the smouldering embers of the burned ships, and with the lights of the two fleets that would not retire, but lay at anchor within two miles of each other, determined to renew the combat with the coming day. The night was busily employed by both in repairing their damages. Leaks were stopped, sails renewed, tackle spliced, arms cleaned for further service, and then only the exhausted men were allowed to snatch the rest which they so needed. At the break of day De Ruyter signalled all the captains of his fleet to come on board, that he might learn in what position he found himself. There were now about fifty ships, Tromp with about thirteen of his squadron having drifted out of sight. Presently, however, he appeared in full trim on a third ship, the two former ones having been necessarily abandoned. The English, scarcely fifty strong, lay about a mile and a half to the westward. They still had the weather-gage, and might again easily have declined the combat, if Monk had not been of so determined a spirit. He approached first, and voluntarily gave up the advantage of the wind, in order to come to closer quarters. The two fleets ran past each other several times under a very torrent of shot and shell.

The wind was no longer violent; the sea had regained its composure, so that the English could this time employ their guns with full effect. And now there happened a curious incident. As the fleets sailed past each other, and were busily repairing their damages before returning to the charge, the wind suddenly calmed, and neither could approach the other. Tromp found himself suddenly with five or six ships on one side of the English fleet, and De Ruyter with the rest of the Dutch fleet on the other. The Admiral wondered what had become of his colleague, but when at eleven the wind freshened again, he once more gave the order to run past the enemy. He had not sailed half way along the line, when suddenly his practised eye detected a confusion amongst the English left wing, and a terrific cannonade told him that some of his ships must have charged the English without his orders. He signalled his squadron to divide into two detachments, one going southward to attack the enemy in the rear, while he advanced to support the straitened friends. What he had expected proved true. Tromp with his small flock of half-a-dozen men-of-war, none of which were of the largest size, had rashly hurled himself against the enemy's squadron with a bold intention of breaking through. The English closed round him. His Vice-Admiral was killed, and barely half his officers were alive when De Ruyter prevented his total destruction. On his own ship one man in every three was killed or wounded, and on every other the proportion, although less, was still dreadful. De Ruyter's skilful manœuvre forced the English to retire and re-form at a distance, but four of Tromp's ships had been so disabled that they had to be sent home.

The battle was now renewed with great fierceness, and Monk began to discover that the Dutch were too strong for him. Ship after ship hoisted signals of distress or disappeared in the waves. De Ruyter was also severely damaged, and had his flag-staff shot down, but he kept his fleet well together, and gave the English not a moment's rest. Monk signalled a retreat, and stood out for the mouth of the Thames about seven at night, when De Ruyter was preparing for a final general charge. The whole of the night and the following day the flight and the pursuit continued. The English Admiral had placed his most disabled ships in front, and formed an impenetrable bulwark with his own and those that were still seaworthy. Vice-Admirals Van Nes and De Liefde tried in vain to draw him into combat. He answered their fire, but continued his way to the Thames, crowding his masts from deck to sky with wetted spare sails. As has been mentioned before, the English vessels were more swiftly built and high rigged, but they had suffered terribly. Monk, seeing that he was encumbered with many a ship scarcely worth saving, set fire to them, after having taken out the men, and abandoned them to the destructive elements. But slowly the whole of the Dutch fleet was drawing round in pursuit. 'And so,' says Bishop Burnet in his History, 'they must all have been taken, sunk, or burned, if Prince Rupert, being yet in the Channel, and hearing that they were engaged by the continued roaring of guns, had not made all possible haste to get to them.' This happened shortly after two. About that time the Dutch sailors on the look-out descried a fleet of war, some sixteen to twenty vessels strong, steering towards them. De Ruyter, judging that it could be no one but Rupert, signalled to Tromp to alter his course and meet him, while he continued the pursuit.

About five o'clock in the afternoon, while the chase was thus at its hottest, and rendered more dangerous by the sand banks that were now near, the 'Royal Prince,' the largest and finest vessel in the whole English fleet, carrying one hundred guns and six hundred and twenty men, commanded by Sir George Ayscue himself, suddenly made signals of distress. Monk signalled back that he could not stay to give assistance, and that Sir George must act as he found best. The 'Royal Prince' had struck on the Galloper Sands. In the hurry of the moment all was done to get her afloat, but in vain. Tromp was at her at once, and a flaming fire-ship approached her on each side. Ayscue's lot was hard. He had fought like a lion. There were a hundred and fifty dead on his ship, and it was not by his counsel that the fleet retired. But seeing himself deserted, and surrounded by an enemy bent on his destruction, he hauled down the Admiral's flag and surrendered. Tromp, who was now on his fourth ship, sent his captain to take Ayscue and his superior officers prisoners. The English sailors were indignant and refused to leave the ship. They were forced into the boats, but crept through the open port-holes back into the ship, until the guns were drawn in and the holes closed. As soon as the fine vessel was empty and lightened, she floated, and Tromp ordered her to be sent in triumph to Holland. But De Ruyter was wiser. Knowing that so heavy a prize would become dangerous, and that he could spare no ship to take her home, he ordered her to be burned at once. Tromp scowled and hesitated, for it was his prize, but well knowing De Ruyter's strength of will, he obeyed. In the sight of the whole Dutch fleet and of its own men, the splendid vessel was consumed by the flames. It was the anniversary of that day, a year before, when Admiral Opdam had been hurled into the air in the midst of his enemies; and as the powder stores of the 'Royal Prince' caught fire, and she was lifted out of the ocean as by some mighty hand and thrown down again in fragments, a ringing cheer went up from among the Dutch sailors.

In the meantime, Prince Rupert had come up with Monk towards the evening with streaming banners, blowing trumpets, and beating drums. So says Colliber, and he adds that there was an immediate renewal of the fight; but this is evidently a mistake. De Ruyter, who could not prevent the junction, saw at once that a heavy day's fighting was still before him, for it was not probable that Monk would continue his flight after this reinforcement. He therefore signalled the fleet to stand towards the east with furled sails, for fear of the sands, and having thus drifted during the night, a council of war, at break of day, determined on a renewal of the fight, and the captains were signalled on board. In his own homely language, De Ruyter exhorted them to stand by him this day, as they had already done. 'My lords the States, the fathers of our land, our own relations, our wives and children, whatever we hold dearest, must urge us to retain the laurel wreath which we have already won, or we shall die from hunger, misery, and stench in the English prisons.' The fleets thereupon prepared for the engagement that was to decide the issue between them. Whatever difference in strength there might have been in the first two days had now disappeared. De Ruyter's fleet had dwindled down to sixty-four men-of-war, every one of which had sadly suffered in the previous day's battles. Sickness, wounds, and death had reduced the number of his men by half, and the incessant work had reduced the strength of even those to a very low ebb. Monk and Rupert together, on the other hand, were now sixty-one vessels strong. There were several of these that carried fifteen to twenty guns more than De Ruyter's largest ship, and the prince's squadron of about twenty fresh men-of-war, who had not fired a shot and were eager for the combat, seemed certainly to incline the balance of superior strength towards the British forces.

It was about eight o'clock in the morning of Whit-Monday, the 14th of June, when the fight was renewed. De Ruyter's Vice-Admiral De Liefde led the way, and, coming alongside the 'London,' commanded by Robert Holmes, Rupert's Vice-Admiral, settled so closely by her side that the yard-arms almost touched. The one carried sixty-six pieces of cannon, the other eighty-five, and during the running of one glass these two poured the most deadly and destructive fire into each other, while the rest of the two fleets gradually engaged around this point. The Prince of Monaco and his brother, Count de Guiche, both celebrated generals in the French army, had received De Ruyter's permission to remain on his deck during the action. The Count was wounded by a splinter in the arm, and both he and his brother confessed that they had never witnessed anything so dreadful in the whole of their career, and that the horrors of a battle on land were not to be compared with it. Indeed, the fury on both sides seemed to have increased rather than diminished. Three times De Ruyter charged and broke through the English fleet. His ship was terribly injured, but with unflagging courage he returned to the charge, while it seemed as though his Vice-Admirals had all determined to outvie him in bravery. Tromp was almost mad. He changed from ship to ship, as Colliber says, 'by a sort of Pythagorean transmigration, and sought revenge in a variety of shapes.' Every vessel from which he waved his flag crashed into the enemy with renewed fury, and caused Monk to ask, in bewilderment, whether there were half-a-dozen Tromps on the Dutch fleet.

About three in the afternoon De Ruyter executed a masterly manœuvre. He had divided his fleet into two halves. Tromp and himself were southward of the English fleet, Van Nes and Evertsen to the northward, when at a given sign, both rushed simultaneously at the British centre. Prince Rupert lost his mainmast and bowsprit, Monk received two dangerous shots in the powder stores, and got his mast so damaged that he had to back out. Two men-of-war, the 'Bull' and the 'Essex,' were boarded by Captain Pouw; another, the 'Clove-tree' ('Nagelboom'), a ship taken from the Dutch in the previous year, and a fourth, the 'Convertine,' were also captured, while the Dutch historians state that two others of the White Squadron were seen sinking about six o'clock at night. The English fleet indeed became divided. The White Squadron stood northward, the Red and the Blue southward towards the English coast, while De Ruyter having hoisted a signal of general pursuit went after Rupert himself. 'This fourth day,' says Vice-Admiral Jordan, 'at seven at night, most of our great ships disabled in masts, yards, rigging, the want of men to ply our guns, and powder and shot nearly all spent, forced our retreat, in which the "Black Bull" and the "Essex," falling aboard each other, and one to leeward which I suppose was the "Convertine," are in the hands of the enemy.' The English were very grateful, and the Dutch almost disposed to quarrel with heaven for marvellously interfering with the pursuit. At seven or thereabouts a dense fog spread over the water, and De Ruyter seeing that a further approach to the sands would be highly dangerous, assembled his fleet and returned home.

King Charles II. was at church attending divine service when Sir Daniel Hanney came in from Monk and related the engagement. The King stopped the service, and hearing from Sir Daniel that Monk had obtained a victory, he commanded that public thanksgiving should immediately be given, 'which,' says honest Burnet, 'was a horrid mockery of God and a lying to the world.' The people very soon discovered the mistake. They saw the bonfires and heard the bells, but they knew 'that it was rather a deliverance than a triumph.' Vice-Admiral Jordan confessed that they had to submit to an all-seeing Providence who knows what is best for us, and he piously praised God for wonderfully preserving him in the awfullest battle that was ever fought at sea. The Dutch historians speak of seventeen English ships that were burnt or sunk, besides the six that were taken; they counted about 3,000 prisoners, and estimated the English dead at between five and six thousand, while their own losses were given out as not exceeding six men-of-war, and two thousand killed and wounded. What the truth of this is, it would be idle to enquire, as no authentic documents or returns exist in this country from that period. But that the fleet had suffered terribly, and that the loss of the 'Royal Prince' grievously afflicted the nation, may be safely assumed from the expressions that were used by many contemporary writers. One of them said that the destruction of the 'Royal Prince' was a national loss, and to be universally deplored; another was indignant that a Vice-Admiral should have been compelled to surrender, and Evelyn, writing in his diary on the 17th of June, said, 'I went on shore at Sheerness, but here I beheld the sad spectacle, more than half that gallant bulwark of the kingdom miserably shattered; hardly a vessel entire, but appearing rather so many wrecks, and hulls, so cruelly had the Dutch mangled us.'

In Holland, on the contrary, there reigned quite a different spirit. The people could at first scarcely believe their ears. While the battle lasted there had been the most eager and anxious expectation, and as ship after ship came running into port, dragged by its own boats, with shattered masts, riddled with shot, and half sinking, and the sailors, when asked how the fighting was getting on, shook their heads dismally, and said it was a bad job, the rumour began to fly through the towns that the fleet had once more been beaten, and that the English would soon be there.

But when De Ruyter at last appeared at the head of his fleet, bringing with him half-a-dozen English ships and lots of prisoners, there could be no longer a doubt who had won, and the nation abandoned itself to the greatest and most heart-felt joy. The States General issued a proclamation announcing the victory, and ordering a solemn day of thanksgiving on the 30th of June. On that day the churches were crowded, the bells were tolled, bonfires were lit, the guns of fleet and army fired a salute, and there was enough beer drunk to have drowned every sailor twice over. But amidst all these festivities De Ruyter, knowing that there was more work before him yet, went back to the fleet, and hurried the repairing of it with every possible despatch. The body of Sir William Berkeley in the meantime had been carefully embalmed, and sent over to England to be buried by the side of his ancestors, and Sir George Ayscue was treated with every respect, although confined in the castle of Louvesteyn. He was now enabled to look at those plump, heavy fellows against whom he had fought so often, and he could not but acknowledge that they were a sturdy race, and when he was told that nineteen days after this terrific battle another fleet of sixty men-of-war was again ready, he exclaimed, 'Indeed, you have a prompt nation.' But it is useful to notice here, how soon the wind of fortune may change, and how admirable was that modesty of De Ruyter's that would not allow him to boast of so splendid a victory, knowing that, after all, he was not the chief cause of it.

The battle had lasted till the 14th of June. On the 6th of July a fleet of 88 men-of-war, 4,700 cannon, and 23,000 men ran out of the different harbours with the intention of attempting a landing somewhere on the English coast, as it was surmised that the English could not possibly be ready. No more they were, but a landing did not take place for all that. Want of pilots, terrific storms, and several other mishaps prevented the immediate execution of this plan, and in the meantime the English were getting ready. On the 1st of August Monk and Rupert ran out of the Thames with 89 men-of-war, and on the 3rd the two fleets hove in sight between the North Foreland and Dunkerque, and anchored towards the evening within two miles of each other, knowing that next day must bring as fierce and perhaps as long a battle as the former. Both De Ruyter and Monk had divided their fleets into three squadrons, John Evertsen and Sir Thomas Allen having the two vanguards, De Ruyter and Monk the centres, and Tromp being opposed to Sir Jeremy Smith. The morning was splendid, and it would be difficult to imagine a more magnificent sight than the two far-stretching lines of men-of-war drawing slowly and deliberately towards each other. It was almost a complete calm. What little wind there was favoured the English, and enabled them to advance at their leisure. This proved of fatal consequence to the Dutch.

Sir Thomas Allen attacked Evertsen with great impetuosity about twelve o'clock. Monk immediately sent him a large reinforcement, whereupon De Ruyter endeavoured to come to Evertsen's assistance, but found that there was not sufficient wind. An hour elapsed before he could engage the English Admiral, and even then many of his ships were lagging behind, while Tromp could not or would not come up at all, and was lying nearly two miles off. Evertsen's squadron got into most awful hot water. From all sides the shot and shell seemed to come raining down on his decks. While he was standing on the forecastle, giving his commands, a ball took away both his legs, and he fell down dead. His Vice-Admiral De Vries was shot down and killed in the same manner. The other Vice-Admiral, Coender, was covered with wounds, and expired shortly afterwards. Banckers, than whom a pluckier fellow did not exist, got so entangled among the English that he had to leave his ship in a small boat and row to another. His ship was taken, but immediately burned, as nothing could have kept it afloat. So many disasters coming in the short space of one hour, stunned the warriors of Friesland. Bereft of all their Admirals and half the Captains, the sailors became mutinous, and forced the officers to retreat.

De Ruyter, seeing this, turned his own guns against them, but in vain. He found himself opposed to the united fury of the first and second English squadrons, with scarcely one squadron of his own. But he weathered the storm manfully. The three largest ships in the English fleet, the 'General' of eighty, the 'Royal Charles' of eighty-two, and the 'Sovereign' of one hundred guns, now attacked him in turn. What his own ship, the 'Seven Provinces,' must have suffered may be imagined, when it is known that all of them were obliged to retire. Mr. Pepys, who, as clerk to the London Admiralty, heard a great deal about the details of the fight, said that the Duke of Albemarle saw De Ruyter coming to have it out with him. 'Now,' says he (chewing tobacco all the while), 'will this fellow come and give me two broadsides, and then he shall run;' but it seems he held him to it two hours, till the Duke himself was forced to retreat to refit, and was towed off; De Ruyter stayed for him till he came back again to fight. One in the ship said to the Duke, 'Sir, methinks De Ruyter has given us more than two broadsides;' whereupon the Duke answered, 'Well, but you shall find him run by-and-by.' And so he did, but it was no wonder. For no sooner had the smoke of this terrific combat cleared up somewhat, when the Duke saw his immense advantage. The Frisian squadron was retreating, and, for some unexplained reason, Tromp, who had first remained out of the fight without firing a shot, was now nowhere to be found, having, on his own hand, without orders, engaged Sir Jeremy Smith's blue squadron, and separated himself entirely from the rest of the fleet. This conduct, for which no historian has been, as yet, able to give a sufficient explanation, has thrown a dark blot on the life of that great son of a great father. There is no doubt that he thereby contributed mainly to the defeat; and although he pleaded that he defeated Admiral Smith, and fought bravely, you will see, when I come to describe his life, that he must have acted from base and almost incredible motives. Prince Rupert, who was here in his element, redoubled his fury against De Ruyter. The English fleet ranged itself in the form of a half-moon, with the Dutch as centre. There was now a danger that even the fugitives might be overtaken by the enemy, and the Dutch Admiral, therefore, retreated slowly to protect them. His Vice-Admiral, Van Nes, stood faithfully by him, and displayed a manly courage under the adverse circumstances, both ships being so full of dead and wounded that the guns could not be properly served.

The evening fell slowly over the dense and sulphur-laden atmosphere. The night was a restless one, for the British fires could be seen not very far ahead. The exhausted condition of the men scarcely allowed the sails and rigging to be repaired; and it was with the greatest difficulty that a careful watch could be kept. When the morning came the situation was, indeed, all but hopeless. The English surrounded De Ruyter on three sides; a dozen ships alone were with him, and, although every mast-head bore an anxious look-out, no Tromp, no Banckers, no other fleet could be discovered. The sailors were half dead with fatigue, the marines were put to the guns, but even they were exhausted. Many of them lay like dead men, sleeping among the dead, and it was necessary to pull their hair, or pinch their limbs, to wake them out of their slumber. The fight was renewed, from the English side at least, as soon as there was sufficient light, and a slow retreat towards the coast was all that remained to the Dutch Admiral. The greater part of his ships had anchored within a mile of him, but were so disheartened, that, notwithstanding his signal, they made all sail home. Van Nes alone remained by him, and came on to his deck. De Ruyter was stern and sad, but determined. 'What are we to do with our handful of ships? I wish I was dead.' 'So do I,' said Van Nes; 'but we cannot always die when we like; let us promise not to part company wherever we go.' They had been seated in the cabin, and as they mounted to the deck, a cannon-ball crashed through the window and took away the chairs that had borne them but a moment ago. The two Admirals regarded each other in silence, and parted, with a warm shake of the hand, to perform their share in that dreadful day's work. Monk confessed, in one of his letters, that he now entertained the hope of taking De Ruyter prisoner, and carrying him to England, after having burned his ship. A fire-ship was sent off and bore down upon him with such correctness that his destruction seemed inevitable. Everyone on board felt a shiver go through him, but De Ruyter's voice reassured them all. At his command, half the men flew into the yards, the other half manned four boats. Steady and clear came his order to lee the helm and clew the sails to starboard. The 'Seven Provinces,' like a docile horse, turned round with a stately movement, and the dreaded enemy shot past her stern. A ringing cheer went up from the men, a broadside made her reel and shiver, and the four sloops pursued her with volley after volley of musketry.

But the danger was by no means past. As they approached the Dutch coast, and Monk saw that pursuit in those dangerous sands would soon be impossible, he ordered a final and general attack, still hoping to reduce De Ruyter to extremity. From a thousand guns there burst over the unhappy man's head a storm of shot and shell, of musketry and fireballs, such as even he had never heard before. The sailors left their posts bewildered, the marines threw down their arms, and made certain that their last hour had come. To answer such fire was useless. The enemy was hidden in a dense cloud; the sun was invisible, they could scarcely see themselves, and every timber in the ships creaked, and burst, and splintered. It was then that De Ruyter felt his fate too great, and himself too weak, to bear it. He was overwhelmed. 'O God!' he exclaimed, in the hearing of his son-in-law, 'why am I so wretched? is there then amongst so many thousand bullets not one that could snatch me away!' His son rebuked him, and with a few pointed words recalled him to his position and his duty. 'Why,' he said, 'do you speak with such despair? if you desire death alone, nothing is easier than to turn round, run into the midst of the enemy, and seek a destruction which cannot fail us.' The Admiral saw his error, and somewhat regained his spirits, for the end was near. The water, in which he alone knew his way, became more and more shallow, the English fleet stood away to seaward, and Vice-Admiral Banckers, who had somewhat repaired in the meantime, was again sent after them with eighteen of the least damaged ships to protect those men-of-war which had gone astray during the battle, and might be intercepted by the hostile fleet.

Complete though the English victory was, the Republic suffered more in point of honour than in the actual loss of ships. Thanks to De Ruyter's determination, two ships only had fallen into British hands, and from all sides the Admiral's conduct was put beyond question. Although the States-General could not compliment him, they notified to him that they were certain he had acted for the best, while some French officers who had been on board all the time protested that in this retreat he had displayed an almost superhuman skill and courage; and the King of France was so struck with his behaviour that he wrote him a letter with his own hand, and invested him with the order of St. Michael. That De Ruyter should have been indignant against Tromp, and should have attributed to him a great part of his defeat, is but natural, and the States-General, without inquiring into the details of that Admiral's conduct, were so convinced of De Ruyter's honesty, that they almost unanimously recalled Tromp, removed him from his ship and the fleet, and grudgingly allowed him to retire to his estates in the neighbourhood of Utrecht.

But although his strength and energies had been taxed to the utmost, De Ruyter scarcely allowed himself time to pay a hurried visit to his wife and family in Amsterdam, before he again returned to Texel to hurry on the repairs of the fleet. Before another month had elapsed, he was again at sea, on the 5th of September, at the head of eighty men-of-war. He was destined, however, during the latter months of this year to taste the cup of bitterness to the full. Although the English fleet appeared off Boulogne on the 11th, unfavourable weather prevented the engagement which he so eagerly sought. A contagious and dangerous disease broke out in the fleet, and while De Ruyter was one day standing on deck by the side of a gun, a piece of burning fuze entered his throat and caused so painful a wound that he was in a few days reduced to a most alarming condition, and had to be transported to his own house. His wife and all his children were ill. The previous month had bereaved him of his youngest daughter Anna, a charming little girl of eleven, 'of ingenuous mind, and greatly inclined to virtue,' to whom he had been tenderly attached. It was at one moment feared that he too would succumb to illness, but after a period of absolute rest, he slowly recovered, and was enabled by degrees to row about on the Y, where part of the fleet was then at anchor.

Now you must know that immediately after that defeat in August of the previous year, when the Dutch fleet was too much shattered to come out, the English Admiral Holmes, the same who had gone on that African expedition, was sent to the road of Vlie, where it was known that a fleet of Dutch merchantmen was lying for shelter. A ketch was sent up the road to discover what there really was, and returned with the intelligence that there were two hundred merchantmen richly laden, and only two men-of-war. Holmes immediately sent off the 'Pembroke' frigate, and five fire-ships, with about a dozen sloops full of armed men. The fire-ships came floating down upon the men-of-war, who, not being able to defend themselves, cut their cables and retired. Then Holmes had it all his own way. One hundred and forty merchantmen were burned with all the riches they contained, while a company of soldiers landed on the island of Ter Schelling, and reduced a considerable part of the dwellings to ashes and ruins. The damage was estimated at millions of money, and the greatest consternation prevailed throughout Holland. Now our old friend Pensionary De Witt had an idea of his own, which he had tried to execute ever since the beginning of the first war, but which had never yet succeeded. When Sir Robert Holmes played him this trick, however, and the people began to clamour, saying that

DE WITT AND DE RUYTER CONSULTING THE MAP OF LONDON.

he was an incapable Minister, and that they must either have a right-down good victory or peace, for that they could not afford to be beaten all over the sea, and in their own harbours as well, De Witt said to himself that now the time for his little plan had come.

Negotiations for peace were already being carried on at Breda, and the Pensionary, who had some very long-headed and clever correspondents in London, who kept him informed about every little thing that took place, knew perfectly well that King Charles, fully relying upon the conclusion of peace, had taken the money which Parliament had voted for the fleet, and spent it in giving splendid dinners and suppers. The correspondents wrote over to say that there were not half-a-dozen good ships afloat, and that if De Witt could only send a good fleet across it might do something better than Sir Robert Holmes. Then De Witt sent for the gentlemen who were making peace at Breda, and told them to draw it out as long as possible, for that he was going to play the English a trick. Then he sent for De Ruyter, and showed him these letters, and the map of London, and how few ships, castles, or soldiers there were about; and then the two of them, in high glee, had a chuckle over the plan. It was kept very dark. Cornelis de Witt, the Pensionary's brother, was sent on board as Public Commissioner; but although the States appointed him they had not the slightest idea what was going to be done. On the 14th of June, while the gentlemen at Breda were quietly discussing the articles of peace, De Ruyter sailed out with fifty-one men-of-war, three frigates, and fourteen fire-ships. On the evening of the 17th the fleet anchored in the mouth of the Thames, a council of general officers was called, and the object of the expedition made known to them. Seventeen of the lightest and strongest men-of-war were selected and put under Admirals Van Ghent, De Liefde, and Vlug, with orders to sail up the Thames and the Medway, take Sheerness Fort, and destroy of the British fleet what they could. Van Ghent and De Witt went on to the 'Agatha,' and at four o'clock on the morning of the 19th of June they were off.

The navigation of the Thames—so full of sands and dangerous shoals—was no easy matter, especially as, perhaps, a fleet might be quietly waiting for them. They had been told that there were some rich ships lying near Gravesend, and thither Van Ghent now cautiously steered. The first tide brought him to The Middle, the second about two miles east of The Hope, or that part of the river where it suddenly bends before reaching Gravesend. But here the wind slackened, the evening came on, and, although the ships could be seen in the distance, they were obliged to cast anchor. Next morning the English ships had disappeared higher up, and Van Ghent sailed back to the mouth of the Medway, where other ten men-of-war, from De Ruyter, joined him. In the afternoon of the 20th they were opposite Sheerness. Van Ghent ordered two yachts and half-a-dozen sloops to sail up the river and carefully sound the depths. Meanwhile the 'Peace,' of 40, the 'Haarlem,' of 46, and the 'Utrecht,' of 36, were ordered to attack Sheerness Fort. After a bombardment of about two hours, 800 men, under Colonel Dolman, landed with the intention of storming the fort, but the garrison took to their heels. The flag was torn down, and when as much of the stores and guns as could be transported were shipped into the fleet, the fort was blown up.

I need not tell you that at this moment the terror in London was extreme, nor that Monk hurried down and found nothing done for the defence of the river, except a chain, which had been drawn across the water, and upheld by masts sunk in the bed, opposite the village of Gillingham. In all hurry he threw up some batteries, reinforced Upnor Castle, sunk five ships before the chain, posted the 'Unity' in front of the chain, and the 'Carolus Quintus,' the 'Matthias,' and the 'Monmouth' behind it. Seven ships had been sunk across the river, eight would have blocked the passage, but through the small opening the Dutch fleet passed up one by one. They had weighed anchor from Sheerness at seven o'clock on the 22nd, favoured by a fresh NE. wind and spring tide. The Dutch 'Protection' of fifty guns led the way, and attacked the 'Unity' lying before the chain, but her Captain Tobyas not being strong enough, Captain Brakel of the 'Peace,' who was under arrest for some neglect of duty, asked permission to help him, and break the chain with his ship. Van Ghent allowed it. The 'Peace' sailed coolly up to the 'Unity,' gave her a broadside, and boarded her in about a quarter of an hour. Meanwhile, Monk was giving furious fire out of his batteries on land, when a fire-ship, the 'Susan,' sailed against the chain, and another coming up almost at the same moment the chain snapped. One of the fire ships ran alongside the 'Matthias,' and she catching fire blew up into the air with an awful crash. The 'Carolus Quintus' was now also taken, and the two land batteries, being exposed to a cross fire, surrendered. The passage was now free, and Van Ghent came up with the whole squadron, but the only ships that fell into their hands were the unrigged 'Royal Charles' and the 'Mary.' De Ruyter had also come up in the meantime and received the Admiral's flag from the 'Royal Charles.' On the following morning the squadron sailed up to Upnor Castle, where some more vessels were said to be ready for burning. Under a heavy fire from the Castle and several batteries, the 'Loyal London,' the 'Princess,' the 'Royal Oak,' and the 'Great James' were set fire to and burned. The 'Royal Charles' was commanded by a certain Captain Douglas, a Scotch gentleman, who seems to have possessed somewhat more than the average valour and stubbornness of his nation. Though everyone fled when the 'Charles' was in flames, he remained, for he had orders to defend and not to leave her. 'It shall never be said that a Douglas quitted his post without order,' said he, and was burned to death—a melancholy instance of misguided and thoughtless heroism. At three o'clock in the afternoon De Ruyter thought it better to retreat, as he could not get up any higher, and the tide might leave him in danger. Towards evening, therefore, the Dutch fleet returned to the mouth of the Thames with flying colours, carrying the 'Royal Charles' and the 'Unity' in their midst. The damage they had done was not so very great, but the terror which was spread throughout London, and the indignation against the Government, most certainly hastened and favourably influenced the conclusion of peace.

MICHIEL ADRIANSZOON DE RUYTER.

PART IV.

AFTER so many exciting and exhausting scenes it was but right that the Admiral, who had now reached his sixty-first year, should have a holiday. Had he consulted his own feelings only, he would have retired to some quiet country spot and spent the remainder of his days in that rest which he so richly deserved. But four years was all that his country allowed him, and these were the only years in the whole of his busy life when he may be said to have enjoyed uninterruptedly the fruits of his labour. I told you that he had bought a house in Amsterdam, and it was here that he now lived in the quietest possible manner. The house was not large, nor the situation in any way equal to his reputation. After the success of the Thames expedition, I need scarcely say that he was overwhelmed with compliments and congratulations. The States of Holland presented him with a splendid gold vase; the States-General received him at a full sitting, and voted their thanks. Every man of note, every foreign prince or ambassador who visited Holland, was proud to make his acquaintance; the King of Denmark sent him a very flattering letter requesting to have his picture, which the Admiral, not daring to refuse so pleasing an order, had painted at once and sent over to Copenhagen. Young Engel de Ruyter, his son, who had just been made captain, and had arrived in England with his ship to fetch the Dutch ambassador, was received by Charles and his Court with the greatest possible kindness. The king knighted him on the 1st of August, 1668, for the sake of his great father.

And yet everybody who went to Amsterdam to see the celebrated man, and expected to find him in a splendid palace, was strangely disappointed. Indeed, the Dutch of those days were a simple people. They could make plenty of money, and they could spend it too in their own fashion—that is, they gave large sums away to the poor, and paid still larger to continue an honourable war; but to spend it in such splendour and magnificence as the Court of the French or English kings of that time presented—of that they had no idea. It may be interesting to you to read what Sir William Temple, the famous statesman, thought of them. 'The other circumstance I mentioned,' he says, 'as an occasion of their greatness, was the simplicity and modesty of their magistrates in their way of living, which is so general, that I never knew one among them exceed the common frugal popular fare; and so great that of the two chief officers in my time, Vice-Admiral de Ruyter and the Pensioner De Witt (one generally esteemed by foreign nations as great a seaman, and the other as great a statesman, as any of their age), I never saw the first in clothes better than the commonest sea-captain, nor with above one man following him, nor in a coach ; and in his own house, neither was the size, building, furniture, or entertainment at all exceeding the use of every common merchant and tradesman in his town. For the Pensioner De Witt, who had the great influence in the Government, the whole train and expense of his domestique went very equal with other common deputies or Ministers of the State ; his habit grave, and plain, and popular; his table what only served turn for his family or a friend ; his train (besides commissaries and clerks, kept for him, in an office adjoining to his house, at the public charge) was only one man, who performed all the menial services of his house at home ; and upon his visits of ceremony, putting on a plain livery cloak, attending his coach abroad ; for upon other occasions, he was seen usually in the streets on foot and alone, like the commonest burgher of the town. Nor was this manner of life affected, or used only by these particular men, but was the general fashion and mode among all the magistrates of the State. The way to office and authority lies through those qualities which acquire the general esteem of the people; no man is exempt from the danger and current of laws ; no great riches are seen to enter by public payments into private purses, either to raise families, or to feed the prodigal expenses of vain, extravagant, and luxurious men; but all public moneys are applied to the safety, greatness, or honour of the State; and the magistrates themselves bear an equal share in all the burdens they impose.' (Vol. i. 116.)

De Ruyter's life indeed was as simple as it could well be. He declined all invitations to balls and parties, and nothing pleased him better than to sit at his window overlooking the harbour of Amsterdam, and read aloud from some instructive book, while his wife, his niece, and some of his grown-up children were engaged in some useful pursuit. It would have pleased him greatly if he could have continued so quiet a life for the rest of his days; but, as I have already mentioned, he was scarcely four years at home when he was once more called upon to defend the honour of his country. When the peace had been signed at Breda between Holland and England, De Witt thought he could do a good stroke of business. Sir William Temple had been sent over as special ambassador to the Hague, and these two statesmen very soon found that they could not help liking each other, and became friends. Thereupon De Witt confessed to Temple that he stood in great fear of the King of France, who, it was certain, would not rest until he had conquered not only Holland but England too. Temple had long thought the same thing, so between the two of them they concocted a treaty which they got Sweden and some of the smaller German States to join in, wherein each promised the other that all should faithfully help to defend whichever of them was first attacked by France. This was the famous Triple League. King Louis of France laughed when he heard of it, and let it go on for a couple of years. But one day when he had made all his plans, he managed to tempt the English king with such deceitful offers and such alluring baits that the unfaithful Charles, without saying a word to De Witt or even to Temple, concluded a secret treaty with Louis, wherein he promised to assist France as faithfully in destroying the Dutch Republic as he had already promised the Dutch to assist them in resisting France. Although both Louis and Charles desired to keep this secret for some time, De Witt soon found out that there was something amiss. Presently Sir William Temple was recalled, and Sir George Downing, whom everybody hated, was sent in his stead. A few days afterwards Sir Robert Holmes made a most unwarranted attack upon the Dutch Smyrna fleet, the value of which was considered nearly two millions sterling; and although he was defeated after a fight of two days, it was at once plain to De Witt and De Ruyter that Charles had broken faith somehow, and that another war was at hand.

On the 27th of March, 1672, without much explanation or comment, both England and France declared war, and a French army entered Flanders, headed by the most celebrated general of the age. When the other subscribers to the Triple League found that England was not going to keep her word, they also drew back, and the little Republic stood alone. Never had so small a country been opposed by such formidable enemies. It seemed as though the whole world was against her. But De Witt was full of courage, and De Ruyter, to whom he looked at this moment, shook him heartily by the hand and promised to stand by him. It was their plan to run out at once with as big a fleet as could be got, do something bold either in the Thames or some other French or English port and so get the advantage over the combined enemy. Had they done so it would undoubtedly have assisted them greatly, for they would have prevented the English and French fleets from joining, and might have opposed them one after the other. Before the end of April De Ruyter was already at sea with about ten ships. But want of money, want of men, and want of that confident enthusiasm without which no war can be successfully carried on, delayed the completion of their measures. From day to day, De Ruyter waited for the necessary ships, but it was not until the 12th of May that the fixed number had been reached. The Admiral immediately sailed over to the Downs, hoping to find the English alone. He came too late. They had gone. A heavy fog and a terrific storm prevented him from pursuing the Duke of York until a Swedish captain informed him that he had sailed through two fleets as they were lying between the Isle of Wight and Portsmouth, and that their junction was no longer to be prevented. There was nothing for it now but to keep close together and wait until they could find a good time and place for battle.

It would be difficult to conceive a more embarrassing position than that in which the veteran Admiral now found himself. He was at the head of the only fleet of his country. He knew that, if he lost it, his enemies were powerful enough and rich enough to overwhelm him. A foreign army was marching forward into the heart of the country, the intelligence he had received spoke of the combined fleets as superior to his own, and while cruising up and down the mouth of the Thames a letter came from De Witt in which that statesman seemed clearly to insinuate what he dared not openly say to his old heroic friend, that it would be wiser to retire than to risk a battle the consequences of which might be so awful. The Pensionary's brother was on board the Admiral's ship as Commissioner from the States, and nobody could have blamed him if he had determined to retire after the receipt of that letter. But De Ruyter was so positively determined to fight that De Witt had not the courage to do less; the Pensionary's letter was quietly put away, the different commanders summoned on board the 'Seven Provinces,' and the resolution to do or die was firmly maintained by all, though each one had already faced danger and death in a thousand forms, and knew what it meant. Early in the morning of the 7th June, 1672, the foremost advance yachts informed the Admiral that the English fleet was in sight. As the sun rose and shone upon the fair English coast, the combined fleet could be seen covering the whole of

Solebay with a vast and glittering crowd of sail. De Ruyter had entertained some hopes of coming upon them unawares, but the sound of guns, drums, and trumpets that floated across the waves taught him that he had been perceived, and a great commotion in the fleet was plainly visible. Even then it would have been possible for De Ruyter to surprise his enemy, who was totally unprepared, but the wind fell, and he could scarcely advance.

In appearance the combined fleet was decidedly more imposing than the Dutch; in reality, it was very much stronger. The Dutch Admiral commanded seventy-five men-of-war and frigates, with four thousand five hundred cannon and twenty thousand men. The allied fleet, on the other hand, consisted of ninety men-of war, while it exceeded the Dutch by six hundred cannon and thirteen thousand men. Nor was this all. The seven largest English ships carried seven hundred guns and five thousand four hundred men between them. The seven largest Dutch had one hundred and sixty guns and one thousand four hundred men less The 'Royal James,' the 'Royal Prince,' and the 'London' carried over a hundred guns each; the 'Seven Provinces' of De Ruyter, the largest in the fleet, only eighty-two; and I need scarcely tell you that one of these immense vessels, of which the guns were tremendously powerful, were not only worth two, but three or four smaller ones. The Duke of York, a brave but somewhat negligent soldier, commanded in chief, and it seems that he had no idea that

De Ruyter was so near. His Vice-Admiral, Robert Montagu, Earl of Sandwich, had warned him that Solebay was about the worst place to anchor in with such a wind, but the Duke thought he knew better. He snubbed poor Sandwich, and asked him whether this advice was prompted by prudence or cowardice. The Earl never said another word, but determined that the fleet should not be lost because the head of it was foolish, he ran out towards the evening and anchored in front of the bay. Many of the English and French officers went ashore to have some fun; and although history does not say anything about it, I am inclined to believe that some of them got drunk. At any rate, when next morning they were awoke by the Earl's drums and trumpets, a good many of them could not get aboard their ships, and had to watch the battle from dry land, although very large sums were offered for boats.

It was between seven and eight o'clock when the fleets had approached sufficiently near to exchange fire. De Ruyter had divided his forces into three squadrons—one under himself, Banckers on his left, and Van Ghent on his right. Banckers was opposed to the White Squadron, half French, half English, under the French Admiral d'Estrées. De Ruyter saw himself confronted by the Red Squadron under the Duke of York, while Van Ghent and the Earl of Sandwich approached each other with equal determination, although neither of them was destined to survive the engagement. The Dutch fleet approached in one long unbroken straight line, each squadron being led by six men-of-war and six fire-ships. The Admiral had secretly retired to his cabin. He felt all the importance of the moment and its possible consequences, and as the despondency of the authorities at home and the great danger of his country could not fail somewhat to damp his spirits, he made use of the moments before the battle to beseech his God in fervent prayer to inspire him with the necessary courage and wisdom to perform his arduous task. While thus engaged he was warned that his commands were looked for. With elastic step and cheerful face he mounted the deck, cast one glance at the enemy, and turning to the master of the 'Seven Provinces,' he pointed to the Duke of York's ship, the 'Royal Prince,' with the words '*Skipper Zeger, that's our man.*' Zeger looked at the big ship, lifted his cap, and answered, '*We'll let him have it, Sir,*' and steered straight for the Duke. A terrific broadside, discharged almost simultaneously from both vessels, was the commencement of the battle. The calm prevented the smoke from rising, and the two Admirals were soon enveloped in a dense cloud of smoke. For two hours they lay side by side. De Ruyter fired so quickly that his guns discharged nearly as often as his muskets, and the Duke was obliged to go over to the 'London,' his flag having been shot down.

Cornelis de Witt, the Commissioner, endeavoured, by his presence, to influence the men. Although suffering from a violent cold and a sore leg, he determined to remain on deck. An arm-chair, on the velvet cushion of which the arms of the State were embroidered, was brought up. The whole day he sat here, representing the dignity and intrepidity of the Republic, while shells and shot flew about him, and every timber on the vessel strained and shook. An armed guard of twelve soldiers stood round his chair, when one cannon-ball killed three; two were fatally wounded, and one lost his leg. With the utmost calmness, he requested De Ruyter's son-in-law, who commanded them, to throw the bodies overboard, and care for the wounded.

I will not attempt to fully describe this battle, for it would be impossible. But I can give a few incidents, and relate some facts that show the extraordinary fury of the combat. Twice the Duke of York was obliged to change his ship. He fought with his accustomed bravery, but he was obliged to confess that De Ruyter out-manœuvred him over and over again, and that although he had fought over thirty battles, he had seen nothing to equal this one. Three Vice-Admirals tried their luck against De Ruyter, and were obliged to turn away. The senior lieutenant of the 'Royal James,' which was burned, had with difficulty been pulled out of the water into the sloop of a fire-ship, and was taken as prisoner on board De Ruyter's ship. The Admiral allowed him to change his clothes and remain in his cabin; but the lieutenant asked permission to remain on deck to watch the fight, as he exclaimed, '*Is this fighting, Sir? It is not yet noon, and we have already done more than in all the four days in 1666.*' It was indeed a most terrific combat. Those on shore were terrified by the horrible noise, although, in consequence of the absence of wind, the fleets were rendered invisible by a dense cloud of smoke. Even the Admirals themselves could at times see no farther than a ship's length ahead, and the signals were frequently not seen. Captain Van Brakel, the same impetuous officer who, being under arrest at Rochester, volunteered to break the chain, left his squadron without orders, and with his ship of sixty guns began a mad and furious combat with the 'Royal James,' of 100 guns. The Earl of Sandwich, seeing him approach with a fire-ship, gave him such a warm reception out of his fifty guns that, as one historian says, 'the sea flew up round about them as though it had been full of whales.' For an hour and a half Brakel lay side by side with his big enemy, and the two pounded away at each other with undiminished fury. Sandwich received reinforcements of men, and so did Brakel; but the latter ship, being very much smaller, was boarded by the English sailors several times, and again cleared by the furious Dutchmen. Three fire-ships had already been sent against the 'Royal James,' but her guns had demolished them in time. She lay in the midst of her enemies. About eleven o'clock, other Dutchmen, having for the moment disposed of their enemies, turned against Sandwich. He cut himself loose from

Brakel, who drifted away in a helpless condition. The 'Royal James' herself was sinking and fearfully damaged. At this moment Vice-Admiral Sweers re-opened fire on one side; Captain Van Ryn approached on the other with a fire-ship. Before the Earl could prevent it, she ran alongside. The hooks were firmly fixed; the men left her, and with a crash a volume of flame leaped out of the ship. In a moment the 'Royal James' caught fire. The crew were struck with a sudden terror. They leaped into the water from all sides. The sight was awful. Of the thousand men which she contained, 600 were lying about on the decks, killed or mutilated, and unable to move. The certain prospect of being scorched to death or drowned made them utter heartrending cries. The sea was covered with men who had jumped overboard, and were escaping from one death to find another. The Earl, and two of his sons, were observed by the Dutch attempting to leave the ship in a boat, when it became overcrowded, capsized, and sank, leaving the Admiral on board to find a horrible death in the flames. His body was afterwards found floating among many others in the bay; but although he was one of the handsomest men of his time, the fire had so scorched and disfigured him that he could only be recognised by his clothes.

The losses on the Dutch side were not less. Admiral Van Ghent was killed on his deck, and the squadron which he commanded was for some time thrown into confusion. All authorities agree in saying that the

French squadron behaved shamefully. Dutch Admiral Banckers, who had been ordered to oppose it, attacked immediately with great fury; but Admiral D'Estrées, who, it is surmised, had received secret instructions from the French king, drew further and further away, and refused to do more than exchange distant shot. De Ruyter, who heard this squadron's cannonading get more and more distant, ordered a grand manœuvre towards the evening, and managed to draw the whole of his fleet in that direction, so as not to leave one squadron separated from the rest. The darkness parted the two fleets without either having been obliged to retire, but the lieutenant of the 'Royal James,' whom I have already mentioned as being a prisoner on board De Ruyter's ship, was so struck with the way in which that Admiral used every ingenuity, and improved even the slightest chance, that he exclaimed, 'Is this an admiral? This is an admiral, a captain, a skipper, a sailor, and a soldier. This man, this hero, is everything at the same time.' Indeed, his wonderful energy and thorough knowledge of all that was required filled his men with courage and trust. Five-and-twenty thousand pounds of powder had been shot away on his ship alone, with 3,500 balls, which, allowing the fight to have lasted full twelve hours, gives him five shots per minute. Amidst such furious slaughter, his men remained as cheerful as their leader, one of them, who had lost his arm at the forecastle, running aft without assistance, and jumping into the hold with the words,

'Get out of the way. Why don't you go and fight? If a man had his head shot off, you should let him go down alone.'

Both parties of course claimed the victory, although a victory was not obtained by either. By their own confession, however, the English lost more ships, more captains, and more men; and although the combined fleet had the advantage of the wind next day and the Dutch remained in sight ready to renew the engagement, the Duke of York prudently abstained, and De Ruyter resolved to go home. When the tidings arrived in Holland that the English and French had not only not landed, as was one time feared, but that they had retired, while one of the most gallant admirals was burned on one of the noblest ships, they accepted the news with joy. And surely some little joy was needed at a moment when the little country was being overwhelmed by a victorious and exultant enemy. All the fortresses that lay on the French and German sides of the Republic had been mastered by the French army. Utrecht, which lies within forty miles of Amsterdam, was in their hands, and it was only by the desperate measure of cutting their dykes and opening their sluices to allow the sea to flow in and inundate the rest of the country, that the French soldiers were prevented from marching with murder, rape, and bloodshed from one unhappy town to another. This of course was in itself the cause of frightful loss to the farmers and townspeople, for it requires but little imagination to picture the scene of whole provinces covered with rich pastures, ample cornfields, heavily laden orchards, and flourishing towns converted into one vast lake, the waters of which swept away and drowned the hope and livelihood of thousands of struggling poor.

In this deplorable situation of his country it was a double satisfaction to De Ruyter to know that he at least had not surrendered the fortresses entrusted to him, but had given a good example for every patriot to follow. Strangely enough, even he had to experience that popular gratitude is more fickle and changeable than the waves and winds with which he had fought all his life. The people, outraged by the presence of the enemy and their own powerlessness, threw all the blame on John De Witt and his brother, who were now as thorough scoundrels as formerly they had been great and admirable men. The elder brother, Pensionary De Witt, was attacked at night as he returned from the council chamber, and all but murdered; but instead of lamenting this disgraceful occurrence, the people rejoiced over it, and said it was a pity he had not been killed right out. They accused the younger brother, the Deputy, of cowardice, of having given orders to De Ruyter while on the fleet not to fight the enemy, and of having so exasperated the Admiral that in a fight between them the Deputy had been wounded in the arm. When De Ruyter heard this he was deeply grieved, and wrote at once to say that, not only had there never been any disagreement between them, but that the

Deputy had shown more eagerness than anyone else on the fleet to follow the enemy and fight; that he had urged it frequently in the council of war with marvellous cleverness, and always behaved in the battle with unexampled bravery. This fine letter remained without effect upon the furious people. They would have it that the brothers were not only the cause of the Republic's smallness and weakness, but also of England's greatness and King Louis' cunning, so that nothing would satisfy them but their death. The most foolish rumours and lies were circulated concerning them, and on the 22nd of August a band of the most senseless and cruel inhabitants of the Hague went to the house where the two brothers were imprisoned, dragged them out of bed and downstairs into the street, trampled on them, and tore them to pieces with a fury that equalled and an ingenuity that excelled the most bloodthirsty brutes. The splendid history of John de Witt and his shocking end are as deeply interesting as anything in history, and some day I may tell you what that little man accomplished in his short life; but I have at present to do with the Admiral only, and he, being a great friend of the two brothers, was deeply shocked when he heard it. 'My poor country!' he exclaimed. 'God forbid that there should be any more such riots!'

Meanwhile he himself was becoming an object of suspicion. He was cruising about in the Channel, and writing home to his wife in Amsterdam that he hoped

'DOES ANYONE KNOW THE ADMIRAL'S HANDWRITING?'

ere long to meet the enemy. But the sympathy which he had expressed for the two murdered brothers was reported among the people, and about a fortnight afterwards Mrs. De Ruyter was warned from Rotterdam that her house might one of those days be attacked and plundered. On Tuesday, the 6th of September, De Ruyter's wife, her daughter and niece, with two female servants, were alone in the house. It was afternoon. The Exchange was going out, when suddenly from all sides hundreds of people of the lowest classes came pouring towards the house, which faced one of the canals. There were sailors from the merchant-ships, with many foreigners amongst them, beggars, loafers, and scores of wives of sailors and soldiers on the fleet. Mrs. De Ruyter, hearing their approach, sent for her son-in-law, who lived a few doors off. He could scarcely get towards her house, being threatened with a fate like that of the two brothers; but when, standing on the steps of the Admiral's house, he asked the mob what they desired, a thousand voices roared out, *that the Admiral had sold the fleet to the French*. The women said *that he was to receive a gold piece for every one of their husbands;* and others again, *that he had been seen the previous day brought into the Hague like a felon, tied hand and foot.*

This the Admiral's wife knew to be a falsehood. She ran into her room, and returned with a letter, which she gave to her son-in-law. 'Does anyone know the Admiral's handwriting?' asked Mr. Smit.

Fifty voices answered, 'Yes.' The letter was handed round, and the words dated from his ship the 'Seven Provinces' were read, wherein he hoped soon again to meet the enemy. This, however, would not satisfy the people, and Smit could with difficulty keep them from entering the house and smashing everything, by reminding them what great services the Admiral had already done. He had meanwhile sent round to the head-quarters of the burgher guard, of which he was captain, for assistance. In half an hour's time a company, fully armed, marched against the house. Other quarters of the town, where the better-educated burghers resided, had also sent a file of cavalry; and there happened to be a river gun-boat being pushed through the canal, the captain of which, being appealed to by Smit, stopped in front of the mob, loaded his guns with small shot, and prepared to fire. Thus threatened by infantry, cavalry, and artillery, the mob promised to retire quietly, and the whole district of the town was cleared. For many days afterwards, however, it was necessary to maintain that watch, and the Admiral requested and received from the Prince of Orange a special bill of protection for his family and his house. Such treatment was not calculated to sweeten the already arduous life of the head of the fleet, but he resolutely remained at his post until the weather became too stormy and uncertain for further manœuvres that year.

But even at home he was not safe. While reposing

in his house at Amsterdam from his fatigues, a vicious-looking fellow with a long knife in his hand rushed into the passage, and would probably have stabbed the Admiral, who came towards him, had not his servant knocked the man down with a ladder. It has never been fully ascertained what was the cause of this outrage, for he was then and up to the moment of his death the idol of officers and men, and the deeply respected friend of all those who knew him. Had the times been peaceful abroad, the old hero would probably have remained at home during the winter. But, with the enemy almost at the gates, he was bustling about all day long to look after the defence of the rivers, and keeping up the spirits of his sailors. Although in his sixty-sixth year, he was as active as a young man, and had worked out many a plan to render his fleet next year more formidable than ever. For the new year was looked forward to by the people of Holland with dread and apprehension. The French king, who still occupied part of the country with his army, and the English ambassadors, made such shameful demands that the people refused as one man to make peace. The Prince of Orange said he would rather die in the last ditch than so surrender his country, and the inhabitants began seriously to speak of a plan to pack themselves on board as many ships as they could find, and fly from their merciless foes to some new country and some new climate, where they could still enjoy the liberty for which they had fought so long.

The fleet was now the only hope. The inundated provinces could keep back the French army; but if the French and English fleets defeated that of the Republic, and the army which had been shipped into them were landed, nothing, it was felt, could save the unhappy people from utter destruction. The most gigantic efforts were made to fit out the fleet. The Prince of Orange, who had reappointed De Ruyter as Lieutenant-Admiral-General, managed to heal the breach that had existed between him and Tromp ever since the battle of August, 1666, and the two Admirals shook hands in presence of the Prince, and promised faithfully to sustain each other in the fearful combat for life that was now inevitable. Every person on the fleet was delighted at the reconciliation, for Tromp was as popular with the men as De Ruyter himself. Not only his name, which reminded them of his great father, but his splendid courage and his benevolence made him beloved, and when he submitted to serve under De Ruyter, and in token of inferiority ran with his ship behind the 'Seven Provinces,' lowered his flag, and saluted, it was felt by all that when two such men led them into battle, and resolved to die rather than surrender or retreat, the enemy must be more than human that could defeat them and drive them away from their own shores.

It seems to me better to describe the battles that now took place somewhat more fully when I shall treat of Tromp; for in the little space that is allowed me I have to deal hastily with many important events in the Admiral's life. Three furious battles were now conducted by De Ruyter against his opponents. The allied fleet numbered 145 sail, all told; the Dutch, only 105. The lowest estimate of the English and French men-of-war gives them about 80, while the Dutch had only 52. Moreover, the unnatural allies had an army of over 10,000 men on board, wherewith it was intended to land in Zealand and assist the French king in the total overthrow of the Commonwealth. On the 7th of June, the anniversary of the battle of Solesbay, the first engagement took place, and the Dutch, who, with a little smile at their own weakness, called themselves 'the small handful,' fought as they had never fought before. The result was not decisive, but in a week's time De Ruyter was out again in the Channel. In the second engagement, the English Admiral-in-Chief, Prince Rupert, was obliged to leave his ship, the 'Royal Charles,' and carry his flag to the 'Sovereign;' but as night parted the combatants, it is impossible to say which of the two was defeated. This much is very certain, that the landing in Zealand did not and could not take place. On the 21st of August, the old hero conducted the final battle at the mouth of Texel, near Kykduin. The incessant labours of the two provinces, Holland and Zealand, had somewhat reinforced the fleet, but it was still inferior to that of the allies. The engagement lasted from early morning till nightfall. The inhabitants of the towns on the Dutch coast ran to the churches, the bells were tolled, and the awful thunder of the cannon was listened to with breathless suspense. When the night fell, the Republic had been saved. Old Michiel had beaten the English fleet back, and the renewal of the combat was not again attempted for more than a hundred years.

The fact was that the English people and the English Parliament were getting somewhat ashamed of the part they had lately played. The Dutch ambassadors had been received by the Londoners with great sympathy, and there were many people who asked why a Protestant country like England should assist a Catholic king to bring another Protestant country to ruin. The costliness of the war, the great damage that had been done to the fleet, and the total absence of results, together with the splendid bravery which the English could not help admiring, disposed King Charles and his Ministers to conclude a separate and very honourable peace with the States in February, 1674, leaving France to finish the land part of the business as she liked best. An anonymous English author, who published a life of De Ruyter in 1677, says of him, 'The rare prudence and sagacity shown by this Admiral on various occasions in this war, made him of such vast use to his own country, the ruined greatness of which he seemed to support like an Atlas, and so famous with his enemies, who had been taught by experience that he was not easily conquered, although they had exerted themselves to the utmost to subdue him, that the chances on both sides were very evenly balanced ; so that neither the one had any reason to despair of peace, nor the other to despise the overtures which had been made.' England saw that she had nothing to gain, and that a man like De Ruyter might some day or other give her a sound thrashing. So she withdrew her insolent claims and pretensions to a great extent, and the conditions of peace were such that when the treaty had been signed the people all ran to the church and held a solemn day of thanksgiving for so great and unexpected a blessing.

De Ruyter himself was an object of great curiosity and admiration to the Londoners, and many people were very anxious to see him. The king invited him more than once, and Lords Arlington and Ossory, who visited Amsterdam during the winter and entertained the celebrated sailor at a grand banquet, so pressingly invited him, that but for his aversion to all ceremony and show, especially at a king's Court—he being a thorough republican—he would have gone to London. His son, who went over instead, was received with every mark of attention, and the knighthood with which Charles had honoured him some years before was now confirmed. Meanwhile, the war with France was continued,—although it was not deemed necessary, now that the English were no longer to be feared, to show that energy or make those vast preparations that had hitherto been necessary. It was resolved to divide the fleet in two. Tromp, with one half, was to remain in the Channel, while De Ruyter, with the other, was to go off secretly to the island of Martinique, and suddenly pouncing upon it, seize the two towns and destroy whatever French property there was. But there was no longer a John De Witt at the Hague to concoct these delicious little secret expeditions, so that when De Ruyter arrived at Martinique he found everything ready for his reception. The news that they were coming had been sent across from France a month ago; several ships of war with reinforcements of soldiers had been sent, and, although a landing was tried twice, the fleet had to return to the Dutch ports without having done anything. One Dutch historian says the Admiral came back with much honour, but without the victory; but I should think the Admiral would not have minded the honour, if he could have given the enemy a sound drubbing.

There were other things that showed how great a spirit had passed away when John De Witt was murdered. This is not the place to discuss the question whether he was guilty of any crime or not; but his worst enemies cannot deny that during the time that he was Pensionary there was a firmness, a smartness, a unity about the doings of the States that were now sadly wanting.

In the year 1675 it was resolved to send another fleet to the Mediterranean to assist the Spaniards against the French, and help them in subduing an insurrection in the island of Sicily. When De Ruyter heard that only eighteen men-of-war, with scarcely a thousand guns and four thousand men, were to be sent, he objected; for he knew very well that although the French had not fought well in the English fleet, it was not for want of courage. One of the Councillors then said to him:—

'I hope, Sir Admiral, that you are not going to show the white feather at your time of life.'

'Certainly not,' answered he, 'but I am surprised that you should hold the flag of this country so cheap. You need not ask me. Command, and if you desired me to go with one ship, I should go. Wherever you trust the flag, I am ready to risk my life.'

These words were not said in a spirit of bravado. The veteran was seriously unwell. A joint attack of gravel, toothache, and colic had laid him up; but he said, 'I shall command the expedition, if they were to carry me on board.'. His parting from wife, children, and friends was affecting and sad. More than once he pressed them in his arms and against his heart, saying that he would never see them again; and one of his most intimate friends he shook long and earnestly by the hand, and wished him good-bye for ever, as he felt that he would return to his country no more.

It was certainly a remarkable thing that he had never before set out amid so many misadventures. His health was far from good, and his friends earnestly implored him to stay at home. His old and celebrated ship, the 'Seven Provinces,' had so suffered that he was obliged to go on board the 'Unity.' But the ships had been so badly and carelessly fitted out, that the Admiral for once lost his temper, and wrote the

States a sharp letter, saying that it was a crying shame that the sailmaker had been allowed to fill his purse so dishonestly, as all the sails, cables, ropes, and canvas on his ships were rotten and all but useless. In Spain he was received with all possible honours, for the Spaniards rather liked the idea of having their fighting done for them by those same Dutch who had, some fifty years ago, destroyed more than one of their fleets. At Naples he was entertained like a king; but when he heard that twenty-three Hungarian Protestant divines were working like slaves on the galleys, he sent to the Viceroy and begged him, as a special favour, for which he would attack the French with redoubled vigour, to release these godly men. The Viceroy made many difficulties, said he could not find them, and afterwards that they were not ministers but pirates; but the Admiral would not rest until they had been released. It was only when he had fought one battle with the French fleet and had driven them from the coast, when the Viceroy and his suite came on board to inspect his ship, that he obtained, after repeated questions, the permission to have these men removed. They were rowed on board next day, twenty-six in number, and their wretched appearance, the rags with which they were covered, the sores and vermin on their wasted bodies, spoke eloquently of the good and charitable service which the old Admiral had done to his fellow-Christians.

On the 22nd of April, as the combined Dutch and Spanish fleet was cruising round about Sicily, the

French fleet hove in sight, thirty men-of-war strong, with more than 10,000 men and 2,000 guns. De Ruyter and his ally had only twenty-seven ships, of which the out-fitting was by no means excellent. Nevertheless, with his wonted determination, the Admiral signalled the attack towards the afternoon, when a slight wind from the south gave him the advantage. The smoking crater of Etna overlooked the scene, and the Duke of Vivonne, Marshal of France, had chosen a spot on the mountain to witness the combat. For four hours it seemed as though the sea had changed nature with the volcano, and emulated, by terrific volumes of flame and smoke, the vomitings of the earth. But it was now seen that valour does not always beget valour, for the Spanish squadron, for whose sake the war was really sustained in these waters, hung fire and scarcely advanced. When De Ruyter sent a sloop to ask the reason of this extraordinary conduct, they made the excuse that they had not enough powder on board. Some of these brave captains had boasted of their valour before the fight, and one of them is reported to have uttered the blasphemous words, 'If God's right hand can be conquered by the sword, I ought to have it.' But now neither their swords nor their cannon were made to do anything wonderful. Meanwhile, as De Ruyter stood on his quarter-deck, a bullet took away half his left foot, another at the same moment tore open part of his right leg above the ankle and knocked him down on the lower deck, a height of seven feet. He was for some time unconscious; but having recovered his senses in the cabin, continued to take a lively interest in the battle. Every time the guns went off, he cried, 'Keep courage, boys! keep courage! That's the way to get the victory!'

His sufferings were already great, but he bore his wounds with patience. His prayers and discourses with the preacher breathe the simple and thorough piety with which he had ennobled a long and glorious life. All that doctors and surgeons could do to save his life, all that the strong love of those around him could suggest, was done, but done in vain. Mournfully and silently, in face of an enemy whom they had beaten, the fleet drifted towards the Bay of Syracuse. Fever had set in; the wounds mortified; the patient sank slowly, and hope became gradually less. In the midst of his fevers and dreadful pain he lay smiling, and repeated the words of the 63rd Psalm, 'My soul thirsteth for Thee: my flesh longeth for Thee in a dry and thirsty land, where no water is.' Towards the evening of the 29th of April his condition became alarming. All the commanders immediately came on board. The cabin was filled with admirals and captains of the fleet. Those faithful and tried servants of the State, who had followed their leader into so many a fight and out of it with glory, who had faced death a hundred times by his side, would have laid down their lives if they could have assisted their beloved leader. They wept when they saw the pale lips, that had so often cheered them on, gasping for breath.

Between nine and ten at night, amid solemn silence and deep emotion, the greatest of the great Dutch admirals passed away, in the sixty-seventh year of his age. His body was immediately embalmed; but his lion heart, which it was intended to bury in Syracuse, was refused the consecrated ground. On the 1st of May it was conveyed by the captains to a small mound which rose out of the bay, and there buried; and there it lies alone, surrounded on all sides, and covered at high tide by the element which he had ruled with honour for eight-and-fifty years.

JOHAN EVERTSEN.

AMONGST the famous names in the history of the Dutch Commonwealth, there is not one that is more honourable than the name of Evertsen. The Evertsens were indeed a very remarkable family, and no list of the Dutch Admirals would be complete without some special mention of them. I have chosen Johan as the subject of my biography, not only because he was undoubtedly the greatest of them all, but because he illustrates, in a very striking manner, how a man can work hard all his life, and work to the very best of his great abilities, how he can risk not only his life but all that is dear to him in the great cause, and be repaid time after time by disappointment, by failure, by hatred and mistrust, and rewarded in the end by popular disgrace. On reading his life the boy who has any ambition in him almost feels as though it were useless ever to try being anything great, when a man who tried so hard and so honestly was so abominably treated, were it not that such considerations never do constitute and never should constitute the cause of our acts. They certainly had no influence on Evertsen. He felt, in the latter part of his life, more strongly than ever, that there was a certain duty which he could perform for the public good, and he simply went and did it. He could not help himself. He expected no reward ; indeed, the last time that he had performed a like service he had been treated very much as though he had committed a murder. His family had certainly derived no great gain by it, and this seemed to warn him that it would go thus with him if he ventured out again. 'I desire,' said he, ' to give my life for the Commonwealth, as my father, one of my sons, and four of my brothers have already had the good fortune to die on the bed of honour, in various battles with the enemy.'

In the course of sixty years, nine Evertsens had died in their country's service, eight of them on board ship in battle with the enemy, and one on land. Commodore Johan Evertsen, the patriarch of the tribe, died at sea in 1617. His great-grand-son, Cornelius Evertsen, died in 1773, and in the years that lie between these two dates there had been fifteen men who had borne the name honourably. Four of these attained to the dignity of Admirals of the fleet, one became Lieutenant-General on land, another Lieutenant-Colonel, five others were commanders when scarcely twenty, and fell before they were of age. Indeed they were so brought up to the sea that it would have been marvellous had they taken to any other kind of occupation in those stirring times, when the very babes were awoke in their cradles by the booming of the guns. Johan Evertsen had scarcely left that cradle when his father took him on board to crawl about on the deck. I suppose he was sent to school afterwards and decently educated, although neither his letters nor his conversation point to any very brilliant scholarship. His knowledge of the sea, however, was all that could be desired; for when he was twenty-two years old, in 1622, he appears on the notes of the Zealand Admiralty as commander of a man-of-war. What posts he occupied before that time cannot now be ascertained, for the notes between 1618 and 1623 have either been stolen or lost; and whatever else is told about him must be taken for what it is worth.

It will be remembered that in the earlier days of the Republic the navy was not so regularly employed as afterwards, and that the few men-of-war that were kept on had plenty of work on hand to control the pirates with which in those days the English Channel swarmed. Captain Johan had his full share of these short but sharp fights, and on all occasions carried his flag out with the greatest honour. On the 18th of March, 1636, he found himself, with four small ships, opposed to the Admiral Colaert and the Vice-Admiral Rombout of the Dunkerque fleet. They were men who had earned for themselves a dreadful reputation for boldness, courage, and cruelty. Colaert had taken over a hundred merchantmen; he had already forced twenty-seven men-of-war to surrender to him, and 1,500 cannon had fallen into his hands. He was, therefore, no contemptible enemy to deal with, especially as he was now in command of four large ships armed to the teeth. Colaert, that he might better escape notice, carried the Dutch flag at his mast-head; and when Evertsen saw this, he thought he might as well fight the pirate with his own weapons, and hoisted the English flag. Meanwhile he issued orders to hold everything in readiness for immediate fight, and, taking the helm into his own hands, steered right for Colaert, who, not altogether expecting an attack from an English man-of-war, did not know what to do. When Evertsen had come within a couple of ships' lengths, he suddenly dropped the English and hoisted his own flag of Zealand. Colaert immediately imitated him, and hoisted the Dunkerque arms. Always prepared, the pirate fired first; but Evertsen sailed straight on until his prow crashed into his opponent's stern, and the grappling-irons firmly tied the two ships together: then he opened fire. The pirates, to whom such scenes were no novelty, immediately took to their swords and axes, and swore that not a man of Evertsen's should survive. But Evertsen was as good as they. Turning to his men he cried out that it was here a game of life and death, and that he who gave in first would go down to the bottom. A fearful scuffle then took place between the two crews at the point where the two vessels were joined, while the guns poured their volleys into the opposed hulls. The pirate soon began to find that superior discipline and skill told against him, and when he discovered his ship in a sinking condition, exerted all his energy to get loose from his enemy. Those who had formerly slashed at men now hacked away at ropes and chains; but Evertsen would not let his prey go. As soon as one fastening had been cut off, he managed to fix another. Some of his men went down into the boats and tied ropes to the rudder. Colaert, brought to despair, threatened to set fire to his powder stores, and blow up both ships. 'Blow away,' answered Evertsen, 'I have promised to bring you back with me, and back you must go.' Every offer of the pirate was refused, while inch by inch of his ship was gained ; and even though it showed dangerous symptoms of sinking, Evertsen was so determined to capture the great pirate that he would rather have sunk with him than have returned without him. Overcome by such resolution and courage, Colaert gave way, when he saw no escape, and surrendered. The other ship in the meantime had imitated Evertsen's example, and so beset the pirates that the Vice-Admiral and the third captain were also obliged to surrender, while the fourth only escaped by a favourable wind and the speed of its rowers. The joy in Middelburg when the two notorious chiefs were brought in tied as prisoners, and their ships half destroyed, need not be described. Evertsen was rewarded with a gold medal and chain, with a suitable inscription, to the value of 100*l*., which was no small sum in those days.

In consideration of his great courage and determination, the Admiralty of Zealand made him Vice-Admiral of their fleet ; and as he was at that time only thirty-seven years old, he certainly had every reason to be content with his lot. Two years afterwards, when Tromp so completely defeated the Spanish Admiral D'Oquendo in the Downs, Evertsen commanded a squadron, and in my description of that furious battle you will perhaps remember how the largest of the Spanish ships, the 'Theresa,' was blown up. Before the battle commenced Evertsen had received orders to take the Portuguese Admiral for his part of the business, and take care that he was duly despatched. Now, in order to get some idea of the difference between them, it would not be unfair to compare the Spanish to one of our large steamers that run between Liverpool and New York, and the Dutchman to one of the small excursion boats that ply on the Thames. Don Lopes Docias, the Portuguese Admiral, had a thousand men on board, and two hundred noblemen, with nearly a hundred pieces of cannon; Evertsen carried not more than two hundred men and thirty to thirty-five guns. Nothing daunted, he sailed against the Portuguese squadron with his own, but with his small cannon it was hopeless to destroy so tremendous a ship. Its lowest guns were so high above him that they fired over his deck without touching him. This was an advantage; but, on the other hand, the enemy's deck was so high that the Spanish musketeers could fire down upon his deck almost unhindered. Again and again he tried to fix himself on his big enemy and climb up, but in vain. At last Admiral Tromp sent him some fire-ships.

T

Now was the time. The clumsy Portuguese could not turn quickly enough to get out of the way. The crowd on deck, when it saw the danger approaching, became mad with fear, and prayed for mercy. But Evertsen in answer pounded them more furiously than ever, and with his squadron hung about the great brute like a pack of hounds round a hunted stag. The end was not long in coming. Three flaming ships fixed themselves on to the unfortunate 'Theresa' at once; as the evening fell, and amidst a scene of the most horrible confusion, that great and splendid ship was hurled with all it contained into thousands of fragments.

So awful a scene struck terror in the hearts of the superstitious Spaniards, and they fled on all sides. When Evertsen arrived at Middelburg with his squadron he had six galleons, two frigates, and a very large man-of-war, the 'Salamander,' in tow, all of which were sold by public auction, and the money honestly divided amongst those who had risked their lives to obtain it. It would be tedious to chronicle the events of his life as they occurred, partly because most of these events have already been described in former articles, partly because in these he was not better or worse than those around him. He fought on land, and behaved himself creditably in two or three attempts to take a town by surprise, under the command of Frederick Henry the Stadtholder; and although he was afterwards again employed at sea against the pirates, there is nothing remarkable in his life until the time of the first war with England. It was a thing that had been looked forward to for years by the Dutch; and every captain in the navy when he saw the English sailing past proudly, expecting a salute to the king's flag, had said to himself, 'This can't go on for ever. A day must come when we shall salute no longer;' and probably Evertsen, with the rest of the fighting men, was not sorry that the day had come; for after all, cruising up and down the Channel, and having an occasional brush with a pirate, was rather dull work at the best of times.

The last battle of that first war was about to be fought. In the short space of thirteen months the two hostile fleets had met nine times, and in each encounter over a hundred men-of-war had been engaged in furious contest, but still the question was not decided. Both parties had suffered great losses: but although a war at sea has great disadvantages, it also has something in its favour. There is no escape. When a ship sinks, its crew must either surrender or drown, while the tempest and the waves are frequently more disastrous than the most embittered enemy. On the other hand, whatever harm is done touches the fleet and the fleet only. No cities are plundered, no treasuries broken open, no defenceless inhabitants are ravaged. The horrors of war are heard of, and those who have a brother or kinsman on the fleet, feel acutely the fluctuations of fortune, and picture to themselves the horrors of a defeat. But to that horror there is not added the more dreadful certainty that the same enemy is marching forward and will repeat his cruelties wherever he comes. This to some extent explains how so small a country as Holland could engage in so tremendous an undertaking and continue in it so long. Had the war been waged in the country, nine pitched battles, in which each side put forth its utmost strength, would have altogether exhausted the resources of the little Republic. But nine battles at sea was quite a different thing. The people paid more taxes, and some of them lost their friends, but that was all. They were still rich enough to equip another fleet of a hundred men-of-war, part of which, having been furnished by the province of Zealand, was entrusted to our Evertsen.

Now there have been a good many persons who have charged this Admiral with ambition, and from the way in which they speak of him, one would almost imagine that in being ambitious Everstsen had committed a felony. As the word is understood in the ordinary sense, it was certainly not his great failing. De Witt and even Tromp had more of that restless desire to be the head everywhere and in everything than he; but at fifty-three years of age it was but natural that he should look forward to the chief command of the fleet as something he had a right to expect. Curiously enough, although he was the oldest captain in the navy, and certainly one of the cleverest, the post he so coveted was continually before his eyes, but never within his grasp. He fought hard enough for it, but somehow fortune favoured him not. On the 3rd of August, 1653, the fleet ran out for the last time under Tromp, to effect a juncture with De Witt, who was being blockaded in the Northern ports. The English fleet lay between the two, and on the 8th the first engagement was fought. Already on that day Evertsen got in for some very hard fighting with his squadron, but the weather was too boisterous to allow the fleets to come very close, and the muskets were not therefore used. It was on the 10th, however, when De Witt had also run out and joined his three colleagues, that the real game began. I may translate an extract from his letter to the States to show you in what manner of plight he was. After telling them how on the 8th he already had six killed and twelve wounded, he continues—

'We received so many shots under water that we were continually obliged to work two pumps. The boisterous state of the weather did not allow us to easily stop the leakages; but while keeping the pumps at work this morning, we have dutifully ranged ourselves, and sailing with our fleet against that of the enemy, we ran through the bulk of them, about sixty or seventy (there being three Admirals' ships and the rest nearly all first-class men-of-war), which so charged us that I had not marvelled at our sinking forthwith; to that end, that I have now more than fifty dead and wounded on board, myself a wound in the back, my captain three wounds, more than twenty shots under water; and further, all our masts, yards, sails, and rigging so utterly destroyed that I ordered Captain Peter Gorcum to remain by me with his ship, that I might be able to save my crew if the ship had sunk.'

Indeed, he was at one moment so completely surrounded by enemies that he had lost all hope. The captain whom he alludes to was his own son, whose wounds threatened at the beginning to be fatal; and he would perhaps have been obliged to surrender, had not the attention of the English been averted at that moment by Tromp, who came up with the rest of the fleet. Evertsen was glad of the relief, and retired, with seventy dead and wounded out of a crew of two hundred, to the Meuse, with De Ruyter and many others. He afterwards frequently blamed himself for not remaining, and there is no doubt that nobody would have blamed him for going on to some other ship. When he was asked why he had not done so, he answered, significantly, 'Because I should then have been obliged to go on board an enemy's ship.' Smart though the sentence sounds, I suppose he meant that no other vessel was near enough to be within hail, while his own wound, the dangerous condition of his son, and of the whole ship, fully warranted his retreat. Meanwhile Tromp had fallen. De Ruyter was already on his way to the Meuse, Evertsen had followed him, and the command of the fleet, which naturally belonged to the latter, came to De Witt, whose conduct I have already related to you in a former article.

The moment the States-General received Evertsen's letter they sent word that he and De Ruyter were to sail again immediately, in whatever vessel they could find, rejoin the fleet, and do whatever was in their power to bring the affairs to a good issue. Although both were exhausted, and the position of the fleet was very uncertain, Evertsen hesitated not a moment, and, without resting, when the evening had already fallen, he put to sea from the Meuze in a small galliot, and sailed in the direction of the late battle. Meanwhile the fleet had run into the Texel harbour, beaten, shattered, and with the body of Admiral Tromp on board.

The real state of affairs immediately became known. The sea was again in English hands, and if the two Admirals were allowed to go they would be taken prisoners. This was De Witt's answer. The States-General at the Hague were frightened at this. They assembled at twelve o'clock at night in a special meeting, and sent a counter-order requesting Evertsen and De Ruyter to come to the Hague at once. The messenger rode for his life, and startled the inhabitants of the villages out of their quiet repose; but when he arrived in Briel, he found that the birds had flown. For two days the little boat tossed about on the ocean in search of the fleet, but without meeting a ship, for the harm had been done, and when they arrived in Texel on the 13th, the collection of shattered hulls required but little explanation.

Evertsen immediately journeyed to the Hague without giving himself rest, for he felt that his reputation was to some extent at stake. The States-General had voted before the beginning of the battle that if Tromp came to die, Evertsen was to be the next in command, and the old man naturally looked forward to the honourable post as his due. He found, however, that the unfortunate circumstance of his retreat out of the battle had lost him his chance. When he arrived again in Texel he found Cornelis De Witt in command; and when he requested that Admiral with some authority to deliver the command to him, he received one of those short and rude answers for which De Witt was so well known. Evertsen saw that he could now get his rights in the Hague alone, but even here he was opposed. The province of Holland considered itself, and in many respects certainly was, the most important and wealthiest of all the seven, especially in maritime matters. When a fleet was to be built, or sailors furnished, or money subscribed, Holland was always foremost, and she naturally liked to have the biggest word in the States-General and on the fleet. Moreover, Holland was tremendously republican, and had always opposed the Prince of Orange becoming Stadtholder. Pensionary John de Witt was one of the members for Holland, and he of course exerted all his great influence, not only to keep the Prince of Orange's party down, but to snub everybody who dared to put himself on equal terms with Holland. You will perhaps wonder that I relate these details to you, but I do this only to show you how small interests and apparently trivial concerns influence the actions of the greatest men. It is certainly very useful to read in history that King Thingummy did so-and-so, or that at a certain date such and such a decree was voted by a Parliament or an Assembly; but it is much more useful to know for what particular reason the king did so, or the Parliament passed their law. Now here were the States of the Netherlands, who, with a Prince of Orange as chief magistrate, would never have gone to war with England. But there was one particular province, and within it one particular town—Amsterdam—and within that town half-a-dozen particular gentlemen, very wealthy, very clever, and uncommonly fond of power, who knew that if the Prince were once admitted it would be all up with them, and, as they feared, with the republic, and so they moved heaven and earth to keep him out of it. To that end wars were carried on, treaties made, and peace concluded, and one half the world kept in a hubbub and a state of ferment, while the other half looked on wondering what it all meant.

Poor John Evertsen got his share of the annoyance. He had been appointed Vice-Admiral by the province of Zealand, and as that province had, next to Holland, the most influence, there naturally was much jealousy between the two. Moreover, Evertsen was a staunch supporter of the Prince, and so when Pensionary De Witt heard that a Zealand Admiral and an Orangeman was asking for the command of the fleet, he opposed him with all his might ; and much to Evertsen's disgust and that of his province he was politely informed that as he had left the fleet before the battle was over, and Admiral De Witt had already got the command, it would be better to leave matters as they were. But this was only the beginning of his mortification. When it was found out that rough and cruel Cornelis De Witt could not get on at all as commander of the fleet, and that he was detested by everyone, the province of Zealand again requested the appointment of Evertsen ; but Holland opposed it, and Wassenaer, a cavalry officer who turned sea-sick when the wind was at all brisk, received the appointment. Worse than this, however, was the nomination of De Ruyter as Vice-Admiral of Holland, and, in virtue of his office, second in command, for De Ruyter was a much younger man than Evertsen ; and although De Ruyter had served under him for more than twenty-two years, Evertsen was suddenly informed that in the event of Wassenaer being killed, he should have to go for orders either to De Witt or to De Ruyter. It is no wonder that the old fellow forgot his manners for once in a way, and broke out into such a storm of angry words and reproaches that the man at the helm began to look out for a life-buoy, fearing that if the Admiral kept on very much longer the ship would go down with all hands.

As far as De Witt was concerned, Evertsen refused point blank ever to go near what he called 'a thrice-unlicked bear,' it being doubtful whether he considered him thrice unlicked or equal to three bears. The Provincial States, his friends, and even the States-General tried to alter his decision; but although he consented to serve on the same fleet, he sternly refused ever to receive one single command from Cornelis. When De With fell in the battle of the Sound, I dare say Evertsen was as sorry as anyone else that the country had lost so brave a soldier; but he ever looked upon his promotion and the general behaviour towards himself as a piece of gross injustice. Even towards De Ruyter he could not help showing some of the same spirit, and you will remember that I told how, on being appointed Commander-in-Chief, De Ruyter was treated with great respect by everyone but the Zealand Admiral. De Ruyter, however, was large-minded, and Evertsen was honest enough to acknowledge that he was a great genius and better than himself.

If the Admiral felt himself wronged by being so continually pushed in the background, the Provincial States who had appointed him felt this much more, and worked hard to get him promoted. For ten years, from 1654 to 1664, they backed him up in everything he did, and liberally praised him for his conduct of the war in the Baltic. Then, as you know, the second war between England and the Netherlands threatened to break out, and a fleet was equipped. Now or never was the time. Zealand had played second fiddle long enough; in a great war like this she must, she should be, treated with the respect due to her station. In a very complimentary address the Provincial States appointed Evertsen Lieutenant-Admiral of their fleet 'for his heroic courage, his long experience, and his rare sagacity at sea.' At last, then, the veteran had reached the pinnacle of ambition. There was only one other of equal rank in the fleet, and on him the command must naturally fall, if that other (Wassenaer) came to die. The gentlemen at Middelburg were already chuckling over their victory, and ordering a splendid banquet with turtle-soup and green peas and all the rest of it, when they heard that the province of Holland was going to outwit them after all. And so it did. Within a few weeks of Evertsen's promotion, the States of Holland startled the whole country by coolly announcing that they had thought it advisable to appoint three more Lieutenant-Admirals, being Cortenaer, De Ruyter, and Meppel. Such a thing had never happened before, and although all sorts of reasons, excuses, and arguments were brought forward, nobody for one moment doubted that it was simply done that Evertsen might never have the chief command of the fleet. That the Admiral himself, and the Provincial States who had appointed him felt thoroughly indignant and tried their utmost to annul the extraordinary decree, need scarcely be said, nor that John de Witt and his party were too strong and too knowing to be thwarted. But heavy was to be the punishment that awaited the Republic for such trifling and trivial conduct in so important an hour.

Immense preparations had been made at this beginning of a new war to turn out a fleet that should ensure success. Never had so splendid an assembly of noble ships sailed out of the Dutch ports, but never had there been so much confusion, jealousy, anger, and want of confidence between the various commanders. The haggling had borne fruit. In order to shut out the best man from the chief command, a land soldier had been appointed; and in order that the blunder might be perfect, a whole list of instructions had been put in his hand, drawn up by the States-General at the Hague, who knew no more about fighting at sea than a sailor knows about the digging of siege-trenches. On the 24th of May, 1665, one hundred and three men-of-war, with four thousand eight hundred cannon and twenty-one thousand men, put out to sea under Wassenaer van Obdam, the noble cavalry colonel, but it was not until the 11th of June that the English fleet hove in sight. A better fleet or a nobler group of commanders England had never put forward. There was the Duke of York, the king's brother; at whose side the wise and venerable William Penn proffered his well-considered advice. Under him came the gallant Prince Rupert, the handsome and high-spirited Earl of Sandwich, John Lawson, George Ayscue, Christopher Mengs, and a list of captains whose features were tanned by a dozen climates and half a hundred engagements. The fleet consisted of one hundred and nine men-of-war, four thousand two hundred guns, and between twenty-one thousand and twenty-two thousand men. There was therefore no great difference between the respective strengths of the two opponents, and each looked forward to the battle with confidence.

The spirits of the Netherlanders were high, all the more because the people had some misgivings about Wassenaer, which they were very eager to have proved foolish. But Wassenaer, being wise, waited his time. The States, being foolish, got impatient, and ordered him to sail across to England at once, and give battle at any and every cost. Wassenaer never said a word, but the expression on his face showed that he was deeply wounded. He ordered all his valuables and plate to be carried on board, and without waiting for wind or tide ran out to sea, followed by the fleet. In an express order of the States he had been commanded to divide it in *seven* squadrons, each squadron being led by a Vice-Admiral of experience and reputation. This was a great blunder. Every Admiral of those days, and every Admiral since, has held that no fleet should be divided into more than three, or at the utmost four squadrons. But the Province of Holland was so afraid of old John Evertsen getting the command of all or a great portion of the fleet, that they must needs invent an order of battle of their own. Wassenaer, having been insulted, had no other wish than to fight, and prove to the States that he was no coward. On the evening of the 12th of June the fleets, which had lain in sight of each other, had approached so closely that a battle for the following morning looked inevitable. No council of war was held. Wassenaer was miserable. For two days the wind had been in his favour, but he had not attacked. On the morning of the 13th it suddenly turned in favour of the English. The Dutch were by no means prepared. The commanders lay all in a group, instead of each at the head of his squadron, when suddenly, as they expected a signal to keep on the defensive, Wassenaer, in the most unaccountable manner, signalled the attack and led the way.

There was no help for it. The English had noticed the movement, and were advancing in splendid style in the shape of a half-moon. A kind of confused movement of the Dutch was the response. The great number of squadrons, the want of confidence in their leader, the want of unity in their actions, and the unfortunate position which Wassenaer had taken up, so that half the fleet could not see his signals, rendered the beginning of the battle already disastrous. The two long lines ran past each other, amidst a heavy fire. The wind being in favour of the English, and their guns of heavier calibre, the Dutch fleet suffered considerable damage. At five o'clock in the morning, the fleets, having passed once, tacked about and repeated the manœuvre, when one of the new Lieutenant-Admirals, Cortenaer, was mortally wounded. The news spread through the fleet with rapidity, and somewhat damped the ardour of the sailors, for it was known that Cortenaer had gone into action with gloomy and serious misgivings of a total defeat. The fleets, having tacked about, attacked each other with energy ; but the want of order among the Dutch, the forwardness of some captains, the backwardness of others, and the reluctance of a few to join in at all, caused on more than one spot so dense a cluster of ships, that none could turn about and manœuvre with ease, while all offered a good aim to the enemy's fire. It is said that some ships did not fire at all, and that after the battle the plugs were found still sticking in the mouths of their cannon. The English of course saw their advantage and blazed away at their opponents with hearty good will. Wassenaer fought well, but time after time he allowed the best of chances to slip by him. At last the Earl of Sandwich, seeing a break in the Dutch line about one o'clock, rushed in with his squadron and divided them. The battle now became furious. Wassenaer, finding that matters went against him, ran deliberately alongside the Duke of York's 'Royal Charles,' and commenced a desperate duel of broadsides. The Royal Duke standing on his own deck was bespattered with the blood of three young noblemen, who had joined the fleet as volunteers, and were killed by his side. At one moment he was so hard pressed, that Wassenaer seemed on the point of entering, when another vessel came to the rescue, and opened fire on the other side. Thus beset, Wassenaer looked round for help, when with an awful crash and a huge column of flame and smoke, in which the mangled bodies of men were mixed with the débris of the ship, the 'Eendragt' was hurled into the air, the Admiral-in-Chief being blown to pieces with the rest of the crew.

The battle was at an end at once. Terror possessed the hearts of most captains, indignant rage and sullen determination but those of a few. The cowardly captain of Cortenaer's ship, still carrying the Admiral's flag, turned without orders and fled. Some in fear, others in astonishment, followed. The existing confusion increased. There was no head: everybody looked to his Admiral, but no Admiral could look to his chief. Many a ship, beset on all sides by the English, defended itself against overwhelming numbers, but was forced to surrender or be destroyed by fire. In this terrible hour John Evertsen hoisted the Admiral's flag, and ordered the fleet to draw round him in a half-circle, but he was unable to stay the general rout. Although his ship had already received seventeen shot under water and had nearly sixty dead and wounded, while more than fifteen thousand pounds of powder had been shot away, he turned against the English. Young Tromp and his own brother, Cornelis Evertsen, both Vice-Admirals, and some twenty others, endeavoured to oppose the overwhelming host, but in vain. At the approach of darkness the Dutch fleet had been utterly scattered and destroyed. John Evertsen, as Chief-Admiral, signalled with fires to retire towards the Meuze; but Tromp, not very ready to acknowledge Evertsen, steered towards Texel, and reached it on the morning of the 14th with about sixty men-of-war, while Evertsen only ran into the Meuze with ten or eleven, and found himself next morning, much to his astonishment, nearly deserted.

Intelligence had already reached the people. The loss of eighteen splendid ships and four thousand men had been exaggerated into twice that number. The people were furious, and by some unaccountable freak fixed their wrath upon Evertsen. A galliot, having been sent out, met him; and the sailors returned with the news that the Admiral looked very well, and that his ship did not seem to have suffered much. Meantime the Admiral had sent a hurried letter to the Hague, complaining of the cowardice of the fleet, describing the battle, and requesting permission to run into the river and go ashore. An answer came back immediately, summoning him to the Hague to appear before the States-General. On the 14th of June he went ashore, hired a carriage and drove towards the Hague. At seven in the evening he passed through Briel, but he had scarcely entered the gate when he was surrounded by a mob of men, women, and children. Excited by the foolish tales of sailors, some of whom blamed him even for the accident to Wassenaer, they assailed him with stones and mud; they tore him from the carriage. The old hero, whose hair had been whitened by five-and-sixty summers, was rudely pushed onward towards the quay. He stumbled and fell. Remonstrances only added to their fury; reason increased their folly. They seized him as he lay, dragged him along the streets with yells of savage delight and murderous excitement, and, having approached the quay, threw the veteran patriot into the water, where they endeavoured to hasten his end by showering upon him a volley of stones. After so great an indignity the old man would fain have died, but the instinct of self-preservation caused him to lift his head above water, and clutch the prow of a vessel hard by. His head was cut in several places; his blood dyed the water; his strength was gone; and the shrieks of the people bewildered his senses. At that moment two Deputies from the States, with the burgomaster and the garrison, came running to the rescue; the mob was dispersed, and the all-but-dying Admiral pulled out of the water, and conducted to a neighbouring house. The whole evening the populace remained in a state of wild and bloodthirsty excitement. Nothing but his life would satisfy them. He was protected by a guard of soldiers, and he was obliged, at two o'clock in the morning, and disguised as a fisherman, to leave the town by the same way he had come, as the road to the Hague was lined with men who were determined to revenge upon him the disaster of the fleet. Such was the state of the people in the whole province of Holland, and it required an escort of soldiers to allow him to reach the Hague in safety.

The Provincial States of Holland, with their Pensionary John De Witt, hearing of his arrival, immediately had his hotel guarded by soldiers, ostensibly to protect him, but really to offer him a fresh indignity.

The States-General being then sitting, the members for Zealand immediately ran to their Admiral, heard his story, went back to the Assembly and prayed that Evertsen might be brought before them. Still suffering from his wounds, and exhausted by what he had undergone, the Admiral appeared before the High Mighty Lords and recounted his deeds. But, if he had hoped for an enthusiastic welcome, he was sorely disappointed. A resolution had already been voted that day whereby all officers whose conduct was open to doubt were to be sent before a court-martial at Texel; and when Evertsen had finished his story, his great enemy, John de Witt, quietly got up and proposed that the Admiral should be sent to Texel that very night. The motion was carried. That very night he was conveyed, in custody of the major of the guard, to the ship 'Middelburg,' where he was to remain until further orders. Thus the old and tried hero was treated by the authorities with as much severity as the coward who had deserted his flag, while the people had endeavoured to take from him the honourable life which the enemy and his God had yet spared him. It is a lasting disgrace to the States, and especially to Holland, that this man's reputation and honour were not more loyally treated. Nobody would judge him. His captains, indeed everyone on the fleet, praised his conduct; his own justification before the Deputies was to them perfectly satisfactory, and the court-martial was split up into factions, as no one would undertake to preside. Seeing that a decision was not to be shortly expected, Evertsen requested permission to go home, as he was still suffering from his wounds. This he received at once, and reached home in July.

The province of Zealand, indignant at such treatment, moved in the States-General that the Admiral should receive a full acquittal, and be thanked for his services; but De Witt once more opposed and defeated the motion. The States remained neutral, but would not allow him to become what he should have been, president of the court-martial. Overwhelmed by so much enmity and injustice, Evertsen retired to his house. He appeared indeed before his own masters, the Provincial States, and was there received with every expression of confidence and respect; but the course of his enemies had so excited the populace throughout the country that they were reluctantly compelled to accept the veteran's resignation, while at the same time his brother Cornelis was appointed to the vacant post. John retired to Flushing, where, still enjoying the title of Lieutenant-Admiral, he was employed by the authorities in preparing a new fleet. A whole year was thus spent in comparative retirement, during which the old man endeavoured to forget the insults, indignities, and injustice which he had undergone. Meanwhile De Ruyter returned from his secret mission, and sailed out at the head of the fleet. The famous battles of that war I have already described to you in De Ruyter's life. The four days' battle was fought, and the younger Evertsen lost his life. The fleet returned victorious, but fearfully damaged. Then old John Evertsen, who could not remain at home, forgot his wrongs, and offered his services once more. 'I desire,' he said, in words we have already quoted, 'the proper time having come, to give my life for the Commonwealth, as my father, one of my sons, and four of my brothers have already had the good fortune to die on the bed of honour, in various battles with the enemy.' Zealand of course gladly accepted his services, and reappointed him Lieutenant-Admiral. Not even now could John De Witt stay his hand. Being in Flushing at the time, he was informed of the appointment, and immediately wrote a sharp and spiteful letter to the States-General, urging them to annul the appointment. For once, however, Evertsen's party triumphed. One of his friends moved that this 'letter be destroyed and not entered in the journal of the proceedings:' and the High Mighty Lords, considering for once that De Witt had gone too far, adopted this course by a silent majority. Evertsen was appointed second in command of the fleet, and leader of the vanguard.

On the 4th of July, 1666, the fleet sailed. A month later the battle was fought. A death-like calm pervaded. Not a ripple stirred the waves. Slowly Evertsen's squadron drifted towards the enemy. It was noon before his first shot opened the battle. Half an hour later the fight raged with terrific fury. The old man had again become young, and cheered his men with energy ; but at three a shot struck him in the leg, and threw him senseless on deck. The next morning he had brought his sixty-six years to an end. His body was buried with that of his brother in one grave, and a splendid marble monument in the Cathedral of Middelburg records in simple language the virtues and heroism of a great and unhappy man.

CORNELIS TROMP.

PART I.

THE name, and some of the deeds, of this man are already familiar to you. He was the son of a great admiral, the constant companion in arms and rival of a still greater; he combined in himself some of the finest qualities of each; he perpetuated the fame which his father had begotten, and he added to the ancient reputation a vigour and a character of his own, thereby becoming one of the singular instances in history, how, in the same profession and with the same means, a son can almost overshadow the greatness of his father, and have transferred to himself the popularity and affection with which the name he bears was received and cherished before he was born.

Old Martin Tromp, though a determined sea-dog, was a very homely man; that is to say, he liked the fireside quite as much as the cabin, and when duty allowed him to be on shore, there was nothing that so delighted him as to spend his days, surrounded by his wife and family, listening to their tales of school-fights or bird catching, and playing with them as gently and tenderly as if he had never shattered a powerful navy, and shaken a mighty empire to its very foundations. It was but natural that he should wish at least one of his sons to enter the profession in which he was already reaping great honours, but he knew from experience that sons do but seldom follow with hearty goodwill the footsteps of their fathers. His eldest son, Cornelis, however, seemed just the kind of lad that would have gone to sea of his own accord, and it was, therefore, with great satisfaction that his father took him on board his own ship at a very early age. Indeed, Cornelis could scarcely help liking the sea. His happy days of boyhood were associated with it, and he had always before him the important position to which his father had already risen. But his father was wise. He determined to make something good of his boy, not merely to help him to a good post, where he need not know much, or do more than draw his salary and eat his dinners. There were plenty of men on the fleet, and plenty of stout, fat-cheeked gentlemen in Amsterdam, or the Hague, who had done so for their own sons, and thought they had done very wisely. For they said to themselves, 'I have worked hard when I was young, I have made a lot of money, I am comfortably off, and I do not see why my son should be obliged to work. I belong to an Admiralty Board, and I will get him a snug, comfortable place.' But old Tromp spoke very differently. He said to himself, 'I have worked hard and risen from nothing. Every man who can work ought to be ashamed if he is lazy, and I will make my son work while I have it in my power, and if he is worth his salt, he will thank me when he gets older.' And so after Cornelis had been playing about his father's ship till he was thirteen or fourteen years old, he was made a common sailor on some other ship, and his father used to laugh heartily when he saw him climbing aloft, with bare head and feet, to reef the sails or keep watch. I dare say young Cornelis did not altogether like it at first, but he soon grew accustomed to it, and when he advanced in age he saw the wisdom of his father's arrangements, for whereas the sailors looked upon the fine and wealthy young officers with contempt, they knew that young Tromp had been one of themselves, knew all their trouble and hardships, and, like De Ruyter and his own father, would see that they were well taken care of.

When his father was appointed Lieutenant-Admiral of the fleet, and fought that famous battle against the Spanish Admiral D'Oquendo in the Downs, young Tromp was scarcely nineteen years old, and is reported to have then made a very fair beginning of his fighting career.

In due time he was promoted to be Lieutenant, and eventually, when he was scarcely twenty-eight, he received command of a man-of-war, and was ordered in 1650 to accompany Admiral Van Galen on his voyage to the Mediterranean, for the suppression of the pirates, who had lately become very troublesome. Now there was a good deal of haughtiness and determination of spirit about him, that was not at all softened either by the higher standing which his father's position naturally gave him, or by the early age at which he was, to a considerable extent, his own master. He treated some of the pirates in a rather off-hand manner I am afraid, and would have been all the better for a little of that prudence which distinguished his father. His first real engagement is of a sufficiently interesting nature to be described at some length. The war with England having broken out, the States-General considered wisely that the English trade might be greatly damaged in the Mediterranean, because the traffic with Turkey and some parts of Italy was almost entirely in their hands. Admiral Van Galen was, therefore, sent expressly overland to Leghorn, where he took the command and sailed away towards Turkey. Commodore Sir Henry Appleton was already lying in Leghorn roads with his men-of-war, and saw Galen depart with serious misgivings as to the nature of his expedition, but as the Dutch had hitherto been very friendly in those parts, he concluded that nothing would be done. On the 6th of September, 1652, Galen descried eight English ships between the islands of Elba and Monte Christo, four being men-of-war and four armed merchantmen. Young Tromp, who led the van, received orders to attack, but the weather was so calm that the real battle had to be postponed till the following day. It was then commenced with great resolution on both sides, Captain Richard Bodley—or, as he wrote his own name, Badiley—endeavouring to protect the ships under his charge. The Dutch were too strong for him, however. One of his ships, the 'Phœnix,' was boarded by young Tromp and taken after a very severe fight, while the rest of the English ships were obliged to take shelter in Porto Longone, one of the harbours of the island of Elba.

I have been unable to discover what Appleton was about all this time, but it is very clear that Van Galen kept Bodley shut up in Porto Longone for five months, the neutrality laws not allowing him to commence an attack from inside. The distance from Elba to the mainland is only seven miles, while the straight line across the sea from Longone to Leghorn does not exceed fifty miles. Bodley and Appleton could, therefore, easily communicate with each other; but being divided, each had perhaps not sufficient faith in the other. Tromp's ship had suffered so much that he was obliged to run towards Corsica; but the day after the fight, having been ordered to land at Elba and convey the Dutch Admiral's compliments to the Spanish Governor, he thought he might as well make the acquaintance of his opponent, and requested permission to call on Bodley. Bodley received him with the utmost civility, and showed by his kind reception how much he valued the visit. He gave the young captain a good dinner in his cabin, drank to the health of Van Galen, whose courage he praised, and greeted on leaving, with a naval salute, the very man whom he would have been but too glad to destroy on the previous day. The 'Maid of Enkhuizen' being in so perilous a condition, was left in Corsica to be repaired, young Tromp taking the captured English 'Phœnix,' with which, in company of Van Galen, he cruised between Leghorn and Elba, now anchoring in one port and now in the other.

This was a thorn in the side of the English. Every time they saw that 'Phœnix' with the English flag, and the Dutch one above it, they determined to have her back again, and after some deliberation among the captains a nice little plan was concocted. Appleton was seemingly in great difficulty. He had received strict orders on no account to disturb the neutrality of the Grand Duke's port. But a certain Captain Cox who commanded the 'Bonaventura' was a hot-headed, irritable man, and does not seem to have suited himself very easily to the rigorous neutrality that Appleton was trying to observe; wherever he had a chance he chased the Dutch sloops, took away their water, and so annoyed them that scarcely a day went by without complaints being sent to the Duke. Then Cox swore he would burn the 'Phœnix.' Appleton besought him to do nothing of the kind, called him an insolent fellow who gave everybody trouble, and altogether had a great quarrel with the irascible captain. Happily about the 25th of November Bodley came over from Elba and showed Appleton an order whereby he was appointed Commander-in-

Chief, and Appleton was therefore relieved of all responsibility. Captain Cox hearing this, immediately pressed his idea of retaking the 'Phœnix' upon Bodley, who considering it rather a good joke gave his permission. Just about this time the Dutch had brought in a merchantman laden with fish, and sold it. They were making themselves merry over the success, and having no suspicion, kept but indifferent watch on their ships. The crew of the 'Phœnix' were specially confident, as she was 'then in the Road, riding the outermost ship, with the English colours under hers.'

Captain Cox in the 'Elizabeth's' shallop, Lieutenant Yonge in the 'Sampson's' pinnace with thirty-four men, and Lieutenant Symmes in the 'Bonaventura's' pinnace with thirty-four more, set out in the middle of the night on the adventure. It was pitch dark, and as no lights dared be used, the three boats lost each other several times, but as the first faint streaks of the morning tinged the horizon they came together and rowed forward. The men were well armed with pistols and axes, and bags of flour to throw in the faces of the Dutch in order to confuse them. Everything being arranged, Captain Cox led the way, went forward and cut the cable, while Yonge and Symmes, drawing along each side, climbed on deck, and after a sharp but short scuffle overpowered the men, not, however, without losing Lieutenant Yonge and two of the men. Tromp was quietly sleeping in his cabin when he was awakened by the

THE ENGLISH BOARDING THE 'PHOENIX.'

noise. Without giving himself time to dress, he jumped out of bed, snatched a couple of pistols, ran on deck, and saw the English swarming over the ship. Each of his pistols brought down a man, but seeing that resistance was useless he rushed below, and having awoke his officers jumped out of the cabin window into the sea, and swam about until he was picked up by one of the Dutch boats. Thus master of the 'Phœnix,' the English made sail for Naples, while those who were not required on deck repaired to the cabin to divide the booty, as had been promised before the enterprise. While they were in the midst of this, Captain Cox entered, drove them out of the cabin, telling them that it and all that was in it belonged to him; at the same time putting all the money in his own pocket and keeping it for his private use.

You will readily understand that the Duke of Tuscany was very angry at this violation of the neutrality of his port, and having sent for Appleton, had that officer confined for several days in the castle, although Bodley was in reality responsible. At last the complaints of the Dutch, and the angry feeling between them and the English became so high, that the Duke would have no more of it, and commanded both of them to get out of his port. Thereupon the Duke's secretary and the two hostile Admirals came together in the palace, and a sort of treaty was drawn up, whereby the Dutch promised to sail away first, and the English afterwards, and whichever could catch or escape the other, might do so. But no sooner had this been arranged than Bodley thought he could play the Dutch a trick. He privately arranged with Appleton that they should both prepare as fast as they could, and that when ready Bodley should send a messenger to Appleton, whereupon the latter sailing out of the Bay of Leghorn, and Bodley coming up from Elba at the same moment, the Dutch would get between two fires and be beaten. This was all very well. Appleton prepared himself, and in due time in the night of the 12th of January one of Bodley's lieutenants came to him and ordered him to run out early in the morning, for that all was ready. But to run out was not without danger, for Van Galen, with the whole strength of the enemy, consisting of sixteen men-of-war, a fire-ship, and several stout merchant-ships (which were offered a share of the booty if they would engage), lay ready before the harbour to intercept them. Cornelis Tromp, who now commanded the 'Moon,' was very eager to engage, for having just been appointed Rear-Admiral, he had a natural desire to distinguish himself in his new capacity.

Bodley kept true to his word, and at the moment that Appleton was ready to slip his cables, appeared in the distance with every intention of attacking the Dutch. Van Galen, however, had his weather-eye open. He immediately weighed anchor and stood out for Bodley, as though he would have attacked the handful with the whole of his force. But this was only a ruse. Appleton seeing the bay clear also made sail in order to join Bodley, but he had scarcely approached half way when suddenly young Tromp with his squadron turned round, tacked about, and without the slightest warning fell upon Appleton. The combat was furious while it lasted, but it could not under the circumstances last very long. The 'Bonaventura,' a ship of 44 guns, led the van, and seeing that there was no help for it, her captain bravely began by pouring a broadside into Van Galen, who was advancing towards her. She had not, however, fired more than twenty guns when a shot penetrated her powder stores. A terrific crash, a sky filled for one moment with flame and smoke, and a hundred and fifty mangled bodies dropping into the water amid the blazing wreck,—such was the beginning of that fight. At the same time two Dutch ships, the 'Sun' and the 'Julius Cæsar,' ran alongside Appleton and began a heavy fire. Appleton looked round and called the 'Sampson' to his assistance; but Tromp, who had now arrived, sailed up to the 'Sampson' and engaged her, while the other vessels of the squadron, each singling out an antagonist, imitated his example. In a few moments the fight was general, and Bodley, who was trying all he could to get up, had the mortification to find that the slackness of the wind prevented him from making sufficient way. The blowing up of the 'Bonaventura' had for one moment paralysed the English, but presently recovering, they felt that their only escape from a similar fate lay in resolute resistance.

But Tromp was in earnest this time. Having engaged the 'Sampson,' but finding in her greater valour and opposition than his impatience could endure, he called his fire-ship, and directing it to board her on the other side, so harassed her, that being between two dangers the crew knew not from which to escape. The fire-ship got its grappling-irons firmly fixed; a slight blaze broke out immediately after; Tromp drew off, knowing what would come, and while the men in the 'Sampson' were cutting and hacking, and pumping, and running about in mad despair, the flames burst out and licked round the ship, climbed into the rigging, ran along the sails, and enveloped her in a few minutes with its scorching arms. With many a heartrending cry the men jumped into the water, and were picked up by Tromp's boats, while those whom too much pride or too little confidence had kept upon the decks were presently hurled into the air and destroyed. By this time Bodley had been able to come up with his squadron at least within range, but the smoke and the confusion probably prevented him from seeing who was most in want of assistance. Appleton was the only one who had as yet fought with some luck. He had returned the fire of the two vessels that had boarded him with interest, and carrying much heavier guns so damaged them that they became disabled and lay by his side without firing a shot, and, as he says, calling for quarter.

But Bodley has quite a different story. Having described how he sailed round and round the three ships, and first poured a broadside into the 'Julius Cæsar' and then into the 'Sun,' he says, 'In all this time there appears not a man upon the "Leopard's" upper deck, that I could discern; and being extreamly troubled to see the "Leopard" manag'd no better, I call'd to man the Pinace, and, the Lord my great witnesse knoweth, with a full resolution to have gone on board her with my boat, verily believing the captain had been killed and chiefe officers. But although Capt. Appleton now saith the two ships on bord him call'd for quarter, or he knoweth not for what; those ships untill I was gone fir'd five times as many Guns as the "Leopard" did in my sight; for I never saw her shoot but once in halfe an hour's time: I say the withdrawing of the "Leopard's" men within doors and hatches, and their not appearing to let goe an anchor in any time, nor doing anything else towards their owne preservation, caus'd me to think some part of the "Leopard" might be in the enemies possession, and so was diverted from going into my boat.'

The fact was that Bodley saw he had come too late. Five English ships had either blown up or sunk, and one was just settling down as he approached, and he therefore thought himself perfectly justified in flying, where his presence could not assist his colleague and might endanger himself. He had sent off a fire-ship to burn Van Galen, but not being able to accompany it, it was so riddled with shot from the Dutch Admiral's ship that it sunk. A sad catastrophe had in the meantime taken place on that vessel. As Van Galen was standing on his deck, a shot struck and tore away his foot. Being greatly excited by the combat, he could not for some time be persuaded to have his wound dressed, and continued all the while to give his orders and encourage his men. Having become very weak by loss of blood, the leg was at last amputated above the knee. But the operation came too late: although it had been undergone with the greatest fortitude, the Admiral rapidly sank. He desired to be carried on deck in his bed to witness the engagement; he drank a glass of wine, and broke the empty glass on the deck with the words, 'The English king's murderers will have to pay for it, after all,' —words that curiously illustrate the spirit with which he and his men were animated. Not long afterwards he expired, and his loss occasioned great distress on the fleet.

The battle, however, had now gone too far to be influenced by this circumstance. Bodley had sailed away with his ships, and Appleton had been left behind in a sore plight, for young Tromp and another vessel running alongside him began to fire with more violence, while those two ships that had cried quarter, seeing him left alone, began again to fire. After two hours' fighting, his stern beaten in, his tiller shot in pieces, fourteen guns made unserviceable, the ship every way pitifully torn, almost half his men disabled, and himself and some of his officers wounded, the men resolved to fight no longer. Appleton, filled with true dogged resolution, forced them time after time into their quarters, and offered them a hundred crowns for every shot. The gunners were firing away when a cry arose, 'The enemy are on the poop!' Appleton called the gunners to him and ordered them privately to blow up the ship. As they were running to execute this order the men rushed at them to prevent it. Appleton coming up with a cutlass in his hand would have rescued them, had not his own men seized him, and so rudely wrenched his weapon from him that his shoulder was put out of joint. The Dutch having in the meantime poured into the ship, Appleton was seized; but as he refused quarter, he would have been put to death but for the entreaties of his men. Of the seven ships he had commanded in the harbour, six fell into Dutch hands or were destroyed, while the seventh having broken through the line escaped with Bodley's squadron to England.

When Tromp returned to Holland with his squadron, he found that he was no longer young Tromp, for in the meantime that tremendous battle had been fought off the Texel, in which his father had given the example which every Admiral but his son afterwards followed. He was received with every mark of popularity and approbation, and the Admiralty of Amsterdam promoted him immediately to the rank of Rear-Admiral, partly in reward of his services, partly in recognition of his father's great talents and heroism. To have become an Admiral at the age of thirty-four, was certainly not the lot of everyone; but to be an Admiral of the most influential and energetic Board, with all the weight and talent of John de Witt and the city of Amsterdam to support him and push him on, was indeed a stroke of luck that might have somewhat turned his head. It is pleasant to know that Tromp remained as simple as his father, and that he was everywhere looked upon by the men as the worthy successor to the title of 'Bestevaer.' It cannot be denied, however, that he wanted some of the old man's rare calmness and prudence, and that both in battle and in daily life he was at times carried away by his ardour to do and say things which he was afterwards compelled to retract or regret. Nor does this failing seem to have been softened, as it generally is, by advancing age. It is unnecessary and would be tedious to relate his different expeditions to Africa and the Mediterranean, for they contain nothing of a very extraordinary character. It was in the second war between England and the Netherlands, that he really began his career.

In 1665, when it became evident that peace could no longer be maintained, the preparation for war became general. Tromp was raised to the post of Vice-Admiral and put in command of the squadron of the Province of Holland. The details of the disastrous battle that opened this war I have already described to you in the life of Evertsen, and you will recollect how Admiral Wassenaer van Opdam, being hurt by an admonition from the States, began the engagement at the worst moment; how Admiral Cortenaer's ship blew up, and he, Wassenaer, and a third Admiral were killed; how many ships, losing hope and following others who had lost honour and courage, turned and fled. Tromp was furious, and if his orders had been executed, the thorough defeat of the Dutch must have been considerably lessened. With John and Cornelis Evertsen and a small knot of faithful and heroic men, he turned a resolute face to the enemy, and, having at one moment come very near old Evertsen, he entreated him, through his trumpet, to cast anchor and perish rather than retreat any longer. But Evertsen wisely answered that this would be folly, as the fugitive ships could not thereby be brought to a stand. Tromp seems to have got disgusted at this. Although Evertsen was really entitled to carry the Admiral's flag, Tromp towards evening hoisted one of his own, and, contrary to the previous arrangement, signalled the vessels under his command to follow him to Texel. There is no doubt that had he acted otherwise, many of the ships which he now protected would have fallen into English hands, and even as it was he experienced great difficulty in so opposing the pursuing enemy that the harbour of refuge might be reached without too great a loss. The troubles and sufferings of that night cannot be easily described, for there was no actual heroism, there were no astounding deeds of courage, there was nothing that could have excited the most sanguine heart with the hope of success. It was the sad and mournful task of remaining as barrier between the shattered wreck of the country's only hope, and the merciless victor whose lights danced with a kind of fiendish gaiety upon the darkling waves for miles and miles around. When the morning sun rose upon the calm and placid sea, the enemy had retired, and sixty ships were lying before the mouth of the Texel, many of the captains congratulating themselves, with smiling faces, that they had escaped the danger so far. Tromp, on the other hand, paced his deck with gloomy brow and called them contemptible cowards, whom he vowed to heaven he would make an example of.

At this moment, a yacht with the Deputies of the States-General ran out to the fleet and sent for Tromp to come on board. Tromp came, looking as black as thunder. The moment he set foot on deck, he began his complaints, to which the Deputies listened with due respect. They then requested him by authority to remain at sea with the fleet for some time longer, notwithstanding the damage he might sustain, merely in order to show that the fleet was not altogether overcome. 'Never, gentlemen!' he burst out. 'I shall never again remain at sea with such a parcel of rogues. I can do nothing with captains that have treated me so infamously, and I do entreat you to come and look at the fleet and convince yourselves that but a few of my ships have done their duty.' Notwithstanding their entreaties and orders,

Tromp returned to his own ship, hoisted the signal to run in, and, setting the example himself, dropped anchor in the Zuyder Zee on the 14th of June, 1665. Immediately afterwards, he invited the deputies to follow him on a tour through the fleet, in order to inspect each ship, and it was then found that but a few of them could have been in that hot and close contest in which it should have been the ambition of each captain to lead all the rest and eclipse even his own former deeds. The vessels of Tromp, the younger Evertsen, and half-a-dozen others were terribly damaged; some few had received serious hurts, but nearly thirty vessels had evidently chosen flight without having been under fire. The Deputies acknowledged the justice of Tromp's indignation, and he repeated his intention of throwing up his office and devoting himself entirely to the punishment of the cowards.

Having landed, he insisted upon a court-martial, but finding that there was some difficulty in the Hague about it, he took the somewhat unusual step of leaving the fleet and travelling to the Hague to urge the matter on the High Mighty Lords. Having at last obtained his wish, he proceeded with the most rigorous inquiry. Nobody was spared. The fiercest and most searching light was turned upon every man; what had been done in the confusion of battle was repeated amidst the undisturbed tranquillity of a harbour, and what had been said in the heat of excitement was calmly reflected on by discerning judges.

The captains who had so lately smiled and congratulated themselves, looked aghast. There was a panic in the fleet. There were days of anxious suspense, there were hours of repentance for many a man who felt that he had not thoroughly done his duty. At last the verdict was made known—three captains were sentenced to be shot within view of the whole fleet; three others were condemned to be disgraced and to have their swords broken by the executioner; two were condemned to exile and declared unfit for service; while the infamous captain of Cortenaer's ship, who had headed the flight after the death of that Admiral, was sentenced to witness the executions with a halter round his neck, and to be for ever expelled the country. A wholesome fear ran through the fleet when these sentences were really carried out, and it was afterwards acknowledged that discipline had become so lax under the worthy cavalry colonel that some such example was greatly needed.

With all this, however, our Tromp had made himself many enemies. The States-General, and especially John De Witt among them, were highly displeased that he had dared to run into the Zuyder Zee with his fleet contrary to their orders as conveyed by the Deputies. The result of it was very soon apparent. Although the province of Holland had promoted him to the post of Lieutenant-Admiral, John De Witt took care to let him feel his displeasure. Instead of supporting his claim to the chief command of the fleet, De Witt got himself and two colleagues appointed as Commissioners. Within four-and-twenty hours after De Ruyter had landed from his expedition to the African coast, he was appointed to the chief command of the fleet, and Tromp, who had already made preparations for sailing, had to put up with a secondary post. This, as you may imagine, was anything but pleasant for so strong-willed and haughty a man, and he immediately resolved not to put up with it. It was a very fortunate thing that De Ruyter's name, already so popular, inspired the whole Dutch navy with joyous sentiments, for the behaviour of Tromp on this occasion might have been the cause of a very serious disaster. Having upbraided the Deputies and especially De Witt with their high-handed measure, he declared that he could neither think of serving under De Ruyter nor of going to sea under such circumstances, as it was not likely that when he had worked hard to get the fleet ready, he would assist some one else in getting all the credit of it. In vain the Commissioners tried to argue him into a better state of mind; nothing would suit him but to resign, and resign he did, never doubting that the States-General rather than lose him would reappoint him to his post.

Not so, however. A letter came back from the Hague, in which the High Mighty Lords, while expressing their displeasure and astonishment at his undutiful and indiscreet behaviour, ordered the Commissioners by no means to stop the progress of the fleet, but let it run out, whether Tromp commanded it or not. The Admiral, seeing that it was necessary to pocket his pride, gave in, and accepted a post under De Ruyter, who had not yet arrived. In the meantime, however, his example of insubordination had produced a bad effect upon his men. They refused to weigh the anchor, except for the Prince of Orange, made a great noise, and in many other ways disobeyed the commands of their superior officers. When mess-time came the mutiny increased, and the greater part of the men pushed into the cabin and clamoured for more meat, thinking that when the Admiral was trying to make better terms for himself they had a right to do the same. The ringleaders were immediately seized, a court-martial was held, and two of the worst were condemned to cast lots for the gallows. In view of the whole fleet they were put in a boat. A tin plate was then brought, covered over with a napkin, under which there were two pieces of paper, one of which had a gallows on it and the other a cypher. The man who drew the paper with the gallows was at once seized, and hung by his neck at the yard-arm, while the other was stripped and first flogged at the side of the Admiral's ship. While he was being rowed to the next, a mixture of salt, pepper, and gunpowder was rubbed into the wounds, and a second flogging laid on the top of that, so that by the time he had been flogged all round the fleet, he had good cause to forswear all mutiny in future.

De Ruyter, having now arrived from Ems, rowed immediately to Tromp's ship, and was received by the Admiral with every token of respect if not of cordiality. Tromp was too honest not to confess that De Ruyter was a greater man than himself, but there could not be very much love between them after what had happened, and the events which followed will show you that the younger man was carried away by his spite somewhat too rashly.

It was not until the spring of the following year that the English fleet again encountered the Dutch; but then, both parties having had ample time to prepare themselves, the collision resulted in that terrific battle of four days, the details of which I have already described. That on this occasion Tromp displayed marvellous courage and energy is shown sufficiently by the fact that he changed his ship six times, having been compelled each time to abandon the one on which he was. He poured such volleys into the enemy wherever he was that the Duke of York, on noticing his flag waving from more than one mast, is reported to have said, 'How is this? Are there, then, six Tromps on the Dutch fleet?' On the first day he put himself at the head of his squadron, and with a boldness that would have been highly blamable but for its success, he charged and broke through the English line. He was immediately surrounded by his enemies. One of his ships was burned and sank; his Vice-Admiral was killed, two of his ships were reduced to the last extremity, and he could only keep the enemy away from him by thundering on all sides, so that his ship looked at times as if on fire. De Ruyter, not knowing what had become of him, for it had been done without his orders, and concluding that the terrific cannonade must come from Tromp, summoned his whole force, broke in upon the English, and liberated him after a severe struggle.

On the third day, Tromp, being in the van, fell upon the 'Royal Prince' of 92 guns, which had run aground on the Galloper Sands, and having compelled Sir George Ayscue and his crew to surrender, was going to throw all the guns overboard, get her afloat, and tow the magnificent ship as his prize behind him, when a positive order came from De Ruyter to burn the ship, as she must necessarily fetter the movements of the fleet. Tromp received the order with grinding teeth, but he was too much of a sailor to dare to disobey such orders, and he had the splendid prize burned. But he never forgave De Ruyter for what he considered nothing but an act of deliberate and malignant rancour. It is absurd to think that so noble-minded a man as De Ruyter should have stooped to such paltry means of revenge, the more so as the next day's battle proved but too plainly that all the activity and quickness of movement possible was needed. In the morning of the last day, Tromp, rushing into the midst of the enemy with his usual fury, was so tremendously damaged that he had to retire in an almost sinking condition, and employed nearly half the day in stopping his leakages. When he was ready he once more joined the combat, and contributed much to the day's victory. The fleet was received by the whole country with loud acclamations, and it must have been no small part of the brave men's reward to feel how their services were appreciated. But the danger was not past, and repose at such a moment would have been almost as bad as cowardice. After nineteen days of the most active preparations, the fleet was again ready, and ran into the Channel.

The ill-feeling between the two Admirals, however, had been by no means softened. De Ruyter could not altogether excuse Tromp from rashness and temerity; Tromp, on the other hand, felt that but for De Ruyter the honours of the victory would be his. It will remain an unsolved mystery whether Tromp was actuated by these and similar motives in his conduct during the battle which followed. Like every great man, he had at that time, and has now, his friends and his enemies; and a long and profitless war has been waged about the question whether the Admiral was so carried away by his passion as to turn traitor or not. This is what happened. John Evertsen commanded the van, De Ruyter had taken the centre, and Tromp was in charge of the rear, an arrangement which seems to have satisfied neither his ambition nor his energetic valour. There was almost a dead calm. Evertsen's division approached the English but slowly, and it was noon before the combat had in reality begun. De Ruyter, seeing that Evertsen might get into great danger if not supported immediately, made all sail and ran towards him; but Tromp remained two miles below him with furled sails, and seemed apparently in no hurry whatever to rush into the fight as usual. The battle had already lasted an hour. The Admirals Evertsen and Coenders were killed. Their division, having been thrown into confusion, fell back. Monk, who had engaged De Ruyter, and was on the point of retiring for a while, no sooner saw this than he immediately renewed his attack with increased fury. De Ruyter's division had already greatly suffered, and when he saw himself thus opposed to the bulk of the English, he looked in vain for Tromp.

Not long after De Ruyter's manœuvres Tromp also weighed anchor; and there can be no doubt that the science of war in those days, and the plan of the Chief Admiral, plainly indicated united action, whereby each leader of a division, although singling out his own part of the enemy, should so dispose of his forces as to be always ready to assist where assistance was necessary. Instead, however, of doing this, Tromp allowed a vast space to come between the centre and his own division, while he directed his fire exclusively to the squadron with the blue flag, commanded by Jeremy Smith. It is true that Tromp sustained this fight against Smith with great valour. He managed to separate the blue squadron from the rest of the fleet. The 'Resolution,' a fine vessel of 64 guns, was burned, and Smith was obliged to retire, or, what is quite as likely, being in command of the smallest squadron, Smith thought it good policy to retire, drawing Tromp away with him out of the battle, and thereby securing his own safety while weakening the enemy. What was the result? Evertsen's division, very much weakened and without Evertsen, assisted De Ruyter as much as it could, but he, having to bear the whole brunt of the English fleet, with his ship so damaged that it would scarcely answer the helm, and half his men killed or wounded, saw himself forced, although much against his will, to retire towards the Dutch shores. From hour to hour he still entertained the hope that Tromp would arrive with his ships that must be comparatively fresh. But the night fell and no Tromp was to be heard of or seen. The sun rose, and as far as the eye could reach the English flag alone fluttered in the breeze. There was nothing for it but to retreat again. During the whole of that anxious day the destruction of the fleet was only prevented by the utmost exertions, and when De Ruyter and his faithful followers dropped anchor in the Wielingen, they were ready to consider their escape a miracle. The whole of the night and the next day Tromp was looked for in vain. It was known that Monk was cruising up and down, and everyone felt certain that he had been captured with the whole of his squadron. But on the evening of the 5th of August the division arrived safely in port and dropped anchor.

Tromp had evidently expected a whole string of

compliments from his Commander and the States, but when he arrived on the quarter deck of the 'Seven Provinces,' the flag-ship, De Ruyter, who was there to receive him, assailed the whole staff with the most biting reproaches. No one had ever seen him in such a passion, and Pensionary de Witt, who was by his side, confessed afterwards that he was sorry to see De Ruyter so vehement in the presence of the common sailors not only against Tromp, but against the Vice-Admiral and Rear-Admiral of his division, and against some other captains, whose duty in any case was only to follow their flag. De Ruyter charged Tromp with desertion and accused him of being the sole and only cause of their defeat. The high-spirited and haughty Tromp could ill brook such reproaches, and an angry quarrel was the result. Tromp excused himself by saying that 'when I had once separated Smith from the rest, I thought it more advisable to pursue this advantage, for had I at that time tacked about and, notwithstanding the calm, sailed to De Ruyter's assistance, both he and the enemy would have thought I was defeated and in flight, which would have thrown our own fleet into confusion and encouraged the enemy.'

He so far obeyed the deputies that he went several times to the 'Seven Provinces' to take part in the council of war, but hearing that De Ruyter had openly blamed him even in writing, he penned what must be considered a foolish and ill-advised letter to their High Mighty Lords, in which he recounts his acts, and complains in very bitter language of De Ruyter accuses him of neglecting his duty, of partiality and jealousy against himself, and requests, in a haughty tone, restitution of his honour or his demission. 'It is insufferable,' he writes, 'that I should be called a rogue and the cause of the defeat, because Almighty God has given me, with less force, an advantage over the enemy, and him (De Ruyter) with greater forces, a disadvantage. This is not a time to employ rogues in the service of the States, and if I have not done well now, I never intend to do any better;' and much more in the same angry strain, ill-suited to the dignified character of the legislators or his own position as their servant. Now you will remember that there had already been some quarrel between him and the States. They were highly offended by the tone and contents of the letter. They remembered how in 1657 he had returned without orders with his squadron to port, how in 1665 he had not only neglected to follow Evertsen, but, in spite of positive orders, ran into port; how he showed his arbitrary disposition in various ways, and had more than once during the four days' battle executed manœuvres for which he received no orders and which imperilled the success of the battle and the safety of the fleet. De Witt knew at the same time that he was a friend of the Stadtholder's, and that it was henceforth impossible that both he and De Ruyter could remain in command of the fleet. It was secretly resolved, therefore, to cancel Tromp's appointment and dismiss him.

He was called to the Hague. He arrived, ignorant of his fate, on the 23rd of August, and without a vestige of his former anger. A few days had been sufficient to make him feel the folly of his conduct and the regret of a noble mind. Fearing that he had gone too far, he declared his readiness to give De Ruyter such satisfactory proofs of his submission and obedience as the States should desire; he even offered to resign the command of his squadron to another for this voyage, and be content to follow in a ship by himself as the Admiral's personal assistant. But the decision of the States was inexorable. The large-minded confession and offer might have softened many members, but not John de Witt. Taking Tromp's changeful and violent character into consideration, and the great difficulty with which he controlled his temper, they adhered to their resolution, and dismissed him from his office; but, knowing his popularity on the fleet, they ordered him to remain in the Hague until further orders on pain of being considered in mutiny against the State. His office was given to W. Joseph van Ghent, a colonel of marines, and the great son of a great father was thus in one moment reduced to the character of a private citizen. Count D'Estrades, the French ambassador, thinking that this was a favourable opportunity for procuring his services, offered him the post of Admiral of the French fleet, and a yearly salary of 50,000 francs (2,000*l.*). Tromp answered, 'I am flattered by such offers from so great a king as Louis XIV., but if

I accepted them, I should only prove that my country was justified in humiliating an officer who could abandon it. Let my fortitude in misfortune alone reproach her with her conduct; honour and duty alike command me to remain.' After having waited in the Hague until the fleet had again run out, he obtained permission to retire to his estate, Trompenburg, near Utrecht, where he remained for years in the most profound and impenetrable seclusion, and it was only at the personal request of the Prince of Orange, and to avert the national ruin, that he consented to come forward and enter his second naval career.

CORNELIS TROMP.

PART II.

To some extent both Tromp and Evertsen may be considered martyrs to their own patriotic feelings. Both Admirals had been educated in the firm belief that the great Prince of Orange, William the Silent, had saved the country from utter destruction and ruin, and that it would again go to ruin if no prince of that house occupied the post of Stadtholder. Neither Tromp nor Evertsen could ever be brought to speak lightly of this matter, or consider it as of secondary importance; and it was for this reason that they encountered the vigorous opposition of the strict Republican party, so ably and successfully led by Pensionary John de Witt. But even John de Witt's success could not last for ever. He had played a prominent and successful part in the administration of affairs for more than twenty years, and there was no Court in Europe where his name was not well known and deservedly respected. But a day came when all his intrigues, his schemes, his nice calculations, were suddenly overthrown. As I have already told you, the Netherlands, small though they were, had been, and were at the moment of which I speak, attacked by the two most powerful countries in the world, France and England. The French and English fleets combined, and the result was that famous battle of Solebay, which I described in De Ruyter's life. But the whole country was overrun by a foreign army, town after town surrendered to the enemy, and it really looked as though in a few weeks everybody would be drowned or brought under a foreign yoke. All this time William of Orange, a clever young prince of twenty-two, splendidly educated, and displaying great talents both as general and statesman, had his hands tied, and could do nothing, because it had pleased De Witt and his party to vote that he should never enter office. But first one province (Zealand), then other, and a third, annulled the absurd edict, and in a few days the Prince was Stadtholder.

Then De Witt in some way or other showed his displeasure, and the people became furious. It has indeed been said that they were bribed by the Prince, some say by Tromp and by other men whom De Witt had eagerly opposed, but of this there is no proof. Enough that the mob went to the house where the Pensionary and his brother were lodging, dragged them out of bed into the street, and murdered them with every kind of cruelty and torture that they could devise. It is quite certain that Tromp was in the Hague on that day, and there are various reports as to his behaviour. One says that one of the murderers meeting him in the street showed him the velvet mantle of the Pensionary, whereupon Tromp told him it was very good. Another seeing him a spectator of the massacre, asked him what he thought of it. According to one account he answered, 'That is the way to do it,' but according to another, he pressed his hat over his eyes and turned away. The shouts of the sailors at the same time showed that, notwithstanding his retirement, he was still popular with the people, for one bawled out, 'These are the rogues who would prepare no fleet against Cromwell, but allowed the old Admiral Tromp to be so scandalously murdered. This dog,' pointing to the body of John, 'thought he could do the same with his son, our Cornelis, but he could not get that done.' Then swinging some of the bloody clothes over his head, he cried,

'Hurrah for Tromp; De Witt goes under.
Who likes not this may go to thunder.'

The town being during the whole of that day in the most intense commotion, the civic guard was called out to repress the riot, and if possible to save the lives of the unhappy brothers. This was impossible, and it turned out that the guard itself was against De Witt, for on passing the hotel where Tromp and a friend of his lay out of the window, they made a demonstration in his favour, with which, however, he seemed by no means pleased.

It is too horrible even to suppose that a man like Tromp, who, however passionate and injudiciously hasty he may have been, cannot be accused throughout a long life of one deliberate act of cruelty or vengeance, should have calmly plotted or given even the slightest encouragement to this abominable outrage; but it is by no means unlikely that when the deed was done, when that strong enemy with his enormous influence had been swept out of the way, Tromp felt a great relief, and seemed to be entering upon a new life. It must have been very, very hard for him to remain unemployed and useless at a moment when the country was in danger, when every one of his friends and colleagues was fighting for the good cause and earning fame. At last, then, the Prince had come to his own again, and the time had come when his friends and supporters could speak out more freely and openly. William of Orange was a man of deep feeling, and gratitude was very strong in him. He liked Tromp, and knew how he and his father had stuck up for the family with manly courage. Being at the same time at a great loss for officers wherewith to oppose the invading French, he appointed him, in November 1672, commander of a regiment of marines, which had been posted somewhere near Arnheim, but both the Prince and Tromp knew that this could not last long, and that if the latter was to remain in the country's service it must be as Admiral. The Prince, however, knew too much of the value of discipline to make light of Tromp's previous disobediences. Van Ghent—the colonel who had been appointed Admiral in his stead—having been killed in the late battle, there was really no one else to fill the post but Tromp; and the probability is that he asked the Prince, who in virtue of his office had the chief administration of the navy, to give him his old squadron.

The Prince was naturally very willing to do this, but he made it an indispensable condition that Tromp should first reconcile himself with De Ruyter, and consent not only to forget entirely what had passed between them, but in all future battles strictly to obey the Lieutenant-Admiral, and consider him in all respects as the first person in the fleet, to whom alone he should look for orders. Having after some difficulty consented to this, the Prince invited them both to dinner, when in his presence they shook hands and promised henceforth to live as brothers. This reconciliation between the greatest and the most beloved Admirals in the fleet caused a universal and genuine enthusiasm; and when after great exertions, in which Tromp himself mounted the watch on deck at night with his officers, in order to give the men some rest, he joined the fleet with his ship the 'Golden Lion,' and duly saluted the 'Seven Provinces,' there was not a sailor in the fleet who did not feel his heart leap with joy and confidence at the happy re-union. Once more to describe the battles that now took place between the two nations would be useless. Tromp behaved with his usual courage. From early morning till noon he thundered away in his ship the 'Golden Lion,' until it was found in a sinking condition. He then went over to the 'Prince on Horse,' which suffered in an equal degree. At seven o'clock at night, having lost the mainmast, he was obliged to change into the 'Amsterdam,' in which, as he writes, he finished the dance; but next morning he writes another letter to his sister from a fourth ship, the 'Comet Star,' so that the finishing of the dance probably finished the ship too.

The last battle between the two fleets was, perhaps, the most furious of all. Tromp commanded as usual the rear-division, and soon after the commencement of the battle he tackled the Blue squadron, which was opposed to his own and commanded by Admiral Spragg. Dutch Vice-Admiral Sweers and English Vice-Admiral John Kempthorn got into a cloud almost immediately, whereupon Den Haen and Lord Ossory followed their example. But neither the combat of the Vice-Admirals nor that of the Rear-Admirals could be compared with the two leaders. As by common consent they approached each other without firing a shot until the distance could be reached by an ordinary pistol, and then the 'Golden Lion' of 82 guns, and the 'Royal Prince' of 100, poured volley after volley into each other for four mortal hours. Spragg had begun the contest with confidence, for it is reported that he had promised not to return to England without Tromp, dead or alive. But fortune was against him. His fire was aimed too high, and it is marvellous to relate that Tromp had not one killed or wounded during those four hours. Spragg, on the other hand, was so damaged that he had to exchange into the 'St. George,' his ship counting over 700 killed and wounded. A furious contest now began to rage for the mastless hull of the 'Royal Prince.' But Spragg, Kempthorn, and fifteen or sixteen other ships gathered round her, and offered a terrific resistance. Tromp's ship was surrounded, his yards and topmasts were shattered, his very cabin smashed, and he was obliged to retreat. Having now changed his ship for the 'Comet,' he again opposed the approaching Spragg. A large fire-ship having nearly touched him, was happily intercepted by one of his own, both being together consumed in one blaze. At the same time Tromp, running alongside the front of the enemy, again espied the hull of the 'Royal Prince,' and rushed towards his prey. A second furious contest for the body of the slain monarch now began. Fireship after fireship was let loose against the raging Admiral, but in vain; he evaded them all. Thereupon Spragg once more opposed himself to Tromp's fire, but in a short time he was rendered helpless. The English Admiral, not desirous to leave the fight a second time, commanded his sloop to be prepared, and rowed towards the 'Royal Charles,' on board which vessel he intended to continue the battle. But scarcely had he left the disabled 'George,' when a well-aimed shot from the 'Comet' pierced the sloop through and through. In vain the Admiral immediately ordered his men to put back. Before the 'George' could be reached the sloop filled and sank, and the English Commander disappeared beneath the waves. So melancholy an occurrence was not calculated to increase the valour of the Blue squadron, but Kempthorn and Ossory continued to defend themselves for three hours, until Prince Rupert came to their assistance. Another general attack on both sides commenced at eight o'clock, and lasted till dark. Had the French Admiral D'Estrées, who commanded the White Squadron, performed his duty as well as the English, there is but little doubt that the Dutch would have been defeated. But having received secret orders from his king to remain passive in order that the Dutch and English might do each other as much harm as possible, he lay at some distance, spectator of the fight, pretending not to understand Prince Rupert's imperative signals, and giving out that he was reserving his strength for the next day. At last the Prince, finding that a victory could not be obtained, gave the signal to retire, shortly after which De Ruyter did the same, and both fleets returned to their coasts.

Great was the indignation in England against D'Estrées, and the French in general. The French Vice-Admiral, De Mantel, who had fought well, and who knew nothing about secret instructions, accused him of cowardice. But De Mantel was recalled and locked up in the Bastille, while the intrigues of the French Ambassador in London so prevailed upon the easy temper of the king that an open rupture was prevented. The people saw, however, that an alliance with so hollow and hypocritical a nation could bring them no advantage; and soon afterwards, the partnership being dissolved, peace was concluded with the Netherlands, and the sea for years afterwards freed from such bloody conflicts. But the result of the last battle, in which, although no decisive victory had been obtained, an invasion was defeated, and a very serious loss inflicted upon the English, was marvellous. The courage of the miserable people of Holland, almost ready to give way under so many misfortunes, rebounded with the news; and the retaking of several towns and success in several small engagements inspired them with new courage to continue the unequal contest. England being no longer unfriendly, it was thought wise to make some attempt upon France itself, so as to draw away from the Netherlands part of the large army and some of the experienced generals who had assembled in the very centre of the country. The fleet was therefore divided into equal halves. De Ruyter was sent off to the French colonies in Martinique, and Tromp received secret orders to harass the French coast with his fleet of thirty-six men-of-war, having on board a small army of about 4,000 men. The French army having been obliged to retreat from many of its positions in the provinces of Utrecht, Gelderland, and Overyssel, did so in its usual barbarous style. Not a town or village was spared. Pillaging, robbing, violence, were the order of the day. Exorbitant sums were extorted from the already afflicted inhabitants, and the many injustices cried to heaven for revenge. It was high time to give these gentlemen a good lesson.

On the 23rd of June, 1674, the Dutch fleet anchored in front of Belleisle, about six miles from the coast of Brittany. Tromp, and Count Horn, the commander of the troops, having reconnoitred the coast, ordered the soldiers next day to effect a landing. The French had thrown up breastworks and opened a heavy fire from the very strong castle that defends the island, but the Dutch soldiers landed, drove the French into their entrenched positions, and besieged them. The next day the whole island was given over to the soldiers. Everything that was of value to the fleet, especially all the live stock, cows, sheep, pigs, was driven away, and the inhabitants reduced to such straits that they humbly requested Tromp to be allowed to send out some fishing boats, as they were in want of food, a request which Tromp somewhat sternly refused. The castle being too strong for a successful attack, however, it was considered wiser to retire from the island and make another attempt at the mouth of the Loire, which was also unprotected. The fleet therefore weighed anchor early in the morning, and sailed away towards the island of Noirmantiers, which is situated quite close to the mouth of the river, and only divided from the mainland by a creek which is almost dry at low water. The whole French coast had been thrown into a state of violent alarm. Six thousand country people had been armed, the militia had been called out, while four hundred country gentlemen of the neighbourhood had assembled on horseback to form a sort of cavalry regiment, and oppose the enemy until the regular army should have time to arrive.

Tromp immediately set out in a sloop with some of his staff and reconnoitred the island. The French had thrown up several breastworks and batteries, from which they opened a heavy fire. The boats too that contained the advance of the landing forces were thrown by the surge against some rocks that were covered with water, and all but upset. But the soldiers jumped out up to their waists into the sea, and rushed to the shore under the very heavy fire which they could not answer. The breastworks were taken; the castle, with about twenty pieces of artillery, was surrendered, and the island cleared of the French. The forces commanded by Tromp were too small, however, to be able to do anything more than alarm the coast. The fishing fleets were seized and destroyed, and several men-of-war chased ashore and burned. All the seaports on that coast becoming seriously alarmed, and believing that their turn was sure to come next, made the most extensive efforts for defence. But Tromp saw that he was not capable of doing more harm, and resolved to quit the island. The houses were pillaged, the castle blown up, and having imposed a fine of about 2,000*l*., for the payment of which he took several of the richest inhabitants with him, the fleet weighed anchor and sailed to Cadiz. For some reason or other, however, nothing of importance was done. The French fleet and army had besieged three Spanish towns for a considerable time, but at the approach of the Dutch fleet they withdrew, and retired to their own harbours, where it was not advisable to attack them. Indeed, Tromp got into some difficulty through the latter part of this expedition, for as he had not received orders to assist Spain or go to the Mediterranean, the States-General and the Prince were very angry with him, recalled him immediately, and refused him for many years afterwards the expenses which he was entitled to. Another instance how, with the best intentions in the world, a great man may exceed his duty, and do himself and his country harm instead of good.

The rebuff which he received on this account was smoothed over, however, by a very pleasant occurrence. When he arrived in the Hague he found a distinguished party of English noblemen there, who received him with the most flattering expressions of their esteem and admiration. They were the Earls of Arlington and Ossory and the youthful Marquis of Danby, who had gone over to the States on some special mission to the Prince. They assured Tromp that his Majesty Charles II. was very anxious not only to see so celebrated an Admiral, but also to confer upon him some signal mark of his favour, and they invited him most pressingly to return with them to London and be presented at Court. You will remember that some such honour had already been bestowed upon his father by Charles I., and although the same honour had been refused by De Ruyter, Tromp, who was of a different disposition, and younger, accepted it. He had rather a curiosity to see the celebrated Court of St. James's, and have an opportunity of conversing with those proud and wealthy noblemen, those beautiful ladies, and the great warriors who had made England's name famous throughout the world. He accordingly sailed for England on January 12, 1675, in the company of several English and Dutch nobles who had fraternized, and were but too willing to continue in London the friendship they had formed in the Hague. The Prince of Orange, who was at that time thinking about a marriage with the Princess Mary, felt rather proud and pleased that the Admiral who had supported him most and of whom he was most fond should be thus treated by King Charles, and he accompanied the festive party to Briele, where they embarked in three yachts which had been sent over for the purpose. They arrived in London on January 15, and were received by the King, the Duke of York, and the other members of the royal family in the most flattering manner. There were several royal coaches with six and eight splendid horses ready at Deptford to convey them to Westminster. The people of London, who were even at that time uncommonly glad to have the chance of a holiday, shut up shop and turned out along the river side to see the great and famous Admiral, who preferred to go to Westminster by water, for the tremendous crowd of people at London Bridge blocked up the streets and rendered them so impassable that nothing but boats could be used. The King conferred upon Tromp the honour of a baronetage of the United Kingdom, the succession to be in the male line, and in default of any children the dignity was to go to his elder brother, Harpert Martinson Tromp, at that time Burgomaster of Delft, and if he died without issue, his younger brother, Adrian Tromp, captain of horse in the States' army, was to be the successor. The letters patent were prepared and handed over to Tromp by the Lord Privy Seal, together with a miniature portrait of the King painted on gold and beautifully set in a circle of diamonds, suspended from a gold chain. It would be tedious to describe all the festivities that were given on his account and the honours with which he was overwhelmed, for everybody seemed determined to make much of him. Enough to say that after a stay of about six weeks he returned to Holland well pleased with his excursion.

The rest which he enjoyed only lasted a year. In 1676 he left for Denmark with the fleet which the States had fitted out for the assistance of that country. Those, however, have made a mistake who represent him as being the commander of that fleet. He was no longer in Dutch service. The King of Denmark was at war with Sweden, and as Sweden was powerful at sea and Denmark rather weak, it had obtained the assistance of the States, who promised a fleet of a dozen ships. At the same time, the King of Denmark felt that he wanted nothing so badly as a great commander, but there was no one in the whole of Europe who seemed so fitted as Tromp. He asked permission from the States, and as there really was nothing for Tromp to do, he was allowed to accept the post of General-Admiral and Councillor of the kingdom. He landed in Copenhagen on May 10, the quay and all the streets to the palace being thronged by an enthusiastic multitude who had flocked together as soon as the news spread that the great Dutch Admiral was about to step on shore. Having been received with much ceremony by the King, he took the oath of fidelity and allegiance to His Majesty, and was immediately invested with the Order of the Elephant. Tromp was rather partial to orders and decorations, but he was still more partial to money, and when he was politely informed that everyone who received this Order had to pay about 400*l.* sterling, he looked very hard at the decoration, and very sour at his purse, muttering to himself that this little animal was rather expensive in its way. The somewhat troublesome elephant may have urged him, perhaps, to make great haste with his preparation, and get away from a capital where he was being let in for hundreds of pounds. At any rate, even during the festivities, he went to the harbour, had a look at the vessels, singled out those which were best, had them fitted out, and Dutch captains appointed to them; and then, having also brought with him about 3,000 Dutch sailors, sent part of them, in about a week's time, to the Danish Admiral Juel, who was cruising up and down the Baltic.

It seems that the Danish Admiral had received secret instructions to risk no general engagement with the Swedish fleet until Tromp should have joined them, but of these orders the Dutch Vice-Admiral Almonde was not aware. When he saw the Swedish fleet, therefore, he saw no reason why it should not be attacked, and went at it straightway in the usual Dutch fashion. The number of ships on both sides was about equal, but the Danes, keeping in the background, and the Swedes returning the fire with good effect, very soon obliged Almonde to retire, indignant at what he considered the Danish cowardice, about which he wrote, in no measured terms, to the States-General, and to Tromp, who was still in Copenhagen superintending the preparation of the fleet. As soon as Tromp heard the news, he decided to set out at once with seven ships, which alone were ready, rather than again expose the Dutch squadron to such disgraceful treatment. He joined the fleet on June 7. and the Swedes were chased and brought to a stand late at night on the 11th, some miles south of the island Oland. The next morning the battle was begun, but the result, which was anxiously looked for on both sides, and might have remained doubtful for a considerable time, was brought about by a lamentable accident. Tromp, who commanded a fine vessel, the 'Christian V.,' had singled out the Swedish Admiral Creutz, whose ship, the 'Three Crowns,' was one of the most beautiful ships that had ever ridden the Northern Seas. A tremendous combat seemed to be about to begin, and the Swedish Admiral had given orders that his cannon should be changed from side to side so that he might fire them all from one part of the vessel without having to tack about. Suddenly, however, while Tromp had only fired a couple of broadsides, and the Swedish Admiral was in the act of answering, the latter's ship was seen to reel to one side like a drunken man. The yards touched the water. Cries and confusion filled the vessel, when with a tremendous crash it was torn asunder and immediately buried under the waves. The crew had executed the orders, but it had been forgotten to tell them that while one half the guns were being fired, the other half should be fastened to the other side. They remained loose. The discharge of the one half sent the other sixty-seven flying over to the same side, and the ship, being thus overbalanced, capsized. Frightful confusion followed, for Tromp was just pouring another broadside into her. Somebody dropped a match into the powder, and what happened afterwards can only be slightly imagined by those who have been blown up themselves. The Admiral and the entire crew of 1,100 men perished in the waves within a few moments, only thirty-six men and a couple of officers being saved by Tromp's sloops. This awful calamity spread dismay among the Swedes, for in his letter to the States Tromp says that immediately afterwards they turned with one accord and took flight. Tromp immediately signalled a general pursuit. He himself pursuing the Vice-Admiral Uggla, brought him to a stand and obliged him to fight. For nearly two hours the two Admirals were engaged in fierce fight. What losses were sustained by Uggla were never known; but Tromp had one captain killed, two others wounded dangerously, and over a hundred of his men killed or wounded.

At last the mainmast of the Swedish Admiral was sent overboard. He called for quarter and hauled down his flag. Tromp signalled that he accepted his surrender, and sent out boats to take the brave Admiral and his officers prisoners. But at this moment 'a villainous fire-ship captain' suddenly ran along the other side of the Swedish Vice-Admiral. Tromp's men's signalled, and shouted, and beckoned that the ship had surrendered, but in vain. The fireman either would not or could not understand these signs, and set fire to the ship. Tromp's sloops could scarcely hold fifty, her own were all destroyed, and so this second vessel was in a very short time demolished, and 600 men brought to an end which they certainly had not deserved. After this second calamity a panic seized the Swedes. They fled in confusion. The third flag-ship, of eighty-six guns, sank in mid-sea. Three men-of-war and one yacht were captured, one flying Swede struck a rock and went down with all hands, while three others ran ashore and were abandoned by their crews. Great was the joy for this victory in Denmark, and no wonder, for the Danes were getting all their fighting done for them for nothing, and their gratitude was of a rather cheap kind. The King certainly praised Tromp to the skies, and made him Earl of Selzburg, but as Selzburg happened to lie in the province of Bleing, which had been taken from the Swedes, and was only kept from them by an army, Tromp's earldom or county was of very little use to him.

The Danish King, now convinced that with so powerful a fleet to back him up, he might attempt greater things, resolved to recapture the province of Schonen, which had been taken from him by the Swedes. Tromp received orders to sail to the south side of the island, and take the city of Ydstad if he could. Having arrived in front of the capital on July 6, he sent a trumpeter to summon the city, but received a refusal. The next day, therefore, he sent two detachments of seven ships. Five of these approached the town as closely as the shallowness of the harbour permitted, and bombarded it with such vehemence during a couple of hours, that not a man dared to make his appearance on the ramparts. Three thousand men were now disembarked, and having been divided, were drawn up on each side of the town. The governor thought that he could prevent their landing or their attack by sending a force of 700 men to meet them; but the guns from the men-of-war played with such terrible effect upon the shore, that the Swedes were obliged to retire, after having lost about 150 men. The Danes now effected their landing, and immediately threw up an entrenched camp close to the town Admiral Tromp then ordered all his troops ashore, and having reconnoitred the ground in person, commanded everything to be in readiness for a general attack next morning. Next morning, however, when he had again summoned the town to surrender, a number of the inhabitants entered the camp, and told him that the Swedes had abandoned the town during the night, having before their departure, however, undermined the principal streets. Tromp took the warning, had the mines drawn, and threw a considerable garrison into the town, in order to prevent the Swedes from getting possession of it again. On July 18, 1676, the King of Denmark embarked 18,000 men, cavalry and infantry, in a fleet of 500 vessels, and landed the next day on the coast of Schonen, between Elsinburg and Landscoon, accompanied by the prince, his brother, and the generals of his army. Having been informed that the Swedish troops were marching on Vistad, he disembarked all his troops, artillery, and engines of war, sent off one detachment to invest Elsinburg, which surrendered to him after very little resistance, the castle only holding out until the 14th, when, seeing no hope of assistance, it surrendered at discretion.

The Danish King, finding himself more prosperous by sea than by land, and knowing that Tromp's reputation and experience were the main cause of this, backed up as they were by the Dutch fleet, exerted himself to the utmost to retain the friendship of the Republic, and consequently its assistance. There was some hesitation on the part of the States, however, for they did not like spending money wholesale for other people. The King, hearing of this, determined upon sending an ambassador to them who could attack them on their weak side, and it may be noted as a strange fact that Tromp was singled out for this post, and sailed for the Hague in December, 1676, accredited as Envoy Extraordinary to the High Mighty Lords. His position in his own country at this time must have been rather strange even to himself, for he was one day received by the States with all the solemnity and dignity with which they always received ambassadors from foreign States, and on the next day he was admitted to their sitting to take the oath of allegiance in his new capacity of head of the fleet. His return to the Netherlands was rather fortunate for him, for the Prince Stadtholder could now fulfil the promise which he had made some years ago. Du Ruyter had been killed in the Mediterranean the previous year, and at the reconciliation of those two the prince had promised that dignity to Tromp as soon as it became vacant. There being now no John de Witt to oppose him, Tromp found himself at last rewarded for his steadfast adherence to the House of Orange by the highest post in the country under the Stadtholder himself, and as he was a more ambitious and impetuous man than De Ruyter, he attached a great deal of importance to these honours, the possession of which gratified him not a little.

His mission to the States was equally successful. They resolved to send another squadron to the assistance of the Danes, and allow him to remain in the King's service for another year, with liberty to recruit 1,500 men in the provinces in addition to those already employed on the Danish fleet; but when the ships were ready to sail, a difficulty, little enough to others, but seemingly great to Tromp, somewhat ruffled his spirits. He naturally concluded that being now Lieutenant-Admiral-General and chief of the fleet, he should have the command of the squadron, and Lieutenant-Admiral Bastians under him, but this the States would not allow. Much though he tried, and talked, and wrote, the States would not allow their squadron to be commanded by a Danish Admiral; and as Tromp went out as such, he had to be content to remain on board the flag-ship as a private person, without being able to give an order to anyone. The States-General had by this time come to see that it was no use holding themselves too cheap, and wherever they came or assisted they made it one condition that proper respect should be paid to the flag which had won such a splendid reputation. So, when the Dutch squadron arrived at Copenhagen, Admiral Bastians insisted on having the first place on the fleet, and refused to move away from the harbour until this had been granted, saying that it would be disrespectful to the States if he consented to occupy any other. The King at last saw that unless he permitted this, the Dutch squadron might as well go home, and so, although there was furious opposition at Court, the fleet sailed away with Tromp as Admiral-in-Chief, and Bastians as next in rank.

The naval operations, however, were of very slender importance. An attempt to destroy the Swedish fleet in the harbour of Calmar was abandoned after repeated trials. But the land troops, having been disembarked, attacked the town, and overran the whole island of Oland, burning, plundering, and destroying wherever and whatever came in their way, the churches being scarcely excepted from the general conflagration. Tromp got disgusted at this, and returned to Copenhagen as soon as he could, for such a mode of warfare was entirely against his feelings of honour and humanity. With the approach of winter, however, a positive order from the States was received recalling the squadron home; and although the King made the utmost endeavours to retain it, Bastians sailed on the 6th of November, leaving Tromp still in the capital. It was not very long, however, before he found out that the affection and consideration with which he had been treated was as purely selfish as it generally is. A warning had already been given him by his wife, who accompanied him; she told him that the King would throw him over as soon as he found it convenient. He did so now. Finding that all hope of another Dutch squadron had gone, and that his own men were sufficiently taught, he lent an ear to those interested and jealous men who had looked at the great Dutchman from the beginning with envy. So one day in May, 1678, two private secretaries of the King told him in the coolest manner possible that, as the King was going to be left to himself, and he could not think of having his navy commanded by a stranger, he begged to thank him much for his services, and he might go.

Tromp said nothing in reply, but gave an immediate order to have all his things taken out of his ship and packed. He was not the man to curry favour with any one, nor to remain one moment longer than he was wanted. The Dutch sailors, soldiers, and officers on the Danish fleet, when they heard of this treatment, immediately became highly indignant. Old Tromp was as popular as ever, and any injury done to him was resented by them as personal. They were on the verge of mutiny, and could only be induced to remain for the time of their engagement by the united efforts of the Dutch ambassadors and consuls, and of Tromp himself. What the King would have done without them it is difficult now to say, for a fleet, entirely organised on Dutch principles, the ships built by Dutch builders after their own models, commanded by Dutch admirals and captains, manned for a great part with Dutch sailors and soldiers, armed with guns, cannon ball, and powder, and provided with sails and tackle bought in Holland, might dispense with the services of an admiral after he had done his best to teach the Danish commanders their business, but one would at least have expected the dismissal to be accomplished in a more suave manner. Before finally returning to his native country, Tromp accepted an invitation of the Elector of Brandenburg, and commanded his small fleet in the attack that was made upon the island Rugen, opposite Stralsund. The attack was, as usual, successful, and the admiral returned home, to spend the rest of his days in the quiet enjoyment of his well-earned wealth and reputation at his country seat near Utrecht.

He was only fifty-eight years old, and to all appearance could live another twenty years without feeling the hand of time press upon him too heavily. Thirteen years passed away quietly in that strange building which, somewhat in the form of a man-of-war, rises out of a broad moat of pure water, on which the swan floats gently round and round. In 1691, the Stadtholder having become King of England, declared war against France, and the sea was once more to be the scene of battle. England and Holland were now united; the two fleets so long opposed were at last to join and attack a common enemy, and both countries looked forward with confidence to success when William appointed Tromp Admiral-in-Chief of the combined fleet. We know not how proud the old man must have felt when he was thus put at the head of the first navy of the world, for he was never destined to occupy the post. On the 29th of May he was attacked by a severe illness, which in a few hours closed his great and interesting life, in Amsterdam. On the 6th of June his body was placed in a yacht and conveyed to Delft, where the grave of his father had been opened to receive him. One marble covers the dust of both.

A Catalogue

OF

HENRY S. KING & CO.'S

PUBLICATIONS.

LONDON:
65, CORNHILL, AND 12, PATERNOSTER ROW.
1873.

MARCH, 1873.

Henry S. King & Co.'s Publications.

THE RELIGIOUS HISTORY OF IRELAND:
PRIMITIVE, PAPAL, AND PROTESTANT,
INCLUDING THE EVANGELICAL MISSIONS, CATHOLIC AGITATIONS, AND CHURCH PROGRESS OF THE LAST HALF CENTURY.

By JAMES GODKIN,
Author of "Ireland, her Churches," etc.

1 vol. 8vo.   [*Preparing.*

IRELAND IN 1872.
A TOUR OF OBSERVATION, WITH REMARKS ON IRISH PUBLIC QUESTIONS.
By Dr. JAMES MACAULAY.

Crown 8vo. 7s. 6d.

MEMOIR AND LETTERS OF SARA COLERIDGE.

2 vols. crown 8vo. With Portraits.   [*In the press.*

LOMBARD STREET. A Description of the Money Market.
By WALTER BAGEHOT.

Large crown 8vo.   [*In the press.*

THE GREAT DUTCH ADMIRALS.
By JACOB DE LIEFDE.

Crown 8vo. Illustrated. Price 5s.

POLITICAL WOMEN.
By SUTHERLAND MENZIES.

2 vols. post 8vo.   [*In the press.*

65, *Cornhill;* & 12, *Paternoster Row, London.*

EGYPT AS IT IS.

By Herr HEINRICH STEPHAN,
The German Postmaster-General.

Crown 8vo. With a new Map of the Country. *[Preparing.*

IMPERIAL GERMANY.

By FREDERIC MARTIN,
Author of "The Statesman's Year Book," &c. *[Preparing.*

THE GOVERNMENT OF THE NATIONAL DEFENCE.

By JULES FAVRE. *[Preparing.*

'ILÂM ĔN NÂS. Historical Tales and Anecdotes of the Times of the Early Khalifahs.

Translated from the Originals by Mrs. GODFREY CLERK,
Author of "The Antipodes and Round the World."

Crown 8vo. *[In the press.*

IN STRANGE COMPANY;
Or, The NOTE BOOK of a ROVING CORRESPONDENT.

By JAMES GREENWOOD,
"The Amateur Casual."

Crown 8vo. *[Preparing.*

NEWMARKET AND ARABIA:

An Examination of the Descent of Racers and Coursers.

By ROGER D. UPTON.

Crown 8vo. Illustrated. *[Preparing.*

65, Cornhill; & 12, Paternoster Row, London.

THE RECONCILIATION OF RELIGION AND SCIENCE.

Being Essays by the Rev. J. W. FOWLE, M.A.

1 vol., 8vo. [*In the press.*

THEOLOGY AND MORALITY.

Being Essays by the Rev. J. LLEWELLYN DAVIES.

1 vol., 8vo. [*Preparing.*

A VOLUME OF ESSAYS.

Edited by the Most Reverend ARCHBISHOP MANNING.

[*Preparing.*

FIELD AND FOREST RAMBLES OF A NATURALIST IN NEW BRUNSWICK.

WITH NOTES AND OBSERVATIONS ON THE NATURAL HISTORY OF EASTERN CANADA.

By A. LEITH ADAMS, M.A., &c.,
Author of "Wanderings of a Naturalist in India," &c., &c.

In 8vo, cloth. Illustrated. 14s.

THE FAYOUM; OR, ARTISTS IN EGYPT.

By J. LENOIR. Translated by Mrs. CASHEL HOEY.

Crown 8vo, cloth. Illustrated. [*In the press.*

TENT LIFE WITH ENGLISH GYPSIES IN NORWAY.

By HUBERT SMITH.

In 8vo, cloth. 12 Illustrations. Price 21s. [*Just out.*

THE GATEWAY TO THE POLYNIA;
OR, A VOYAGE TO SPITZBERGEN.
By Captain JOHN C. WELLS, R.N.

In 8vo, cloth. Profusely illustrated. [*In the press.*]

A WINTER IN MOROCCO.
By AMELIA PERRIER.

Large crown 8vo. Illustrated. [*In the press.*]

AN AUTUMN TOUR IN THE UNITED STATES AND CANADA.
By Lieut.-Colonel JULIUS GEORGE MEDLEY.

Crown 8vo. Price 5s. [*In the press.*]

BOKHARA: ITS HISTORY AND CONQUEST.
By Professor ARMINIUS VÀMBÈRY,
Of the University of Pesth, Author of "Travels in Central Asia," &c.

Demy 8vo. 18s.

"We conclude with a cordial recommendation of this valuable book. In former years, Mr. Vambery gave ample proofs of his powers as an observant, easy, and vivid writer. In the present work his moderation, scholarship, insight, and occasionally very impressive style have raised him to the dignity of an historian."—*Saturday Review.*

"Almost every page abounds with composition of peculiar merit, as well as with an account of some thrilling event more exciting than any to be found in an ordinary work of fiction."—*Morning Post.*

"A work compiled from many rare, private, and unavailable manuscripts and records, which consequently cannot fail to prove a mine of delightful Eastern lore to the Oriental scholar."—*Liverpool Albion.*

ECHOES OF A FAMOUS YEAR.
By HARRIET PARR,
Author of "The Life of Jeanne d'Arc," "In the Silver Age," &c.

Crown 8vo. 8s. 6d.

"A graceful and touching, as well as truthful account of the Franco-Prussian War. Those who are in the habit of reading books to children will find this at once instructive and delightful."—*Public Opinion.*

"Miss Parr has the great gift of charming simplicity of style; and if children are not interested in her book, many of their seniors will be."—*British Quarterly Review.*

OVER VOLCANOES;

Or, THROUGH FRANCE AND SPAIN IN 1871.

By A. KINGSMAN.

Crown 8vo. 10s. 6d.

"The writer's tone is so pleasant, his language is so good, and his spirits are so fresh, buoyant, and exhilarating, that you find yourself inveigled into reading, for the thousand-and-first time, a description of a Spanish bull-fight."—*Illustrated London News.*

"The adventures of our tourists are related with a good deal of pleasantry and humorous dash, which make the narrative agreeable reading."—*Public Opinion.*

"A work which we cordially recommend to such readers as desire to know something of Spain as she is to-day. Indeed, so fresh and original is it, that we could have wished that it had been a bigger book than it is."—*Literary World.*

ALEXIS DE TOCQUEVILLE.

CORRESPONDENCE AND CONVERSATIONS WITH NASSAU W. SENIOR FROM 1833 TO 1859.

EDITED BY MRS. M. C. M. SIMPSON.

2 vols., large post 8vo. 21s.

"Another of those interesting journals in which Mr. Senior has, as it were, crystallized the sayings of some of those many remarkable men with whom he came in contact."—*Morning Post.*

"A book replete with knowledge and thought."—*Quarterly Review.*

"An extremely interesting book, and a singularly good illustration of the value which, even in an age of newspapers and magazines, memoirs have and will always continue to have for the purposes of history."—*Saturday Review.*

JOURNALS KEPT IN FRANCE AND ITALY,

FROM 1848 TO 1852.

WITH A SKETCH OF THE REVOLUTION OF 1848.

By the late NASSAU WILLIAM SENIOR.

Edited by his Daughter, M. C. M. SIMPSON.

In 2 vols., post 8vo. 24s.

"'The present volume gives us conversations with some of the most prominent men in the political history of France and Italy . . . as well as with others whose names are not so familiar or are hidden under initials. Mr. Senior has the art of inspiring all men with frankness, and of persuading them to put themselves unreservedly in his hands without fear of private circulation."—*Athenæum.*

"The book has a genuine historical value."—*Saturday Review.*

"No better, more honest, and more readable view of the state of political society during the existence of the second Republic could well be looked for."—*Examiner.*

65, Cornhill; & 12, Paternoster Row, London.

A MEMOIR OF NATHANIEL HAWTHORNE,

WITH STORIES NOW FIRST PUBLISHED IN THIS COUNTRY.

By H. A. PAGE.

Large post 8vo. 7s. 6d.

"The Memoir is followed by a criticism of Hawthorne as a writer; and the criticism, though we should be inclined to dissent from particular sentiments, is, on the whole, very well written, and exhibits a discriminating enthusiasm for one of the most fascinating of novelists."—*Saturday Review.*

"Seldom has it been our lot to meet with a more appreciative delineation of character than this Memoir of Hawthorne . . . Mr. Page deserves the best thanks of every admirer of Hawthorne for the way in which he has gathered together these relics, and given them to the world, as well as for his admirable portraiture of their author's life and character."—*Morning Post.*

"We sympathise very heartily with an effort of Mr. H. A. Page to make English readers better acquainted with the life and character of Nathaniel Hawthorne . . . He has done full justice to the fine character of the author of 'The Scarlet Letter.'"—*Standard.*

"He has produced a well-written and complete Memoir . . . A model of literary work of art."—*Edinburgh Courant.*

MEMOIRS OF LEONORA CHRISTINA,

DAUGHTER OF CHRISTIAN IV. OF DENMARK:

WRITTEN DURING HER IMPRISONMENT IN THE BLUE TOWER OF THE ROYAL PALACE AT COPENHAGEN, 1663—1685.

TRANSLATED BY F. E. BUNNETT,

Translator of Grimm's "Life of Michael Angelo," &c.

With an Autotype portrait of the Princess. Medium 8vo. 12s. 6d.

"A valuable addition to history."—*Daily News.*

"This remarkable autobiography, in which we gratefully recognize a valuable addition to the tragic romance of history."—*Spectator.*

LIVES OF ENGLISH POPULAR LEADERS.

No. 1. STEPHEN LANGTON.

By C. EDMUND MAURICE.

Crown 8vo. 7s. 6d.

"Mr. Maurice has written a very interesting book, which may be read with equal pleasure and profit."—*Morning Post.*

"The volume contains many interesting details, including some important documents. It will amply repay those who read it, whether as a chapter of the constitutional history of England or as the life of a great Englishman."—*Spectator.*

65, Cornhill; & 12, Paternoster Row, London.

NORMAN MACLEOD, D.D.,

A CONTRIBUTION TOWARDS HIS BIOGRAPHY.

BY ALEXANDER STRAHAN.

Crown 8vo, sewed.   Price One Shilling.

. Reprinted, with numerous Additions and many Illustrations from Sketches by Dr. Macleod, from the *Contemporary Review*.

CABINET PORTRAITS.

BIOGRAPHICAL SKETCHES OF LIVING STATESMEN.

BY T. WEMYSS REID.

1 vol. crown 8vo.   7s. 6d.

"We have never met with a work which we can more unreservedly praise. The sketches are absolutely impartial."—*Athenæum*.

"We can heartily commend his work."—*Standard*.
"The 'Sketches of Statesmen' are drawn with a master hand."—*Yorkshire Post*.

THE ENGLISH CONSTITUTION.

BY WALTER BAGEHOT.

A New Edition, revised and corrected, with an Introductory Dissertation on recent changes and events.   Crown 8vo.   7s. 6d.

"A pleasing and clever study on the department of higher politics."—*Guardian*.
"No writer before him had set out so clearly what the efficient part of the English Constitution really is."—*Pall Mall Gazette*.
"Clear and practical."—*Globe*.

REPUBLICAN SUPERSTITIONS.

ILLUSTRATED BY THE POLITICAL HISTORY OF THE UNITED STATES.

INCLUDING A CORRESPONDENCE WITH M. LOUIS BLANC.

BY MONCURE D. CONWAY.

Crown 8vo.   5s.

"Au moment où j'écris ceci, je reçois d'un écrivain très distingué d'Amérique, M. Conway, une brochure qui est un frappant tableau des maux et des dangers qui résultent aux Etats Unis de l'institution présidentielle."—*M. Louis Blanc* ("De la Dissolution de l'Assemblée. Paris: Ernst Leroux).
"A very able exposure of the most plausible fallacies of Republicanism, by a writer of remarkable vigour and purity of style."—*Standard*.

65, *Cornhill;* & 12, *Paternoster Row, London.*

ESSAYS BY WILLIAM GODWIN,

AUTHOR OF "POLITICAL JUSTICE," ETC.

Never before published. 1 vol. crown 8vo. 7s. 6d.

"Interesting as the frankly expressed thoughts of a remarkable man, and as a contribution to the history of scepticism." —*Extract from the Editor's Preface.*

THE PELICAN PAPERS.

REMINISCENCES AND REMAINS OF A DWELLER IN THE WILDERNESS.

BY JAMES ASHCROFT NOBLE.

Crown 8vo. 6s.

"Written somewhat after the fashion of Mr. Helps' 'Friends in Council.'"—*Examiner.*

"Will well repay perusal by all thoughtful and intelligent readers."—*Liverpool Leader.*

"The 'Pelican Papers' make a very readable volume."—*Civilian.*

SOLDIERING AND SCRIBBLING.

BY ARCHIBALD FORBES,

Of the *Daily News*,

Author of "My Experience of the War between France and Germany."

Crown 8vo. 7s. 6d.

"All who open it will be inclined to read through for the varied entertainment which it affords."—*Daily News.*

"There is a good deal of instruction to outsiders touching military life in this volume."—*Evening Standard.*

"There is not a paper in the book which is not thoroughly readable and worth reading."—*Scotsman.*

BRIEFS AND PAPERS.

BEING SKETCHES OF THE BAR AND THE PRESS.

BY TWO IDLE APPRENTICES.

Crown 8vo. 7s. 6d.

"They are written with spirit and knowledge, and give some curious glimpses into what the majority will regard as strange and unknown territories."—*Daily News.*

"This is one of the best books to while away an hour and cause a generous laugh that we have come across for a long time."—*John Bull.*

65, Cornhill; & 12, Paternoster Row, London.

THE INTERNATIONAL SCIENTIFIC SERIES.

MESSRS. HENRY S. KING & CO. have the pleasure to announce that under this title they are issuing a SERIES of POPULAR TREATISES, embodying the results of the latest investigations in the various departments of Science at present most prominently before the world.

Although these Works are not specially designed for the instruction of beginners, still, as they are intended to address the non-scientific public, they will be, as far as possible, explanatory in character, and free from technicalities. The object of each author will be to bring his subject as near as he can to the general reader.

The volumes will all be crown 8vo size, well printed on good paper, strongly and elegantly bound, and will sell in this country at a price *not exceeding Five Shillings*.

☞ Prospectuses of the Series may be had of the Publishers.

Already published,

THE FORMS OF WATER IN RAIN AND RIVERS, ICE AND GLACIERS.

By J. TYNDALL, LL.D., F.R.S.

With 26 Illustrations. Crown 8vo. 5s.

"One of Professor Tyndall's best scientific treatises."—*Standard.*

"The most recent findings of science and experiment respecting the nature and properties of water in every possible form, are discussed with remarkable brevity, clearness, and fullness of exposition."—*Graphic.*

"With the clearness and brilliancy of language which have won for him his fame, he considers the subject of ice, snow, and glaciers."—*Morning Post.*

"Before starting for Switzerland next summer every one should study 'The forms of water.'"—*Globe.*

"Eloquent and instructive in an eminent degree."—*British Quarterly.*

PHYSICS AND POLITICS;

Or, Thoughts on the Application of the Principles of "Natural Selection" and "Inheritance" to Political Society.

By WALTER BAGEHOT.

Crown 8vo. 4s.

"On the whole we can recommend the book as well deserving to be read by thoughtful students of politics."—*Saturday Review.*

"Able and ingenious."—*Spectator.*

"The book has been well thought out, and the writer speaks without fear."—*National Reformer.*

"Contains many points of interest both to the scientific man and to the mere politician."—*Birmingham Daily Gazette.*

The Volumes now preparing are—

MIND AND BODY: THE THEORIES OF THEIR RELATIONS. By ALEXANDER BAIN, LL.D., Professor of Logic at the University of Aberdeen. Illustrated.

PRINCIPLES OF MENTAL PHYSIOLOGY. With their applications to the Training and Discipline of the Mind, and the Study of its Morbid Conditions. By W. B. CARPENTER, LL.D., M.D., F.R.S., &c. Illustrated.

ON FOOD. By Dr. EDWARD SMITH, F.R.S. Profusely Illustrated.

THE FIRST PRINCIPLES OF THE EXACT SCIENCES EXPLAINED TO THE NON-MATHEMATICAL. By Professor W. KINGDOM CLIFFORD, M.A.

ANIMAL MECHANICS; or, WALKING, SWIMMING, and FLYING. By Dr. J. BELL PETTIGREW, M.D., F.R.S. 125 Illustrations.

65, Cornhill; & 12, Paternoster Row, London.

STREAMS FROM HIDDEN SOURCES.
By B. MONTGOMERIE RANKING.
Crown 8vo. 6s.

THE SECRET OF LONG LIFE.
DEDICATED BY SPECIAL PERMISSION TO LORD ST. LEONARDS.
Second Edition. Large crown 8vo. 5s.

"A charming little volume, written with singular felicity of style and illustration."—*Times.*

"A very pleasant little book, which is always, whether it deal in paradox or earnest, cheerful, genial, scholarly."—*Spectator.*

"The bold and striking character of the whole conception is entitled to the warmest admiration."—*Pall Mall Gazette.*

"We should recommend our readers to get this book . . . because they will be amused by the jovial miscellaneous and cultured gossip with which he strews his pages."—*British Quarterly Review.*

CHANGE OF AIR AND SCENE.
A PHYSICIAN'S HINTS ABOUT DOCTORS, PATIENTS, HYGIÈNE, AND SOCIETY;
WITH NOTES OF EXCURSIONS FOR HEALTH IN THE PYRENEES, AND AMONGST THE WATERING-PLACES OF FRANCE (INLAND AND SEAWARD), SWITZERLAND, CORSICA, AND THE MEDITERRANEAN.

By Dr. ALPHONSE DONNÉ.
Large post 8vo. Price 9s.

"A very readable and serviceable book. . . . The real value of it is to be found in the accurate and minute information given with regard to a large number of places which have gained a reputation on the continent for their mineral waters."—*Pall Mall Gazette.*

"Not only a pleasant book of travel but also a book of considerable value."—*Morning Post.*

"A popular account of some of the most charming health resorts of the Continent; with suggestive hints about keeping well and getting well, which are characterised by a good deal of robust common sense."—*British Quarterly.*

"A singularly pleasant and chatty as well as instructive book about health."—*Guardian.*

"A useful and pleasantly-written book, containing many valuable hints on the general management of health from a shrewd and experienced medical man."—*Graphic.*

MISS YOUMANS' FIRST BOOK OF BOTANY.
DESIGNED TO CULTIVATE THE OBSERVING POWERS OF CHILDREN.
From the Author's latest Stereotyped Edition.
New and Enlarged Edition, with 300 Engravings. Crown 8vo. 5s.

It is but rarely that a school-book appears which is at once so novel in plan, so successful in execution, and so suited to the general want, as to command universal and unqualified approbation, but such has been the case with Miss Youmans' First Book of Botany. Her work is an outgrowth of the most recent scientific views, and has been practically tested by careful trial with juvenile classes, and it has been everywhere welcomed as a timely and invaluable contribution to the improvement of primary education.

65, *Cornhill*; & 12, *Paternoster Row, London.*

AN ESSAY ON THE CULTURE OF THE OBSERVING POWERS OF CHILDREN,

ESPECIALLY IN CONNECTION WITH THE STUDY OF BOTANY.

By ELIZA A. YOUMANS,

Edited, with Notes and a Supplement
By JOSEPH PAYNE, F.C.P.,
Author of "Lectures on the Science and Art of Education," &c.

Crown 8vo. 2s. 6d.

"The little book, now under notice, is expressly designed to make the earliest instruction of children a mental discipline. Miss Youmans presents in her work the ripe results of educational experience reduced to a system, wisely conceiving that an education—even the most elementary—should be regarded as a discipline of the mental powers, and that the facts of external nature supply the most suitable materials for this discipline in the case of children. She has applied that principle to the study of botany. This study, according to her just notions on the subject, is to be fundamentally based on the exercise of the pupil's own powers of observation. He is to see and examine the properties of plants and flowers at first hand, not merely to be informed of what others have seen and examined."—*Pall Mall Gazette.*

THE HISTORY OF THE NATURAL CREATION:

BEING A SERIES OF POPULAR SCIENTIFIC LECTURES ON THE GENERAL THEORY OF PROGRESSION OF SPECIES;

WITH A DISSERTATION ON THE THEORIES OF DARWIN, GOETHE, AND LAMARCK: MORE ESPECIALLY APPLYING THEM TO THE ORIGIN OF MAN, AND TO OTHER FUNDAMENTAL QUESTIONS OF NATURAL SCIENCE CONNECTED THEREWITH.

By Professor ERNST HÆCKEL, of the University of Jena.

8vo. With Woodcuts and Plates. [*Preparing.*

AN ARABIC AND ENGLISH DICTIONARY OF THE KORAN.

By Major J. PENRICE, B.A.

4to. [*Just ready.*

MODERN GOTHIC ARCHITECTURE.

By T. G. JACKSON.

Crown 8vo. [*In the press.*

65, Cornhill; & 12, Paternoster Row, London.

A LEGAL HANDBOOK FOR ARCHITECTS.
By EDWARD JENKINS and JOHN RAYMOND.
Crown 8vo. Price 5s. [*Nearly ready*

CONTEMPORARY ENGLISH PSYCHOLOGY.
From the French of Professor TH. RIBOT.
An Analysis of the Views and Opinions of the following Metaphysicians, as expressed in their Writings.

| JAMES MILL. | JOHN STUART MILL. | HERBERT SPENCER. |
| A. BAIN. | GEORGE H. LEWES. | SAMUEL BAILEY. |

Large post 8vo. [*Preparing.*

PHYSIOLOGY FOR PRACTICAL USE.
By Various Eminent Writers.
Edited by JAMES HINTON.
With 50 Illustrations. [*Preparing.*

HEALTH AND DISEASE
As Influenced by
THE DAILY, SEASONAL, AND OTHER CYCLICAL CHANGES IN THE HUMAN SYSTEM.
By Dr. EDWARD SMITH, F.R.S.
A New Edition. 7s. 6d.

PRACTICAL DIETARY
FOR FAMILIES, SCHOOLS, & THE LABOURING CLASSES.
By Dr. EDWARD SMITH, F.R.S.
A New Edition. Price 3s. 6d.

CONSUMPTION IN ITS EARLY AND REMEDIABLE STAGES.
By Dr. EDWARD SMITH, F.R.S.
A New Edition. 7s. 6d.

65, *Cornhill;* & 12, *Paternoster Row, London.*

A TREATISE ON RELAPSING FEVER.

By R. T. LYONS,

Assistant-Surgeon, Bengal Army.

Small post 8vo. 7s. 6d.

"A practical work thoroughly supported in its views by a series of remarkable cases."—*Standard*.

IN QUEST OF COOLIES.

A SOUTH SEA SKETCH. By JAMES L. A. HOPE.

Second Edition. Crown 8vo, with 15 Illustrations from Sketches by the Author. Price 6s.

"Mr. Hope's description of the natives is graphic and amusing, and the book is altogether well worthy of perusal."—*Standard*.

"Lively and clever sketches."—*Athenæum*.

"This agreeably written and amusingly illustrated volume."—*Public Opinion*.

THE NILE WITHOUT A DRAGOMAN.

By FREDERIC EDEN.

Second Edition. In one vol. Crown 8vo, cloth. 7s. 6d.

"Should any of our readers care to imitate Mr. Eden's example, and wish to see things with their own eyes, and shift for themselves, next winter in Upper Egypt, they will find this book a very agreeable guide."—*Times*.

"We have in these pages the most minute description of life as it appeared on the banks of the Nile; all that could be seen or was worth seeing in nature or in art is here pleasantly and graphically set down. . . . It is a book to read during an autumn holiday."—*Spectator*.

"Gives, within moderate compass, a suggestive description of the charms, curiosities, dangers, and discomforts of the Nile voyage."—*Saturday Review*.

ROUND THE WORLD IN 1870.

A VOLUME OF TRAVELS, WITH MAPS.

By A. D. CARLISLE, B.A.,

Trin. Coll., Camb.

Demy 8vo. 16s.

"Makes one understand how going round the world is to be done in the quickest and pleasantest manner, and how the brightest and most cheerful of travellers did it with eyes wide open and keen attention all on the alert, with ready sympathies, with the happiest facility of hitting upon the most interesting features of nature and the most interesting characteristics of man, and all for its own sake."—*Spectator*.

"We can only commend, which we do very heartily, an eminently sensible and readable book."—*British Quarterly Review*.

65, *Cornhill;* & 12, *Paternoster Row*, London.

Military Works.

THE FRONTAL ATTACK OF INFANTRY.
By Capt. LAYMANN, Instructor of Tactics at the Military College, Neisse. Translated by Colonel EDWARD NEWDIGATE. Crown 8vo, limp cloth. Price 2s. 6d.

"This work has met with special attention in our army."—*Militarin Wochenblatt.*

THE FIRST BAVARIAN ARMY CORPS IN
THE WAR OF 1870–71, UNDER VON DER TANN. Compiled from the Official Records by Capt. HUGO HELVIG. Translated by Capt. G. SALIS SCHWABE. Demy 8vo. With 5 large Maps.

History of the Organisation, Equipment, and War Services of
THE REGIMENT OF BENGAL ARTILLERY.
Compiled from Published Official and other Records, and various private sources, by Major FRANCIS W. STUBBS, Royal (late Bengal) Artillery. Vol. I. will contain WAR SERVICES. The Second Volume will be published separately, and will contain the HISTORY of the ORGANISATION and EQUIPMENT of the REGIMENT. In 2 vols. 8vo. With Maps and Plans. *Preparing.*

THE ABOLITION OF PURCHASE AND THE
ARMY REGULATION BILL OF 1871. By Lieut.-Col. the Hon. A. ANSON, V.C., M.P. Crown 8vo. Price One Shilling.

THE STORY OF THE SUPERSESSIONS.
By Lieut.-Col. the Hon. A. ANSON, V.C., M.P. Cm. 8vo. Price 6d.

ARMY RESERVES AND MILITIA REFORMS.
By Lieut.-Colonel the Hon. C. ANSON. Crown 8vo. Sewed. Price 1s.

ELEMENTARY MILITARY GEOGRAPHY,
RECONNOITRING, AND SKETCHING. Compiled for Non-Commissioned Officers and Soldiers of all Arms. By Lieut. C. E. H. VINCENT, Royal Welsh Fusileers. Small crown 8vo.

65, *Cornhill;* & 12, *Paternoster Row*, London.

MILITARY WORKS—*continued.*

VICTORIES AND DEFEATS.
An Attempt to explain the Causes which have led to them. An Officer's Manual. By Col. R. P. ANDERSON. Demy 8vo. [*In preparation.*

STUDIES IN THE NEW INFANTRY
TACTICS. By Major W. VON SCHEREFF. Translated from the German by Col. LUMLEY GRAHAM. [*Shortly.*

THE OPERATIONS OF THE FIRST ARMY
TO THE CAPITULATION OF METZ. By Major VON SCHELL, with Maps, including one of Metz and of the country around. Translated by Capt. E. O. HOLLIST. In demy 8vo. [*In preparation.*

*** The most important events described in this work are the battles of Spichern, those before Metz on the 14th and 18th August, and (on this point nothing authentic has yet been published) the history of the investment of Metz (battle of Noisseville).

This work, however, possesses a greater importance than that derived from these points, because it represents for the first time from the official documents the generalship of Von Steinmetz. Hitherto we have had no exact reports on the deeds and motives of this celebrated general. This work has the special object of unfolding carefully the relations in which the commander of the First Army acted, the plan of operations which he drew up, and the manner in which he carried it out.

THE OPERATIONS OF THE FIRST ARMY
IN NORTHERN FRANCE AGAINST FAIDHERBE. By Colonel COUNT HERMANN VON WARTENSLEBEN, Chief of the Staff of the First Army. Translated by Colonel C. H. VON WRIGHT. In demy 8vo. Uniform with the above.
[*In preparation.*

THE OPERATIONS OF THE FIRST ARMY,
UNDER GEN. VON GOEBEN. Translated by Col. C. H. VON WRIGHT. With Maps. Demy 8vo.

TACTICAL DEDUCTIONS FROM THE WAR
OF 1870-1. By Captain A. VON BOGUSLAWSKI. Translated by Colonel LUMLEY GRAHAM, late 18th (Royal Irish) Regiment. Demy 8vo. Uniform with the above. Price 7s.

"Major Boguslawski's tactical deductions from the war are, that infantry still preserve their superiority over cavalry, that open order must henceforth be the main principles of all drill, and that the chassepot is the best of all small arms for precision.... We must, without delay, impress brain and forethought into the British Service; and we cannot commence the good work too soon, or better, than by placing the two books ('The Operations of the German Armies' and 'Tactical Deductions') we have here criticised, in every military library, and introducing them as class-books in every tactical school."—*United Service Gazette.*

65, *Cornhill;* & 12, *Paternoster Row, London.*

MILITARY WORKS—*continued.*

THE OPERATIONS OF THE GERMAN
ARMIES IN FRANCE, FROM SEDAN TO THE END OF THE WAR OF 1870-1. With Large Official Map. From the Journals of the Head-quarters Staff, by Major WM. BLUME. Translated by E. M. JONES, Major 20th Foot, late Professor of Military History, Sandhurst. Demy 8vo. Price 9s.

"The book is of absolute necessity to the military student. . . . The work is one of high merit and . . . has the advantage of being rendered into fluent English, and is accompanied by an excellent military map."—*United Service Gazette.*

"The work of translation has been well done; the expressive German idioms have been rendered into clear, nervous English without losing any of their original force; and in notes, prefaces, and introductions, much additional information has been given."—*Athenæum.*

"The work of Major von Blume in its English dress forms the most valuable addition to our stock of works upon the war that our press has put forth. Major Blume writes with a clear conciseness much wanting in many of his country's historians, and Major Jones has done himself and his original alike justice by his vigorous yet correct translation of the excellent volume on which he has laboured. Our space forbids our doing more than commending it earnestly as the most authentic and instructive narrative of the second section of the war that has yet appeared."—*Saturday Review.*

THE OPERATIONS OF THE SOUTH ARMY
IN JANUARY AND FEBRUARY, 1871. Compiled from the Official War Documents of the Head-quarters of the Southern Army. By COUNT HERMANN VON WARTENSLEBEN, Colonel in the Prussian General Staff. Translated by Colonel C. H. VON WRIGHT. Demy 8vo, with Maps. Uniform with the above. Price 6s.

HASTY INTRENCHMENTS. By Colonel A.
BRIALMONT. Translated by Lieutenant CHARLES A. EMPSON, R.A. Demy 8vo. Nine Plates. Price 6s.

"A valuable contribution to military literature."—*Athenæum.*

"In seven short chapters it gives plain directions for performing shelter-trenches, with the best method of carrying the necessary tools, and it offers practical illustrations of the use of hasty intrenchments on the field of battle."—*United Service Magazine.*

"It supplies that which our own text-books give but imperfectly, viz., hints as to how a position can best be strengthened by means . . . of such extemporised intrenchments and batteries as can be thrown up by infantry in the space of four or five hours . . . deserves to become a standard military work."—*Standard.*

"A clever treatise, short, practical and clear."—*Investor's Guardian.*

"Clearly and critically written."—*Wellington Gazette.*

THE ARMY OF THE NORTH-GERMAN
CONFEDERATION. A Brief Description of its Organisation, of the different Branches of the Service and their 'Rôle' in War, of its Mode of Fighting, &c. By a PRUSSIAN GENERAL. Translated from the German by Col. EDWARD NEWDIGATE. Demy 8vo. 5s.

⁎ The authorship of this book was erroneously ascribed to the renowned General von Moltke, but there can be little doubt that it was written under his immediate inspiration.

65, Cornhill; & 12, Paternoster Row, London.

MILITARY WORKS—*continued*.

CAVALRY FIELD DUTY. By Major-General VON MIRUS. Translated by Captain FRANK S. RUSSELL, 14th (King's) Hussars. Crown 8vo, limp cloth. 5s.

*** This is the text-book of instruction in the German cavalry, and comprises all the details connected with the military duties of cavalry soldiers on service. The translation is made from a new edition, which contains the modifications introduced consequent on the experiences of the late war. The great interest that students feel in all the German military methods, will, it is believed, render this book especially acceptable at the present time.

STUDIES IN LEADING TROOPS. By Colonel VON VERDY DU VERNOIS. An authorised and accurate Translation by Lieutenant H. J. T. HILDYARD, 71st Foot. Parts I. and II. Demy 8vo. Price 7s. [*Now ready*.

*** General BEAUCHAMP WALKER says of this work:—"I recommend the first two numbers of Colonel von Verdy's 'Studies' to the attentive perusal of my brother officers. They supply a want which I have often felt during my service in this country, namely, a minuter tactical detail of the minor operations of the war than any but the most observant and fortunately placed staff-officer is in a position to give. I have read and re-read them very carefully, I hope with profit, certainly with great interest, and believe that practice, in the sense of these 'Studies,' would be a valuable preparation for manœuvres on a more extended scale."—Berlin, June, 1872.

THE FRANCO-GERMAN WAR, 1870-71. FIRST PART:—HISTORY OF THE WAR TO THE DOWNFALL OF THE EMPIRE. FIRST SECTION:—THE EVENTS IN JULY. Authorised Translation from the German Official Account at the Topographical and Statistical Department of the War Office, by Captain F. C. H. CLARKE, R.A. First Section, with Map. Demy 8vo. 3s.

DISCIPLINE AND DRILL. Four Lectures delivered to the London Scottish Rifle Volunteers. By Captain S. FLOOD PAGE. A New and Cheaper Edition. Price 1s.

"One of the best-known and coolest-headed of the metropolitan regiments, whose adjutant moreover has lately published an admirable collection of lectures addressed by him to the men of his corps."—*Times*.

"The very useful and interesting work. . . . Every Volunteer, officer or private, will be the better for perusing and digesting the plain-spoken truths which Captain Page so firmly, and yet so modestly, puts before them; and we trust that the little book in which they are contained will find its way into all parts of Great Britain."—*Volunteer Service Gazette*.

THE SUBSTANTIVE SENIORITY ARMY LIST. Majors and Captains. By Captain F. B. P. WHITE, 1st W. I. Regiment. 8vo, sewed. 2s. 6d.

65, Cornhill; & 12, Paternoster Row, London.

Books on Indian Subjects.

THE EUROPEAN IN INDIA.

A HAND-BOOK OF PRACTICAL INFORMATION FOR THOSE PROCEEDING TO, OR RESIDING IN, THE EAST INDIES,

RELATING TO OUTFITS, ROUTES, TIME FOR DEPARTURE, INDIAN CLIMATE, ETC.

By EDMUND C. P. HULL.

WITH A MEDICAL GUIDE FOR ANGLO-INDIANS.

BEING A COMPENDIUM OF ADVICE TO EUROPEANS IN INDIA, RELATING TO THE PRESERVATION AND REGULATION OF HEALTH.

By R. S. MAIR, M.D., F.R.C.S.E.,
Late Deputy Coroner of Madras.

In 1 vol. Post 8vo. 6s.

"Full of all sorts of useful information to the English settler or traveller in India."—*Standard.*

"One of the most valuable books ever published in India—valuable for its sound information, its careful array of pertinent facts, and its sterling common sense. It is a publisher's as well as an author's 'hit,' for it supplies a want which few persons may have discovered, but which everybody will at once recognise when once the contents of the book have been mastered. The medical part of the work is invaluable."—*Calcutta Guardian.*

EASTERN EXPERIENCES.

By L. BOWRING, C.S.I.,
Lord Canning's Private Secretary, and for many years the Chief Commissioner of Mysore and Coorg.

In 1 vol. Demy 8vo. 16s. Illustrated with Maps and Diagrams.

"An admirable and exhaustive geographical, political, and industrial survey."—*Athenæum.*

"The usefulness of this compact and methodical summary of the most authentic information relating to countries whose welfare is intimately connected with our own, should obtain for Mr. Lewin Bowring's work a good place among treatises of its kind."—*Daily News.*

"Interesting even to the general reader, but more especially so to those who may have a special concern in that portion of our Indian Empire."—*Post.*

"An elaborately got up and carefully compiled work."—*Home News.*

A MEMOIR OF THE INDIAN SURVEYS.

By CLEMENT R. MARKHAM.

Printed by order of Her Majesty's Secretary of State for India in Council.

Imperial 8vo. 10s. 6d.

65, Cornhill; & 12, Paternoster Row, London.

BOOKS ON INDIAN SUBJECTS—*continued.*

WESTERN INDIA BEFORE AND DURING THE MUTINIES.

PICTURES DRAWN FROM LIFE.

BY MAJOR-GEN. SIR GEORGE LE GRAND JACOB, K.C.S.I., C.B.

In 1 vol. Crown 8vo. 7s. 6d.

"The most important contribution to the history of Western India during the Mutinies which has yet, in a popular form, been made public."—*Athenæum.*

"The legacy of a wise veteran, intent on the benefit of his countrymen rather than on the acquisition of fame."—*London and China Express.*

"Few men more competent than himself to speak authoritatively concerning Indian affairs."—*Standard.*

EXCHANGE TABLES OF STERLING AND INDIAN RUPEE CURRENCY,

UPON A NEW AND EXTENDED SYSTEM,

EMBRACING VALUES FROM ONE FARTHING TO ONE HUNDRED THOUSAND POUNDS, AND AT RATES PROGRESSING, IN SIXTEENTHS OF A PENNY, FROM 1s. 9d. TO 2s. 3d. PER RUPEE.

BY DONALD FRASER,

Accountant to the British Indian Steam Navigation Co., Limited.

Royal 8vo. 10s. 6d.

A CATALOGUE OF MAPS OF THE BRITISH POSSESSIONS

IN INDIA AND OTHER PARTS OF ASIA.

Published by order of Her Majesty's Secretary of State for India in Council.

Royal 8vo, sewed. 1s.

A continuation of the above, sewed, price 6d., is now ready.

☞ *Messrs. Henry S. King & Co. are the authorised agents by the Government for the sale of the whole of the Maps enumerated in this Catalogue.*

65, *Cornhill; & 12, Paternoster Row, London.*

Juvenile Books.

BRAVE MEN'S FOOTSTEPS. A Book of Example and Anecdote for Young People. By the Editor of "MEN WHO HAVE RISEN." With Four Illustrations. By C. DOYLE. 3s. 6d.

"The little volume is precisely of the stamp to win the favour of those who, in choosing a gift for a boy, would consult his moral development as well as his temporary pleasure."—*Daily Telegraph.*

"A readable and instructive volume."—*Examiner.*
"No more welcome book for the schoolboy could be imagined."—*Birmingham Daily Gazette.*

THE LITTLE WONDER-HORN. By JEAN INGELOW. A Second Series of "Stories told to a Child." Fifteen Illustrations. Cloth, gilt. 3s. 6d.

"Full of fresh and vigorous fancy: it is worthy of the author of some of the best of our modern verse."—*Standard.*

"We like all the contents of the 'Little Wonder-Horn' very much."—*Athenæum.*
"We recommend it with confidence."—*Pall-Mall Gazette.*

STORIES IN PRECIOUS STONES. By HELEN ZIMMERN. With Six Illustrations. Crown 8vo. 5s.

"A series of pretty tales which are half fantastic, half natural, and pleasantly quaint, as befits stories intended for the young."—*Daily Telegraph.*

"Certainly the book is well worth a perusal, and will not be soon laid down when once taken up."—*Daily Bristol Times.*

GUTTA-PERCHA WILLIE, THE WORKING GENIUS. By GEORGE MACDONALD. With Illustrations. By ARTHUR HUGHES. Crown 8vo. 3s. 6d.

THE TRAVELLING MENAGERIE. By CHARLES CAMDEN, Author of "Hoity Toity." Illustrated by J. MAHONEY. Crown 8vo. 3s. 6d.

PLUCKY FELLOWS. A Book for Boys. By STEPHEN J. MACKENNA. With Six Illustrations. Crown 8vo. Price 3s. 6d.

THE DESERTED SHIP. A Real Story of the Atlantic. By CUPPLES HOWE, Master Mariner. Illustrated by TOWNLEY GREEN. Crown 8vo. 3s. 6d.

65, *Cornhill;* & 12, *Paternoster Row, London.*

JUVENILE BOOKS—*continued.*

GOOD WORDS FOR THE YOUNG.
The Volume for 1872, gilt cloth and gilt edges, 7s. 6d. Containing numerous Contributions by popular authors, and about One Hundred and Fifty Illustrations by the best artists.

JEAN JAROUSSEAU, THE PASTOR OF THE
DESERT. Translated from the French of EUGENE PELLETAN. By Colonel E. P. DE L'HOSTE. In fcap. 8vo, with an Engraved Frontispiece. Price 5s.

"There is a poetical simplicity and picturesqueness; the noblest heroism; unpretentious religion; pure love, and the spectacle of a household brought up in the fear of the Lord. . . . The whole story has an air of quaint antiquity similar to that which invests with a charm more easily felt than described the site of some splendid ruin."—*Illustrated London News.*

"This charming specimen of Eugène Pelletan's tender grace, humour, and high-toned morality."—*Notes and Queries.*

"A touching record of the struggles in the cause of religious liberty of a real man."—*Graphic.*

HOITY TOITY, THE GOOD LITTLE FELLOW.
By CHARLES CAMDEN. Illustrated. Crown 8vo. 3s. 6d.

LILLIPUT REVELS.
By the Author of "LILLIPUT LEVÉE." With Illustrations. Crown 8vo. 3s. 6d. [*Preparing.*

SEEKING HIS FORTUNE, AND OTHER
STORIES. Crown 8vo. Illustrated. [*Preparing.*

THE "ELSIE" SERIES.

ELSIE DINSMORE.
By MARTHA FARQUHARSON. Crown 8vo. Illustrated.

ELSIE'S GIRLHOOD.
A Sequel to "Elsie Dinsmore." By the same Author. Crown 8vo. Illustrated.

ELSIE'S HOLIDAYS AT ROSELANDS.
By the same Author. Crown 8vo. Illustrated.

65, *Cornhill; &* 12, *Paternoster Row, London.*

Poetry.

IMITATIONS FROM THE GERMAN OF SPITTA AND TERSTEGEN.
By Lady DURAND. Crown 8vo. *[In the press.*

EASTERN LEGENDS AND STORIES IN ENGLISH VERSE.
By Lieutenant NORTON POWLETT, Royal Artillery. Crown 8vo. 5s.

EDITH; or, LOVE AND LIFE IN CHESHIRE.
By T. ASHE, Author of the "Sorrows of Hypsipylé," etc. Sewed. Price 6d.

"A really fine poem, full of tender, subtle touches of feeling."—*Manchester News.*

"Pregnant from beginning to end with the results of careful observation and imaginative power."—*Chester Chronicle.*

THE GALLERY OF PIGEONS, AND OTHER POEMS.
By THEOPHILUS MARZIALS. Crown 8vo. *[In the press.*

A NEW VOLUME OF POEMS.
By the Rev. C. TENNYSON TURNER. Crown 8vo. *[In the press.*

ENGLISH SONNETS.
Collected and Arranged by JOHN DENNIS. Small crown 8vo. *[In the press.*

GOETHE'S FAUST.
A New Translation in Rhyme. By the Rev. C. KEGAN PAUL. Crown 8vo. 6s.

WILLIAM CULLEN BRYANT'S POEMS.
Handsomely bound, with Illustrations. A Cheaper Edition. A Pocket Edition. *[Preparing.*

65, *Cornhill;* & 12, *Paternoster Row, London.*

POETRY—*continued.*

CALDERON'S POEMS. The Purgatory of St. Patrick—The Wonderful Magician—Life is a Dream. Translated from the Spanish. By DENIS FLORENCE MACCARTHY.

SONGS FOR SAILORS. By Dr. W. C. BENNETT. Dedicated by Special Request to H.R.H. the Duke of Edinburgh. Crown 8vo. 3s. 6d. With Steel Portrait and Illustrations. An Edition in Illustrated paper Covers. Price 1s.

DR. W. C. BENNETT'S POEMS will be shortly Re-issued, with additions to each part, in Five Parts, at 1s. each.

WALLED IN, AND OTHER POEMS. By the Rev. HENRY J. BULKELY. Crown 8vo. 5s.

THE POETICAL AND PROSE WORKS OF ROBERT BUCHANAN. Preparing for publication, a Collected Edition in 5 vols.

CONTENTS OF VOL. I.—DAUGHTERS OF EVE; UNDERTONES AND ANTIQUES; COUNTRY AND PASTORAL POEMS. [*In the Press.*

SONGS OF LIFE AND DEATH. By JOHN PAYNE, Author of "Intaglios," "Sonnets," "The Masque of Shadows," etc. Crown 8vo. 5s. [*Just out.*

SONGS OF TWO WORLDS. By a NEW WRITER. Fcap. 8vo, cloth, 5s.

"The 'New Writer' is certainly no tyro. No one after reading the first two poems, almost perfect in rhythm and all the graceful reserve of true lyrical strength, can doubt that this book is the result of lengthened thought and assiduous training in poetical form. . . . These poems will assuredly take high rank among the class to which they belong."—*British Quarterly Review, April 1st.*

"If these poems are the mere preludes of a mind growing in power and in inclination for verse, we have in them the promise of a fine poet. . . . The verse describing Socrates has the highest note of critical poetry."—*Spectator, February 17th.*

"No extracts could do justice to the exquisite tones, the felicitous phrasing and delicately wrought harmonies of some of these poems."—*Nonconformist, March 27th.*

"Are we in this book making the acquaintance of a fine and original poet, or of a most artistic imitator? And our deliberate opinion is that the former hypothesis is the right one. It has a purity and delicacy of feeling like morning air."—*Graphic, March 16th.*

65, Cornhill; & 12, Paternoster Row, London.

POETRY—*continued.*

THE INN OF STRANGE MEETINGS, AND
OTHER POEMS. By MORTIMER COLLINS. Crown 8vo. 5s.

"Abounding in quiet humour, in bright fancy, in sweetness and melody of expression, and, at times, in the tenderest touches of pathos."—*Graphic.*

"Mr. Collins has an undercurrent of chivalry and romance beneath the trifling vein of good humoured banter which is the special characteristic of his verse. . . . The 'Inn of Strange Meetings' is a sprightly piece."—*Athenæum.*

EROS AGONISTES. By E. B. D. Crown 8vo. 3s. 6d.

"The author of these verses has written a very touching story of the human heart in the story he tells with such pathos and power, of an affection cherished so long and so secretly. . . . It is not the least merit of these pages that they are everywhere illumined with moral and religious sentiment suggested, not paraded, of the brightest, purest character."—*Standard.*

THE LEGENDS OF ST. PATRICK & OTHER
POEMS. By AUBREY DE VERE. Crown 8vo. 5s.

"Mr. De Vere's versification in his earlier poems is characterised by great sweetness and simplicity. He is master of his instrument, and rarely offends the ear with false notes. Poems such as these scarcely admit of quotation, for their charm is not, and ought not to be, found in isolated passages; but we can promise the patient and thoughtful reader much pleasure in the perusal of this volume."—*Pall-Mall Gazette.*

"We have marked, in almost every page, excellent touches from which we know not how to select. We have but space to commend the varied structure of his verse, the carefulness of his grammar, and his excellent English. All who believe that poetry should raise and not debase the social ideal, all who think that wit should exalt our standard of thought and manners, must welcome this contribution at once to our knowledge of the past and to the science of noble life."—*Saturday Review.*

ASPROMONTE, AND OTHER POEMS. Second
Edition, cloth. 4s. 6d.

"The volume is anonymous, but there is no reason for the author to be ashamed of it. The 'Poems of Italy' are evidently inspired by genuine enthusiasm in the cause espoused; and one of them, 'The Execution of Felice Orsini,' has much poetic merit, the event celebrated being told with dramatic force."—*Athenæum.*

"The verse is fluent and free."—*Spectator.*

THE DREAM AND THE DEED, AND OTHER
POEMS. By PATRICK SCOTT, Author of "Footpaths between Two Worlds," etc. Fcap. 8vo, cloth, 5s.

"A bitter and able satire on the vice and follies of the day, literary, social, and political."—*Standard.*

"Shows real poetic power coupled with evidences of satirical energy."—*Edinburgh Daily Review.*

65, *Cornhill;* & 12, *Paternoster Row, London.*

Fiction.

CHESTERLEIGH. By ANSLEY CONYERS. 3 vols. Crown 8vo. [*Just out.*

SQUIRE SILCHESTER'S WHIM. By MORTIMER COLLINS, Author of "Marquis and Merchant," "The Princess Clarice," &c. Crown 8vo. 3 vols.

SEETA. By Colonel MEADOWS TAYLOR, Author of "Tara," "Ralph Darnell," &c. Crown 8vo. 3 vols.

"The story is well told, native life is admirably described, and the petty intrigues of native rulers, and their hatred of the English, mingled with fear lest the latter should eventually prove the victors, are cleverly depicted."—*Athenæum.*

A New and Cheaper Edition, Illustrated, of
COL. MEADOWS TAYLOR'S INDIAN TALES is preparing for publication.

JOHANNES OLAF. By E. DE WILLE. Translated by F. E. BUNNETT. Crown 8vo. 3 vols.

The author of this story enjoys a high reputation in Germany; and both English and German critics have spoken in terms of the warmest praise of this and her previous stories. She has been called "The 'George Eliot' of Germany."

"The book gives evidence of considerable capacity in every branch of a novelist's faculty. The art of description is fully exhibited; perception of character and capacity for delineating it are obvious; while there is great breadth and comprehensiveness in the plan of the story."—*Morning Post.*

OFF THE SKELLIGS. By JEAN INGELOW. (Her First Romance.) Crown 8vo. In 4 vols.

"Clever and sparkling. . . . The descriptive passages are bright with colour."—*Standard.*
"We read each succeeding volume with increasing interest, going almost to the point of wishing there was a fifth."—*Athenæum.*
"The novel as a whole is a remarkable one, because it is uncompromisingly true to life."—*Daily News.*

HONOR BLAKE: The Story of a Plain Woman. By Mrs. KEATINGE, Author of "English Homes in India," &c. 2 vols. Crown 8vo.

"One of the best novels we have met with for some time."—*Morning Post.*
"The story of 'Honor Blake' is a story which must do good to all, young and old, who read it."—*Daily News.*

65, Cornhill; & 12, Paternoster Row, London.

FICTION—*continued*.

THE DOCTOR'S DILEMMA. By HESBA STRETTON, Author of "Little Meg," &c., &c. Crown 8vo. 3 vols.

THE PRINCESS CLARICE. A Story of 1871. By MORTIMER COLLINS. 2 vols. Crown 8vo.

"Mr. Collins has produced a readable book, amusingly characteristic. There is good description of Devonshire scenery; and lastly there is Clarice, a most successful heroine, who must speak to the reader for herself."—*Athenæum*.

"Very readable and amusing. We would especially give an honourable mention to Mr. Collins's '*vers de société*,' the writing of which has almost become a lost art."—*Pall Mall Gazette*.

"A bright, fresh, and original book, with which we recommend all genuine novel readers to become acquainted at the earliest opportunity."—*Standard*.

THE SPINSTERS OF BLATCHINGTON. By MAR. TRAVERS. 2 vols. Crown 8vo.

"A pretty story. In all respects deserving of a favourable reception."—*Graphic*.

"A book of more than average merits and worth reading."—*Examiner*.

THOMASINA. By the Author of "DOROTHY," "DE CRESSY," etc. 2 vols. Crown 8vo.

"We would liken it to a finished and delicate cabinet picture, in which there is no brilliant colour, and yet all is harmony; in which no line is without its purpose, but all contribute to the unity of the work."—*Athenæum*.

"For the delicacies of character-drawing, for play of incident, and for finish of style, we must refer our readers to the story itself: from the perusal of which they cannot fail to derive both interest and amusement."—*Daily News*.

"This undeniably pleasing story."—*Pall Mall Gazette*.

THE STORY OF SIR EDWARD'S WIFE. By HAMILTON MARSHALL, Author of "For Very Life." 1 vol. Crown 8vo.

"A quiet graceful little story."—*Spectator*.

"There are many clever conceits in it. . . . Mr. Hamilton Marshall proves in 'Sir Edward's Wife' that he can tell a story closely and pleasantly."—*Pall Mall Gazette*.

LINKED AT LAST. By F. E. BUNNETT. 1 vol. Crown 8vo.

"'Linked at Last' contains so much of pretty description, natural incident, and delicate portraiture, that the reader who once takes it up will not be inclined to relinquish it without concluding the volume."—*Morning Post*.

"A very charming story."—*John Bull*.

65, *Cornhill;* & 12, *Paternoster Row, London.*

FICTION—*continued.*

PERPLEXITY. By SYDNEY MOSTYN. 3 vols.
Crown 8vo.

"Written with very considerable power, the plot is original and . . . worked out with great cleverness and sustained interest."—*Standard.*
"Shows much lucidity, much power of portraiture, and no inconsiderable sense of humour."—*Examiner.*
"The literary workmanship is good, and the story forcibly and graphically told."—*Daily News.*

HER TITLE OF HONOUR. By HOLME LEE.
Second Edition. 1 vol. Crown 8vo.

"It is unnecessary to recommend tales of Holme Lee's, for they are well known, and all more or less liked. But this book far exceeds even our favourites—'Sylvan Holt's Daughter,' 'Kathie Brande,' and 'Thorny Hall'—because with the interest of a pathetic story is united the value of a definite and high purpose."—*Spectator.*
"A most exquisitely written story."—*Literary Churchman.*

BRESSANT. A Romance. By JULIAN HAWTHORNE. 2 vols. Crown 8vo. [*Preparing.*

CRUEL AS THE GRAVE. By the Countess VON BOTHMER. 3 vols. Crown 8vo.
"*Jealousy is cruel as the Grave.*"

"The Wise Man's motto is prefixed to an interesting, though somewhat tragic story, by the Countess von Bothmer. . . Her German prince, with his chivalrous affection, his disinterested patriotism, and his soldierlike sense of duty, is no unworthy type of a national character which has lately given the world many instances of old-fashioned heroism."—*Athenæum.*
"An agreeable, unaffected, and eminently readable novel."—*Daily News.*

MEMOIRS OF MRS. LÆTITIA BOOTHBY.
By WILLIAM CLARK RUSSELL, Author of "The Book of Authors." Crown 8vo. 7s. 6d.

"The book is clever and ingenious."—*Saturday Review.*
"One of the most delightful books I have read for a very long while. Very few works of truth or fiction are so thoroughly entertaining from the first page to the last."—*Judy.*
"This is a very clever book, one of the best imitations of the productions of the last century that we have seen."—*Guardian.*

LITTLE HODGE. A Christmas Country Carol. By EDWARD JENKINS, Author of "Ginx's Baby," &c. Illustrated. Crown 8vo. 5s.

"We shall be mistaken if it does not obtain a very wide circle of readers."—*United Service Gazette.*
"Wise and humorous, but yet most pathetic."—*Nonconformist.*
"The pathos of some of the passages is extremely touching."—*Manchester Examiner.*
"One of the most seasonable of Christmas stories."—*Literary World.*

FICTION—*continued.*

GINX'S BABY; HIS BIRTH AND OTHER MISFORTUNES. By EDWARD JENKINS. Twenty-ninth Edition. Crown 8vo. Price 2s.

LORD BANTAM. By EDWARD JENKINS, Author of "Ginx's Baby." Sixth Edition. Crown 8vo. Price 2s.

HERMANN AGHA: An Eastern Narrative. By W. GIFFORD PALGRAVE, Author of "Travels in Central Arabia," &c. Second Edition. 2 vols. Crown 8vo, cloth, extra gilt. 18s.

"Reads like a tale of life, with all its incidents. The young will take to it for its love portions, the older for its descriptions, some in this day for its Arab philosophy."—*Athenæum.*
"The cardinal merit, however, of the story is, to our thinking, the exquisite simplicity and purity of the love portion. There is a positive fragrance as of newly-mown hay about it, as compared with the artificially perfumed passions which are detailed to us with such gusto by our ordinary novel-writers in their endless volumes."—*Observer.*

SEPTIMIUS. A Romance. By NATHANIEL HAW- THORNE. Author of "The Scarlet Letter," "Transformation," &c. Second Edition. 1 vol. Crown 8vo, cloth, extra gilt. 9s.

A peculiar interest attaches to this work. It was the last thing the author wrote, and he may be said to have died as he finished it.

The *Athenæum* says that "the book is full of Hawthorne's most characteristic writing."
"One of the best examples of Hawthorne's writing; every page is impressed with his peculiar view of thought, conveyed in his own familiar way."—*Post.*

PANDURANG HARI; Or, Memoirs of a Hindoo. A Tale of Mahratta Life sixty years ago. With a Preface, by Sir H. BARTLE E. FRERE, G.C.S.I., &c. 2 vols. Crown 8vo.

THE TASMANIAN LILY. By JAMES BONWICK, Author of "Curious Facts of Old Colonial Days," &c. Crown 8vo. Illustrated. [*Preparing.*

A GOOD MATCH. By AMELIA PERRIER, Author of "Mea Culpa." 2 vols.

"Racy and lively."—*Athenæum.*
"As pleasant and readable a novel as we have seen this season."—*Examiner.*
"This clever and amusing novel."—*Pall Mall Gazette.*
"Agreeably written."—*Public Opinion.*

65, *Cornhill;* & 12, *Paternoster Row, London.*

The Cornhill Library of Fiction.

3s. 6d. per Volume.

IT is intended in this Series to produce books of such merit that readers will care to preserve them on their shelves. They are well printed on good paper, handsomely bound, with a Frontispiece, and are sold at the moderate price of 3s. 6d. each.

ROBIN GRAY. By CHARLES GIBBON. With a Frontispiece by HENNESSY.

KITTY. By Miss M. BETHAM-EDWARDS.

READY MONEY MORTIBOY. [*Just out.*

HIRELL. By JOHN SAUNDERS, Author of "Abel Drake's Wife."

ONE OF TWO. By J. HAIN FRISWELL, Author of "The Gentle Life," etc.

GOD'S PROVIDENCE HOUSE. By Mrs. G. L. BANKS.

OTHER STANDARD NOVELS TO FOLLOW.

Forthcoming Novels.

WHAT 'TIS TO LOVE. By the Author of "FLORA ADAIR," "THE VALUE OF FOSTERSTOWN." 3 vols.

CIVIL SERVICE. By J. T. LISTADO, Author of "Maurice Reynhart." 2 vols.

VANESSA. By the Author of "THOMASINA," etc. 2 vols.

A LITTLE WORLD. By GEO. MANVILLE FENN, Author of "The Sapphire Cross," "Mad," etc.

THE QUEEN'S SHILLING. By Capt. ARTHUR GRIFFITHS, Author of "Peccavi; or, Geoffrey Singleton's Mistake." 2 vols.

TOO LATE. By Mrs. NEWMAN. 2 vols. Crown 8vo.

LISETTE'S VENTURE. By Mrs. RUSSELL GRAY. 2 vols. Cr. 8vo.

A WINTER FRIEND. By FREDK. WEDMORE, Author of "A Snapt Gold Ring." 2 vols. Cr. 8vo.

65, Cornhill; & 12, Paternoster Row, London.

Religious.

THE ETERNAL LIFE. Being fourteen sermons. By the Rev. JAS. NOBLE BENNIE, M.A. Crown 8vo.
[Nearly ready.

MISSIONARY ENTERPRISE IN THE EAST. By the Rev. RICHARD COLLINS. Illustrated. Crown 8vo.
[Preparing.

THE REALM OF TRUTH. By Miss E. CARNE. Crown 8vo.
[Preparing.

HYMNS FOR THE CHURCH AND HOME. By the Rev. W. FLEMING STEVENSON, Author of "Praying and Working."
[Preparing.

THE YOUNG LIFE EQUIPPING ITSELF FOR GOD'S SERVICE. Being Four Sermons Preached before the University of Cambridge in November, 1872. By the Rev. J. C. VAUGHAN, D.D., Master of the Temple. Third Edition. Crown 8vo. Price 3s. 6d.

WORDS & WORKS IN A LONDON PARISH. Edited by the Rev. CHARLES ANDERSON, M.A. Demy 8vo. 6s.

LIFE CONFERENCES DELIVERED AT TOULOUSE. By the Rev. PÈRE LACORDAIRE. Crown 8vo. 6s.

THOUGHTS FOR THE TIMES. By the Rev. H. R. HAWEIS, M.A., "Author of Music and Morals," etc. Third Edition. Crown 8vo. 7s. 6d.

CATHOLICISM AND THE VATICAN. With a Narrative of the Old Catholic Congress at Munich. By J. LOWRY WHITTLE, A.M., Trin. Coll., Dublin. Second Edition. Crown 8vo. 7s. 6d.

"A valuable and philosophic contribution to the solution of one of the greatest questions of this stirring age."—*Church Times.*

"We cannot follow the author through his graphic and lucid sketch of the Catholic movement in Germany and of the Munich Congress, at which he was present; but we may cordially recommend his book to all who wish to follow the course of the movement."—*Saturday Review.*

65, *Cornhill;* & 12, *Paternoster Row, London.*

RELIGIOUS—*continued.*

NAZARETH: ITS LIFE AND LESSONS.
By the Author of "THE DIVINE KINGDOM ON EARTH AS IT IS IN HEAVEN." Second Edition. In small 8vo, cloth. 5s.

"In Him was life, and the life was the light of men."

"A singularly reverent and beautiful book; the style in which it is written is not less chaste and attractive than its subject."—*Daily Telegraph.*

"Perhaps one of the most remarkable books recently issued in the whole range of English theology. . . . . Original in design, calm and appreciative in language, noble and elevated in style, this book, we venture to think, will live."—*Churchman's Magazine.*

SCRIPTURE LANDS IN CONNECTION WITH THEIR HISTORY.
By G. S. DREW, M.A., Vicar of Trinity, Lambeth, Author of "Reasons of Faith." Second Edition. Bevelled boards, 8vo. Price 10s. 6d.

"Mr. Drew has invented a new method of illustrating Scripture history—from observation of the countries. Instead of narrating his travels, and referring from time to time to the facts of sacred history belonging to the different countries, he writes an outline history of the Hebrew nation from Abraham downwards, with special reference to the various points in which the geography illustrates the history. The advantages of this plan are obvious. Mr. Drew thus gives us not a mere imitation of 'Sinai and Palestine,' but a view of the same subject from the other side. . . . He is very successful in picturing to his readers the scenes before his own mind. The position of Abraham in Palestine is portrayed, both socially and geographically, with great vigour. Mr. Drew has given an admirable account of the Hebrew sojourn in Egypt, and has done much to popularise the newly-acquired knowledge of Assyria in connection with the two Jewish Kingdoms."—*Saturday Review.*

MEMORIES OF VILLIERSTOWN.
By C. J. S. Crown 8vo. With Frontispiece. 5s.

SIX PRIVY COUNCIL JUDGMENTS—1850-1872.
Annotated by W. G. BROOKE, M.A., Barrister-at-Law. Crown 8vo. 9s.

THE DIVINE KINGDOM ON EARTH AS IT IS IN HEAVEN.
In demy 8vo, bound in cloth. Price 10s. 6d. [*Now ready.*

"Our Commonwealth is in Heaven."

"A high purpose and a devout spirit characterize this work. It is thoughtful and eloquent. . . . The most valuable and suggestive chapter is entitled 'Fulfilments in Life and Ministry of Christ,' which is full of original thinking admirably expressed."—*British Quarterly Review.*

"It is seldom that, in the course of our critical duties, we have to deal with a volume of any size or pretension so entirely valuable and satisfactory as this. Published anonymously as it is, there is no living divine to whom the authorship would not be a credit. . . . Not the least of its merits is the perfect simplicity and clearness, conjoined with a certain massive beauty, of its style."—*Literary Churchman.*

65, *Cornhill;* & 12, *Paternoster Row, London.*

Life & Works of the Rev. Fred. W. Robertson.

NEW AND CHEAPER EDITIONS.

LIFE AND LETTERS. Edited by STOPFORD BROOKE, M.A., Chaplain in Ordinary to the Queen.

In 2 vols., uniform with the Sermons. Price 7s. 6d.

Library Edition, in demy 8vo, with Two Steel Portraits. 12s.

A Popular Edition, in 1 vol. Price 6s.

SERMONS. FOUR SERIES. 4 vols. small crown 8vo, price 3s. 6d. per vol.

EXPOSITORY LECTURES ON ST. PAUL'S EPISTLE TO THE CORINTHIANS. Small crown 8vo. 5s.

AN ANALYSIS OF MR. TENNYSON'S "IN MEMORIAM." (Dedicated by permission to the Poet-Laureate.) Fcap. 8vo. 2s.

THE EDUCATION OF THE HUMAN RACE. Translated from the German of GOTTHOLD EPHRAIM LESSING. Fcap. 8vo. 2s. 6d.

LECTURES & ADDRESSES ON LITERARY AND SOCIAL TOPICS. Small crown 8vo. 3s. 6d. [*Preparing.*

A LECTURE ON FRED. W. ROBERTSON, M.A. By the Rev. F. A. NOBLE, delivered before the Young Men's Christian Association of Pittsburgh, U.S. 1s. 6d.

Sermons by the Rev. Stopford A. Brooke, M.A.,
Chaplain in Ordinary to Her Majesty the Queen.

CHRIST IN MODERN LIFE. Sermons Preached in St. James's Chapel, York Street, London. Third Edition. Crown 8vo. 7s. 6d.

"Nobly fearless and singularly strong. . . . carries our admiration throughout."—*British Quarterly Review.*

FREEDOM IN THE CHURCH OF ENGLAND. Six Sermons suggested by the Voysey Judgment. Second Edition. In 1 vol. Crown 8vo, cloth. 3s. 6d.

"A very fair statement of the views in respect to freedom of thought held by the liberal party in the Church of England."—*Blackwood's Magazine.*

"Interesting and readable, and characterised by great clearness of thought, frankness of statement, and moderation of tone."—*Church Opinion.*

SERMONS Preached in St. James's Chapel, York Street, London. Sixth Edition. Crown 8vo. 6s.

"No one who reads these sermons will wonder that Mr. Brooke is a great power in London, that his chapel is thronged, and his followers large and enthusiastic.

"They are fiery, energetic, impetuous sermons, rich with the treasures of a cultivated imagination."—*Guardian.*

THE LIFE AND WORK OF FREDERICK DENISON MAURICE: A Memorial Sermon. Crown 8vo, sewed. 1s.

65, *Cornhill;* & 12, *Paternoster Row, London.*

www.ingramcontent.com/pod-product-compliance
Lightning Source LLC
Chambersburg PA
CBHW022111290426
44112CB00008B/634